New Solutions in Legal Informatics, Economic Sciences and Mathematics

New Solutions in Legal Informatics, Economic Sciences and Mathematics

Edited by
Munenori Kitahara
Kazuaki Okamura
Hiroshima Shudo University

Volume 6 in a Series of Monographs of Contemporary Social Systems Solutions
Produced by the Faculty of Economic Sciences, Hiroshima Shudo University

Kyushu University Press

Volume 6 in a Series of Monographs of Contemporary Social Systems Solutions
Produced by Hiroshima Shudo University

All rights reserved. No part of this publication may be reproduced or transmitted in any form or by any means, electronic or mechanical, including photocopying and recording, or by any information storage and retrieval system, without the written permission from the publisher.

Copyright © 2015 by Munenori Kitahara and Kazuaki Okamura
7-1-146, Hakozaki, Higashi-ku, Fukuoka-shi, 812-0053, Japan

ISBN978-4-7985-0152-9

Printed in Japan

Preface

Hiroshima Shudo University established the Faculty of Economic Sciences in 1977 and the Graduate School of Economic Sciences in 2001. One goal of this faculty is to unify information sciences and economics and the faculty has endeavored to make progress in the research fields of operations research, computer sciences, mathematical economics and econometrics. While the definition of economic sciences has not been established yet, our specific understanding is that the economic sciences should unite system sciences and qualitative economic analysis and construct new fields relating to the management of the international economy, the financial system, and the national economy, or environmental issues, legal policies in communication.

The Faculty of Economic Sciences is a unique academic institution. There are no other faculties titled as "economic sciences" in Japan. Basically, we pursue analyzing various issues of contemporary economies and social systems, but its uniqueness can be observed in our efforts to balance the traditional economics and information sciences as means of analytical tools.

The Faculty consists of some 30 highly qualified members, whose research interests span a wide range of topics but more or less concern quantitative analytical frameworks. Since 2005 we have been publishing our research results in a form of monographs in English, one or two volumes a year, in order to present our academic contributions to possible readers in the world.

In the past several years, members of this faculty have made plans to expand these new frontiers as follows:
1. Macro-econometric models or micro-models which contain international economics or micro-models.
2. System analysis of financial institutions and international trade.
3. Information sciences, such as network systems or information systems or theory of reliance.
4. System sciences, such as operations research and production system analysis.
5. Research on information society and social systems.
6. Legal informatics, applying information technology to legal fields and solution of legal problems in digital society.

Faculty members have undertaken joint research with the aim of constructing these new fields and to publish our new research as a monograph as follows:
   Quantitative Economic Analysis, International Trade and Finance **(2005)**
   Applied Economic Informatics and Systems Sciences **(2005)**
   Quantitative Analysis of Modern Economy **(2007)**
   System Sciences for Economics and Informatics **(2007)**

*Quantitative Analysis on Contemporary Economic Issues **(2008)**

*Research on Information Society and Social Systems **(2008)**

*Social Systems Solutions by Legal Informatics, Economic Sciences and Computer Sciences **(2009)**

*The New Viewpoints and New Solutions of Economic Sciences in the Information Society **(2010)**

*Social Systems Solutions Applied by Economic Sciences and Mathematical Solutions **(2011)**

*Social Systems Solutions through Economic Sciences **(2012)**

*Legal Informatics, Economic Science and Mathematical Research **(2013)**

In these monographs our aim is to develop new methods and materials for constructing new fields of economics.

The authors of papers in these monographs have participate in building this new faculty and worked to develop new horizons of system sciences, information sciences, economics, economic sciences, computer sciences and legal informatics. We would welcome comments or suggestions in any forms.

The 2014 monograph is also entirely financed by the Faculty of Economic Sciences and is entitled under the title of "New Solutions in Legal Informatics, Economic Science and Mathematics" edited by Munenori Kitahara and Kazuaki Okamura.

This book contains contributions from wide variety of research in information society, information sciences, economic sciences, systems approach to the economic, managerial, mathematical and legal subjects. The focus of most articles is on the recent developments in the relevant. The set of papers in this book reflect both the each theory and wide range of applications to economic and managerial models. The economic sciences is based upon an interdisciplinary education and research area of sciences economics, econometrics, statistics, information sciences, system sciences, application information sciences, operations research and legal informatics.

This book consists of four chapters as follows:

Chapter 1, by *Munenori Kitahara*, refers to a legal justice through a fusion of law and information technology. The author will deal with a relationship between law and information technology. Legal states would require the residents and the organizations of lawful behaviors and business activities. The customers could lawfully purchase goods and services via the Internet by using their own terminal devices. The business entities could carry on the enterprises on the information systems complying with regulations. Because the computers and the information systems would guarantee the legality and the compliance. In other words, the information technologies could lead the customers and the entities to lawful behaviors as well as complying enterprises. This research will aim at realizing the content of law through a fusion of law and information technology. The fusion is composed of information society law, privacy law, data protection law and information security law as well as information technologies, such as privacy enhancing technology, internet communication technology and encryption technology. In the fusion of the information environment, the technologies will guarantee legality of one's behaviors and compliance of organizations with applied laws.

Chapter 2, by *Takeshi Ogawa*, will deal with the literature on Ricardian models. This study reviews existing literature on Ricardian models with joint production, primarily for the schematizable three-good case, and presents new ideas on the definition of secondary products and efficient specialization patterns. The term "secondary product," often encountered in a world of joint production, is difficult to define definitively; this study reconsiders the definition. Further, the three-country, three-good model contains a known possibility of multiple efficient specialization patterns (each country specializing in a different production process). We demonstrate that introducing joint production leads to the possibility of price curves intersecting at the boundary where the specialized goods change.

Chapter 3, by *Kouhei Iyori* will examine on a cellular automata model of an oligopolistic market with network externality. The author describes a cellular automata model of an oligopolistic market with network externality. When consumers buy a product, they sometimes take their neighbors' choices into consideration. We introduce the effect of consumer decisions into a market model and perform computer simulations under various conditions. The results of simulations show that (1) the final state of the market can be classified into four cases; (2) as neighborhood size increases, the rate of the case where products share the market decreases; and (3) the market requires long periods to reach the final state for a certain neighborhood range.

Chapter 4, by *Takashi Yano* and *Hiroyuki Kosaka* will analyze the effects of tariff reduction between Japan and the United States on the Asia-Pacific region. The purpose of this chapter is to develop a multi-country multi-sectoral model and to demonstrate its application. Regarding the model, the following features are included: 1) the model is constructed by using multi-period international input-output tables in constant prices and international dollars, 2) most parameters of the model are econometrically estimated, 3) the monopoly model is incorporated, 4) input coefficient varies over time, 5) sectoral price and output are simultaneously determined. As an application, the effects of tariff reduction between Japan and the United States on the Asia-Pacific region are quantified. Based on the results, the United States would have positive impact while Japan's findings would be negative with respect to output. The main cause of Japan's output decline is the shift in demand from domestic products to U.S. products due to improved U.S. price competitiveness in Japan's market.

Chapter 5 by *Michinori Sakaguchi* and *Masanori Kodama* will deal with the inventory models. Stochastic inventory models with salvaged opportunities at the beginning of each period are constructed in order to research the inventory system with style goods. These inventory models are equipping the notion of demand changes with time in the period. The demand distribution is assumed to be a general continuous distribution. It is attempted to get the way to reduce the expectation of the total inventory cost analytically by differentiating the object function.

We state precisely the optimal policies in the inventory model of single period. There are two threshold levels which are founded by solving equations, and using them the object function would take the minimal value at there.

Chapter 6 by *Setsuko Sakai* and *Tetsuyuki Takahama* will propose a new current-to-pbest strategy. A key issue in interactive evolutionary computation is to reduce fatigue of a user when the use revaluates candidate solutions. In a pairwise comparison, the user compares two solutions at a time and judges which is superior or inferior. It is thought that the fatigue can be reduced by using the pairwise comparison, compared with usual comparisons where all solutions are compared at a time. In this study, interactive differential evolution (interactive DE, IDE) using the pairwise comparison is improved to realize efficient search by introducing adaptive parameter control into IDE. One of the most successful studies on the adaptive parameter control in DE is JADE. In JADE, two parameter values for DE are generated according to a probability density function which is learned by the parameter values in success cases. There are two problems to introduce the parameter control of JADE into IDE. Sufficient number of function evaluations required for the parameter control is not provided in order to avoid the fatigue. The mutation strategy "current-to-pbest" cannot be adopted in IDE because only the order relation between a parent and its child is provided in pairwise comparison. In this chapter, we study an effective parameter control when the number of function evaluations is limited and "current-to-pbest" strategy is not adopted.

Chapter 7 by *Ryoko Wada* and *Yoshio Agaoka* will deal with harmonic polynomials of more degree. There have been many studies for classical harmonic polynomials on Cp. On the other hand, Kostant-Rallis introduced more general denition of harmonic polynomials from the Lie algebraic viewpoint. According to this viewpoint, these classical harmonic polynomials on Cp can be canonically idented with the harmonic polynomials corresponding to the Lie algebra $\mathfrak{so}(p, 1)$, which is the case of real rank 1. In our previous paper we consider some properties of generalized harmonic polynomials in the case $\mathfrak{so}(p, 2)$, which is the case of real rank 2 and show some results about harmonic polynomials of degree ≤ 4. In this paper we consider for these harmonic polynomials of more general degree.

We hope that these articles provide a comprehensive yet lively and up-to-date discussion of the state-of-the-art in information society and social systems. We believe that this book contains a coherent view of the important unifying ideas throughout the many faces of systems approach and a guide to the most significant current areas of approach. We also appreciate that this book should contribute to build the ubiquitous society in Japan. We would like to thank Hiroshima Shudo University and the Faculty of Economic Sciences for financial supports of publishing this monograph. Also we would like to take the opportunity to thank Kyushu University Press for publishing this book and for authors for their contributions.

November, 2014
Munenori Kitahara
Kazuaki Okamura

Contents

Preface i

Chapter 1 Legality and Compliance through Deploying Information Technology
.... *Munenori Kitahara* 1
   1. Introducion 1
   2. Fusion of Law and Information Technology 3
   3. Architecture and Security Standard of Information Technology 4
   4. Instances of the Fusion of Law and Information Technology 6
   5. Conclusions 12

Chapter 2 Three-Good Ricardian Model with Joint Production:
              A Schematic Reconsideration .... *Takeshi Ogawa* 17
   1. Introduction 17
   2. Model Setup 19
   3. Defining Primary and Secondary Products 22
   4. Potential for Use of Price Region Diagrams 27
   5. Principle of Multiple Efficient Patterns of Specialization 35
   6. Conclusion 37

Chapter 3 An Application of Cellular Automata to the Oligopolistic Market
.... *Kouhei Iyori* 47
   1. Introduction 47
   2. Market Model 48
   3. Simulations 50
   4. Discussion 56
   5. Conclusion 57

Chapter 4 Development of a Multi-Country Multi-Sectoral Model
              in International Dollars .... *Takashi Yano and Hiroyuki Kosaka* 59
   1. Introduction 59
   2. Theoretical Structure of the Model 61
   3. Empirical Structure of the Model 68
   4. Application 77
   5. Conclusions 81

Chapter 5   Stochastic Inventory Model with Time-Varying Demand
.... *Michinori Sakaguchi and Masanori Kodama*   85
   1. Introduction 85
   2. Preparation 86
   3. Inventory Model of Single Period 87
   4. Numerical Illustration 95
   5. Model of Two-Period 97

Chapter 6   A Study on Adaptive Parameter Control for Interactive Differential Evolution Using Pairwise Comparison
.... *Setsuko Sakai and Tetsuyuki Takahama*   101
   1. Introduction 101
   2. Related Works 103
   3. Optimization by Differential Evolution 104
   4. JADE 106
   5. Numerical Experiments 109
   6. Conclusion 120

Chapter 7   On Some Properties of Harmonic Polynomials in the Case of $\mathfrak{so}(p, 2)$: Irreducible Decomposition and Integral Formulas
.... *Ryoko Wada and Yoshio Agaoka*   123
   1. Introduction 123
   2. Preliminaries 124
   3. Irreducible Decomposition of $\mathcal{H}_n$ 127
   4. Irreducible Subspaces of $\mathcal{H}_n$ for $n \leq 4$ 134

Contributors 143

Chapter 1

Legality and Compliance through Deploying Information Technology

Munenori Kitahara
Faculty of Economic Sciences, Hiroshima Shudo University
1-1 Ozuka-Higashi 1-chome, Asaminami-ku, Hiroshima, JAPAN 731-3195

Abstract

Legal states would require the residents and the organizations of lawful behaviors and business activities. The customers could lawfully purchase goods and services via the Internet by using their own terminal devices. The business entities could carry on the enterprises on the information systems complying with regulations. Because the computers and the information systems would guarantee the legality and the compliance. In other words, the information technologies could lead the customers and the entities to lawful behaviors as well as complying enterprises.

This research will aim at realizing the content of law through a fusion of law and information technology. The fusion is composed of information society law, privacy law, data protection law and information security law as well as information technologies, such as privacy enhancing technology, internet communication technology and encryption technology. In the fusion of the information environment, the technologies will guarantee legality of one's behaviors and compliance of organizations with applied laws.

Key Words:
Legality, Compliance, Information technology, Fusion, Law, Legal justice, Privacy

1. Introduction

In the system of information society law, the laws have often introduced information technologies into the letter of the laws themselves. That is, the information technologies are defined as legal concepts in the laws. Therefore, performing the law would mean using the information technologies defined in the law. For examples, the electronic customer contract act requires customers of using an electromagnetic method, an electronic information system, e-mail technology and information communication technology. The electronic signature act also introduces an electromagnetic method and encryption technology. The internet minors protection act requires the providers of installing the information blocking and filtering technologies into the devices, which they sell to the minors.

These laws will achieve the purpose of law through letting the parties use an electromagnetic method. The electromagnetic method means a method of using electronic information processing system or other types of information communication technology. The method would be premised on using computer, other terminal devices, network, the Internet, application software, and computer program. The consumers or customers only select the messages and click the icons on the visual browser of the computer in order to purchase goods and services. These computer operations would not make legal issues such as unlawful actions. The reason is why the contents of the law are realized in the systems. That is, the law is programmed into the systems. In other words, the method will guarantee the legality of the computer operations. As the result, the law could maintain the effectiveness of the law itself. At the same time, it can be said that the law could realize the content of the law.

The consumers and customers used the information technologies in order to exercise their own legal rights from the viewpoint of the parties. They could exercise the legal rights and achieve the purpose of the contract with legality.

On the other hand, the information service provider (ISP) provide the IT infrastructure for the organizations and their users. The ISPs must provide the information systems installed with the architecture which will maintain the compliance with the related laws. The ISP should be responsible for implementing an architecture standard and security standard to protect systems, applications, and information and to comply with various regulatory, privacy and data protection requirements. To address those requirements, it might be recommended to deploy various information technologies.

The business entities could carry on the enterprises on the information systems complying with the related legal rules and various regulations. The information systems would have been designed on the rules, regulations and policies. Because the computers and the information systems would guarantee the compliance. In other words, the information technologies could lead the customers and the entities to lawful behaviors as well as complying enterprises.

Under the informational environment as mentioned above, it is necessary for both law and information technology to collaborate in order to achieve the purpose of the law while maintaining the legality and compliance. Moreover, one method should be adopted, how information technology can be imbedded into the letters of the law. The method might be called 'fusion of law and information technology.' The information technology will be given a legal authority through the fusion. As a result, information technology will become to be legally enforceable.

This research has a couple of main purposes. First, this paper will aim at presenting that a legal action will be guaranteed for legality and a system operating for compliance through a fusion of law and information technology. Thus, the author will have to elucidate the meaning and method of the fusion of law and information technology (2). He will examine a traffic accident case which gave this research a crucial insight. This case is a fusion of a road traffic act and an automobile speed control technology (3). Last, the author will examine several cases of a fusion of law and information technology. The former group includes existing fusion cases, and the latter expectable ones (4).

2. Fusion of Law and Information Technology
2.1 The Methodology of Fusion

At the earlier stage, it was conceived for the laws to collaborate with information technology in order to realize the intention of law [1]. Or the law aimed at realizing the purpose of itself though the combination of law and information technology. In a collaboration or combination, the component elements work jointly on an activity in which the component elements are individually distinct.

As for the information society law, information technology has been defined in the letter of the law. In other words, the technologies are embedded into the articles of the law, not vice versa. The two component elements are inseparably fused together. It means that the law would promote the addressees to use some kind of the technologies. That is, the law shall aim at realizing the content of the law itself through the addressees' using those technologies.

In the electronic consumer contracts law, an electronic consumer contract means a contract that is made between a consumer and a business entity by electromagnetic method through a visual browser of a computer in cases where the consumer manifests his/her intention to make an offer or to accept the offer by transmitting his/her intention through his/her computer in accordance with the procedures prepared on this visual browser by the business entity or its designee. In the law, an electromagnetic method means a method using electronic information processing system or other types of information communication technology. In the law, an electronic acceptance notice means an acceptance notice to the offer of a contract which is, among electromagnetic methods, given by means of transmission through a telecommunication line connecting a computer used by the party dispatching the acceptance notice to the offer of the contract with a computer used by the offer or the said contract [2].

In this way, the consumers have only to operate the computer connected with the Internet to conclude an electronic consumers contract to buy goods on the Web. They only did click some messages and icons on the visual browser of the device. In other words, the consumers use the information technologies to exercise their legal right. Moreover, their operations would comply with the contract law. As a result, the information processing system provided their operations with a legality.

2.2 The Concept of Fusion

The method of fusion is to embed information technology into the law. As a matter of fact, the information technologies must be defined in the articles of the law. Then, the information technologies will be given a legal meaning. That is, the information technologies will have a legal authority as the other legal concepts.

Under the informational environment which information technologies are embedded into the letter of law, man would operate a computer, or an information system, and use information technology instead of performing the law as information. The users operate the device according to the messages on a visual browser of a computer. The operating procedures are written in the program of the system.

An electronic consumers contract means a contract that is made between a consumer and a business entity by electromagnetic method. The electromagnetic method would include using electronic devices and applications (computer, visual browser, electromagnetic information processing system, information communication technology). Then, operating these devices would be considered as a legal action. That is, sending an e-mail may be transmitting an offer or acceptance as a legal action. Therefore, the information technologies would be required of a legal standard on the architecture and security [3].

2.3 The Objectives of Fusion

There will be three main objectives in the fusion of law and information technology.

The first objective is to guarantee a legality of consumers', customers', or users' operating procedures. The consumers want to conclude a sales contract on the Web. They have only to press keys or click icons according to the messages on the browser in practice. But, they were certainly performing their legal rights according to the electronic consumers contracts law. The operating procedures will become consistent with the content of the law.

The second one is to guarantee a compliance of ISPs with various regulations. Under a fused IT infrastructure, or informational environment, the organizations could achieve the compliance with various requirements, which would be required the entities in providing and operating the systems.

For the compliance, the architecture of the information systems will be very important. The ISPs should take account of an architecture standard in design and building the systems, which the related laws require. The laws will require the entities of the architecture based on 'security by default,' 'privacy by design,' 'data protection by default,' and 'identity/access management by design.'

The third objective is to put the words 'like cures like' into practice on the Internet through the fusion of law and information technology. That is, 'information technology cures information technology.' A hacker attacks a network with the same information technology as a networking engineer uses to protect the network. Therefore, an information technology could prevent unlawful actions on the Web. Because the information technology has a legal basis through the fusion.

3. Architecture and Security Standard of Information Technology

3.1 The Necessity of the Standards

Under the fused informational environment, the addressees of law have no adequate knowledge of information technologies. The addressees would use the technologies as a customer, consumer, or tax-payer. They do not normally have enough time to follow the progress and change of the information technologies as well as the applications. Most information technologies have been never passed through technology impact assessment. The most important thing is that it is considered as a legal action to use the information technologies and operate the devices. Therefore, law should promulgate an architecture and security standard of information technologies.

3.2 Security Standard

Under the fused informational environment, the requirements of the core IT infrastructure will be presented, which are related to the architecture, user, data, operation from the viewpoints of security, data protection, privacy, compliance, and audit.

With securing an organization's core IT infrastructure at the network, host, and application levels, the threats must be examined, and the security policy must be written and communicated within the entity.

The requirements are related to user management, authentication management, authorization management, access management, data management and provisioning, monitoring and auditing.

3.3 Architecture Standard

To protect system, applications, and information from internal and external threats and to comply with various regulatory, privacy and data protection requirements, organizations implement an "IT general and application-level controls" framework deprived from industry standard frameworks [4]. Identity and access management (IAM) processes and practices can help organizations meet objectives in the area of access control and operational security. IAM is as much an aspect of architecture as it is a collection of technology components, processes, and standard practices. As much as cloud IAM architecture and practices impact the efficiency of internal IT processes, they also play a major role in managing compliance within the enterprise. Properly implemented IAM practices and processes can help improve the effectiveness of the controls identified by compliance frameworks [5].

In the areas of privacy protection, data protection, and information security, the architecture of the information systems which collect, use and disclose personal information, must attain a certain level. The reason why I would refer to the architecture is that I would like to solve such problems through an engineering methodology in design. This methodology is a proactive measure. Those kinds of problems should be solved through a proactive method. Therefore, the ideas of privacy by design through a privacy impact assessment, or a data protection impact assessment would provide the systems with the appropriate architecture level. In the long run, information systems will have to adopt almost the information technologies as described in the previous section.

4. Instances of the Fusion of Law and Information Technology

4.1 The Outline of the Fusion

If the two conditions are met, the fusion will be achieved. The first condition is that the information technology is defined in the letter of the law. The second one is that the law provides the standards of architecture and security. If the information technology is the one which is normally being used, the technology already has the standards.

4.2 Information Technology and Law
4.2.1 E-Mail Technology and the Electronic Consumer Contracts Act

An e-mail technology has been introduced into the Electronic Consumer Contracts Act. The article 2 (definitions) defines the electronic consumer contracts as follows:

"In this Act, an 'electronic consumer contract' means a contract that is made between a consumer and a business entity by electromagnetic method through a visual browser of a computer in cases where the consumer manifests his/her intention to make an offer or to accept the offer by transmitting his/her intention through his/her computer in accordance with the procedures prepared on this visual browser by the business entity or its designee."(1)

"In this Act, 'electromagnetic method' means a method using electronic information processing system or other types of information communication technology."(3)

"In this Act, 'electronic acceptance notice' means an acceptance notice to the offer of a contract which is, among electromagnetic methods, given by means of transmission through a telecommunication line connecting a computer, etc. (meaning a computer, a facsimile device, a telex or a telephone, the same shall apply hereinafter) used by the party dispatching the acceptance notice to the offer of the contract with a computer, etc. used by the offer or of the said contract."(4)

As described above, an electromagnetic method is using electronic information processing system or other types of information communications technology in this act. Transmitting offering and accepting electromagnetic records would use e-mail technologies.

The email technology uses SMTP (Simple Mail Transfer Protocol) and POP (Post Office Protocol) in TCP/IP.

A number of cryptosystems have been adapted to help secure e-mail, a notoriously insecure method of communication. Some of the more popular adaptations include Secure Multipurpose Internet Mail Extensions (S/MIME), Pretty Enhanced Mail (PEM), and Pretty Good Privacy (PGP) [6].

S/MIME builds on the Multipurpose Internet Mail Extensions (MIME) encoding format by adding encryption and authentication via digital signatures based on public cryptosystems. PEM has been proposed by the IETF (Internet Engineering Task Force) as a standard that will function with public key cryptosystems [7].

4.2.2 Authorizing Technology and Law

In 1999 the Unauthorized Computer Access Prohibition Act was established in Japan. The Act provides the punishment of unauthorized computer access and the security measures of access controllers. An unauthorized computer access means an act of making available a restricted specific use by making in operation a specific computer having that access control function through inputting into it, via a telecommunication line, any information or command that can evade the restrictions placed by that access control function on that specific use (art.3(2)), and an act of making available a restricted specific use by making in operation a specific computer, whose specific use is restricted by an access control function installed into another specific computer which is connected, via a telecommunication line, to that specific computer, through inputting into it, via a telecommunication line, any information or command that can evade the restrictions connected (art.3(3)).

The access controller who has added an access control function to a specific computer shall endeavor to properly manage identification codes relating to that access control function and codes used to confirm such identification codes through that access control function, and shall always verify the effectiveness of that access control function, and, when he deems it necessary, shall endeavor to promptly take necessary measures to protect that specific computer from acts of unauthorized computer access, including the upgrading of the access control function concerned (art.5).

Then the access controllers will be required of necessary measures to protect the specific computer systems.

4.2.3 Encryption Technology and Law

Encryption is one technique which can be used to achieve secrecy for the contents of a message, but there are other methods of hiding identities and information including steganography, remailers, account cloning and spoofing [8]. Encryption can provide confidentiality, integrity and authenticity of the information transferred countering the open nature of the electronic documents. Digital signatures can be created by the use of encryption, and these can authenticate the sender of the information.

The Electronic Signatures and Certification Business Act has introduced encryption technologies. The purpose of this Act is to provide the presumption of authentic establishment of electromagnetic records by electronic signatures. In the Act, any electromagnetic record that is made in order to express information shall be presumed to be established authentically if the electronic signature is performed by the principal with respect to information recorded in such electromagnetic record. The authenticity and electronic signature of the electromagnetic record can be verified by the public key cryptosystem.

Japanese electronic signatures act (Act on Electronic Signatures and Certification Business) has the following provisions:

Article 1(Purpose)

The purpose of this Act is to promote the distribution of information by electromagnetic forms and information processing through ensuring the smooth utilization of Electronic Signatures, and thereby to contribute to the improvement of the citizens' quality of life and the sound development of the national economy, by providing the presumption of authentic establishment of electromagnetic records, the accreditation system for designated certification businesses and other necessary matters, with respect to Electronic Signatures.

Article 2(Definitions)

(1) The term "Electronic Signature" as used in this Act means a measure taken with respect to information that can be recorded in an electromagnetic record (a record that is prepared by an electronic form, a magnetic form or any other form not perceivable by human senses and that is used for information processing by computers; hereinafter the same shall apply in this Act), and which falls under both of the following requirements:

(i) A measure to indicate that such information was created by the person who has taken such measure; and

(ii) A measure to confirm whether such information has been altered.

(2) The term "Certification Business" as used in this Act means a service that, in response to either the request of any person who uses the business (hereinafter referred to as the "User") with respect to the Electronic Signature that he/she himself/herself performs or the request of another person, certifies that an item used to confirm that such User performed the Electronic Signature pertains to such User.

(3) The term "Specified Certification Business" as used in this Act means a Certification Business that, among Electronic Signatures, is performed with respect to an Electronic Signature that conforms to the criteria prescribed by ordinance of the competent minister as an Electronic Signature that can be performed by that person in response to the method thereof.

But, in these provisions, we can find no provisions to introduce an encryption technology into the act. The hint can be found in the ordinance for enforcement of the act (art. 2). That is, there is provided of the security of electronic signatures and the difficulty of electromagnetic records. In addition, the difficulty shall be depended upon the factorization in prime numbers of integer, and the calculation of discrete logarithm.

These hints suggest that we are forced to use an encryption technology in order to establish and send electromagnetic records.

The use of encryption seems to give rise to an element of suspicion—it is often assumed that the use of secret codes is associated with the world of spies and industrial espionage. Nevertheless, there are many legitimate purposes of secrecy in general and encryption in particular. Many are connected with business transactions and the desires to keep financial information away from the prying eyes of third parties and to authenticate and prevent repudiation of the communication as between the intended parties to the transaction. In this way, encryption technology is a fundamental element for the development of a global electronic commercial system [9].

4.3 Filtering Technology and Law
4.3.1 Packets Filtering Technology and Law

Packet filtering firewalls are simple networking devices that filter packets by examining every incoming and outgoing packet header. They can selectively filter packets based on values in the packet header, accepting or rejecting packets as needed. These devices can be configured to filter based on IP address, type of packet, port request, and/or other elements present in the packet [10].

In the Act Concerning Environment for Children to Safely Use the Internet, information providers shall be obliged to provide filtering technologies. This Act focuses on measures to protect minors from harmful information and explicitly provides for the direction of future efforts with respect to a vision of the environment for the Internet utilization.

SaaS for email primarily involves cleaning spam, phishing e-mails, and malware included in e-mail from an organization's incoming e-mail stream, and then delivering that clean e-mail security to the organization so that it is effectively not depolluted [11].

This is accomplished by using either Secure Socket Layer (SSL) or Transport Layer Security (TLS) on network communications at the transport layer [12].

4.3.2 Web Content Filtering Technology and Law

In the Cloud, a SaaS provider scans for malware threats and ensures that only clean traffic is delivered to end users. SaaS providers supplement that URL filtering with the examination of HTTP header information, page content, and embedded links to better understand site content. SaaS for web content also involves scanning outbound web traffic for sensitive information (e.g., ID numbers, credit card information, intellectual property) that users could send externally without appropriate authorization (data leakage protection). Web traffic is also scanned for content analysis, file type, and pattern matching to prevent data exfiltration [13].

Content filter effectively protects the organization's systems from misuse and unintentional denial-of-service conditions. A content filter is a software program or a hardware/software appliance that allows administrators to restrict content that comes into a network. The most common application of a content filter is the restriction of access to Web sites with nonbusiness-related material, such as pornography or entertainment. Another application is the restriction of spam e-mail from outside sources. Content filters can consist of small add-on software for the home or office, or major corporate applications [14].

Content filters ensure that employees are not using network resources inappropriately. Unfortunately, these systems require extensive configuration and constant updating of the list of unacceptable destinations or incoming restricted e-mail source addresses. Some newer content filtering applications update the restricted databases automatically, in the same way that some antivirus programs do. These applications match either a list of disapproved or approved Web sites, for example, or key content words, such as *nude* and *sex*. Content creators, of course, work to bypass such restrictions by suppressing these trip words, creating additional problems for networking and security professionals [15].

4.4 Privacy and Data Protection Technology and Law
4.4.1 Privacy-Enhancing Technology and Law

Privacy-enhancing technologies(PET) is a system of ICT measures protecting informational privacy by eliminating or minimizing personal data thereby preventing unnecessary or unwanted processing of personal data, without the loss of the functionality of the information system[16].

The PETs mean the information technologies for limitation in the collection of personal data, information technologies for identification and authentication, information technologies for pseudo-identity, encryption technology, and an audit ability technology. These PETs can be implemented in privacy law and data protection law. Designers of information systems that wish to comply with privacy legislation through technology must be open-minded [17].

4.4.2 Data Audit Technology and Law

The only way to be sure that organizations are processing the various files about the data subjects in compliance with the data protection law is by actual examination of the data [18]. A data auditor will need to examine the personal data from the obtaining, recording or holding of data at one end of its life to the eraser or destruction at the other. After the examination, the auditor can get the meta-data of personal data—where that data comes from, how it is gathered, how it is processed, how it is corrected when necessary, and how and when it is finally deleted.

By implementing a data audit technology, a data controller can grasp a lifetime of personal data, which will contribute to the effectiveness of a data protection act. It might be possible to grasp a personal data flow by attaching a logical IC tag to the personal data. The logical IC tag will play the same role as the header of an IP packet.

Packet filtering firewalls examine every incoming packet header and can selectively filter packets based on header information such as destination address, packet type, and other key information. The firewalls scan network data packets looking for compliance with or violation of the rules of the firewall's database [19].

4.4.3 Do-Not-Track Mechanism and Law

The US Federal Trade Commission (FTC) created standards for a do-not-track mechanism that would allow Web users to opt out of online tracking and the sharing of customer data among online business. In the Do Not Track Me Online Act, the Commission shall promulgate regulations that establish standards for the required use of an online opt-out mechanism to allow a customer to effectively and easily prohibit the collection or use of any covered information and to require a covered entity to respect the choice of such consumer to opt-out of such collection or use (sec.3).

The US largely relies on industry self-regulation to protect Internet privacy. According to the FTC report, both Mozilla Firefox and Microsoft's Internet Explorer implemented a DNT (Do Not Track) feature in the spring of 2011, and shortly after added support got mobile browsing on

Android. Apple's Safari web browser added support for Do Not Track in the summer of 2011. By 2012, they expect that approximately half of Internet users will upgraded to a modern Web browser that supports DNT [20].

There is no explicit regulatory requirement that mandates implementing support for the DNT header. That said, there are legal and compliance-related considerations to keep in mind when designing how to support consumer requests not to be tracked online via browser-based DNT mechanism [21].

In addition to the legislative proposals calling for the creation of Do Not Track, various industry sectors have developed tools to allow consumers to control online tracking. A number of browser vendors announced that their browsers permit consumers to instruct websites not to track their activities across websites. The World Wide Web Consortium("W3") convened a working group to create a universal standard for Do Not Track [22].

4.4.4 Anonymizing Technology and Law

The digital economy relies on the collection of personal data on an ever-increasing scale. Many companies that collect personal information, including social networks, retailers, and service providers, assure customers that their information will be released only in a non-personally identifiable form [23]. In the Statistic Act of Japan, the statistical surveys should be conducted by requesting individuals or juridical persons, or other organizations to report facts for the purpose. The questionnaire information means information collected through the statistical surveys. In the Act, anonymized data means the questionnaire information that is processed so that no particular individuals or juridical persons, or other organizations shall be identified for the purpose of providing it for general use. The administrative organs can produce anonymized data. Moreover, administrative organs may provide the anonymized data to academic organizations for the academic researches. However, no regulations are established, which provide the information technology to anonymize the information, the security and architecture standards.

Anonymization is a technique that enterprises can use to increase the security of data in the public cloud while still allowing the data to be analyzed and used [24]. Data anonymization is the process of changing data that will be used or published in a way that prevents the identification of key information.

4.4.5 De-identifying and Re-identifying Technology and Law

Once data records have been de-identified, they magically become safe to release, with no way of linking them back to individuals [25]. But, any information that distinguishes one person from another can be used for re-identifying anonymous data. So a common practice is for organizations to release and receive person-specific data with all explicit identifiers, such as name, address and telephone number, removed on the assumption that anonymity is maintained because the resulting data look anonymous [26]. Rendering anonymous means the modification of personal data so that the information concerning personal or material circumstances can no longer or only with a disproportionate amount of time, expense and labor be attributed to an identified or identifiable individual (Sec.3(7)BDSG).

With technological advances, personal information is also becoming easier to collect, retain, use, disclose and leverage for a wide range of secondary uses [27]. If organizations do not strongly protect of individuals in the information being sought out, there may be far-reaching implications for both the individuals and the organizations involved. One of the most effective ways to protect the privacy of individuals is through strong de-identification. De-identification, using proper de-identification techniques and re-identification risk management procedures, remains one of the strongest and most important tools in protecting privacy [28].

4.4.6 Aliasing Technology and Law

Aliases can be tailored to specific scenarios, which allows individuals to assume different aliases depending on the context of interaction. Many online users utilize aliases as pseudonyms in order to protect their true identity, such that one alias is used for web forum postings and another for e-mail correspondence [29]. An alias is a unique identifier that is substituted for a phone number, name, or address. This means man can keep his/her private information secure.

This aliasing technology has been adopted in the German data protection law. "Aliasing" shall mean replacing the data subject's name and other identifying features with another identifier in order to make it impossible or extremely difficult to identify the data subject (art. 6(a)).
"Aliasing" means replacing a person's name and other identifying characteristics with a label, in order to preclude identification of the data subject or to render such identification substantially difficult.

5. Conclusions

The main purpose of this research comes forth in finding out a new relationship between law and information technology. The relationship appears in the form of collaboration, combination, and fusion. The two elements have been incompatible with each other. However, it will be nothing but a problem of simultaneity. Because they say that law always follows technology.

Rather than law following technology, I do not think that information technology may follow legal actions in the electromagnetic method. Information technology could neither read nor understand the natural languages which human beings uses every day, and with which law is presented. Therefore, this research is also an attempt for information technology to let understand the content of law.

This research aims at researching the relationships of law and information technology. I could find various affinities between law and information technology in the research through overcoming the previous problems. Moreover, I could find a few of the same characteristics in the information technology as law has.

I would like to explain the reasons why information technologies should be embedded into the law. First, the important features of computer system and network have been adopted in many social systems. Second, the information and networking technologies have ethical and social aspects. Therefore, information technologies could be affiliated to legal norms. Networking technologies, especially, are being used to link the two parties into closer relations with each other. Third, information technologies can guarantee a legality of behaviors. The technologies can contribute for organizations to comply with the laws. The information society can reach to a legal justice.

Are there the legitimacy in that individuals use information technologies in order to exercise the legal rights? An email is only a method of transporting an offer and acceptance notice between the parties in an electronic consumer contract. The information technology would provide no legal reasoning on the contract at all. The way of thinking is to be valid to the other fusion cases.

In the fusion, the more difficult problem is the way how the legislators describe the usage of information technologies in the articles of law. The electronic signatures act might provide an appropriate model. The act will suggest an introduction of the information technology, first of all. Then, the regulations of the law will promulgate the security and architecture of the information technology.

The important features of computer systems are adopted in many social systems in the information society. I could show the idea in that many important features of the technology have been adopted in the real political and social systems. The information systems have been contributing to social systems solutions.

Information security technology includes authentication technology, data protection technology and information filtering technology. These technologies would require the users of an ethical consideration. These technologies might lead the users to an ethical deed. Therefore, I would define that these information technologies are ethical technologies.

Information technologies have been being used in many legal fields. The fact might be an evidence that the information technology has legitimacy from the legal view point. The TCP/IP might, especially, be a law that controls behaviors of the internet users'.

It will be permitted that these technologies are used to realize the contents of laws in place of the laws. That is, this is a fusion of law and information technology. The fusion will aim at realizing legal justice.

There might be certainly various problems about the fusion. First, technologies will regulate technologies. Second, the fusion will force the users to use specific computer systems with the information technologies implemented. Third, the fusion will have to cope with the evolution of technologies. Last, there will be left the problem of standardizing the technologies.

Information society, increasingly, depends on computer systems to behave acceptably in applications with extremely critical requirements, by which she means that the failure of systems to meet their requirements may result in serious consequences.

References

[1] Cf., M.Kitahara, The Collaboration of Law and Information Technology, *Social Systems Solutions applied by Economic Sciences and Mathematical Solutions*, Kyushu Univ. Press 2011, pp. 1ff.

[2] Cf., M. Kitahara, ibid., p.15.

[3] Cf., ibid., pp. 26ff.

[4] Tim Mather/Subra Kumaraswamy/Shahed Latif, *Cloud Security and Privacy*, O'Reilly 2009, pp.73ff.

[5] Tim Mather/Subra Kumaraswamy/Shahed Latif, ibid., p.99.

[6] Cf., National Law Enforcement and Corrections Technology Center, *A Guide for Applying Information Technology in Law Enforcement*, U.S. Department of Justice 2001, p.1.

[7] Cf., Japan National Police Agency, the White Paper on Police, 2012, p.22.

[8] Y. Akdeniz/C. Walker/D.Wall (eds.), *The Internet, Law and Society*, Longman 2000, p.320.

[9] Ibid., p.321.

[10] M.E.Whitman/H.J.Mattord, *Management of Information Security*, 2nd ed., Thomson 2008, p.353.

[11] Tim Mather/Subra Kumaraswamy/Shahed Latif, *Cloud Security and Privacy*, O'Reilly 2009, p.220.

[12] Ibid.

[13] M.E.Whitman/H.J.Mattord, *Reading and Cases in the Management of Information Security*, Course Technology 2006, p.63.

[14] M.E.Whitman/H.J.Mattord, *Management of Information Security*, 2nd ed., Thomson 2008, p.373.

[15] Ibid.

[16] G.W. van Blarkom/J.J. Borking/J.G.E. Olk(eds.), Handbook of Privacy and Privacy-Enhancing Technologies, PISA 2003, p.33.

[17] Ibid.

[18] Cf., R. Morgan/R. Boardman, Data Protection Strategy: Implementing Data Protection Compliance, Sweet and Maxwell 2003, p.33.

[19] M.E.Whitman/H.J.Mattord, *Principles of Information Security*, 3rd ed., Course Technology 2009, pp. 245- 246.

[20] Cf., The Do Not Track Field Guide (https://developer.mozilla.org/en-US/docs/tag/DNT). The US FTC, Protecting Consumer Privacy in an Era of Rapid Change: Recommendations for Businesses and Policymakers, FTC Report March 2012, p.4.

[21] Cf., ibid., The Do Not Track Field Guide.

[22] US FTC, ibid., pp.4-5.

[23] Cf., A. Narayanan / V. Shmatikov, Privacy and Security: Myths and Fallacies of "Personally Identifiable Information," *Communication of the ACM*, Vol.53 No.6, 2010, p.25.

[24] Jeff Sedayao, Enhancing Cloud Security Using Data Anonymization, IT@Intel White

Paper, 2012, p.2.

[25] A. Narayanan / V. Shmatikov, ibid.

[26] Cf., Latanya Sweeney, *k*-Anonymity: A Model for Protecting Privacy, International Journal on Uncertainty, Fuzziness and Knowledge-asked Systems, 10(5), 2002, pp. 557-570.

[27] Cf., Ann Cavoukian/Khaled El Emam, De-identification Protocols: Essential for Protecting Privacy, PbD 2014, pp.1ff.

[28] Ann Cavoukian/Khaled El Emam, ibid., p.1.

[29] Cf., R. Hölzer/B. Malin/L. Sweeney, Email Alias Detection Using Social Network Analysis (http://dataprivacylab.org/dataprivacy/projects/emailalias/paper.pdf).

Chapter 2

Three-Good Ricardian Model with Joint Production: A Schematic Reconsideration

Takeshi Ogawa
Faculty of Economic Sciences, Hiroshima Shudo University
1-1 Ozuka-Higashi 1-chome, Asaminami-ku, Hiroshima, JAPAN 731-3195

Abstract

This study reviews existing literature on Ricardian models with joint production, primarily for the schematizable three-good case, and presents new ideas on the definition of secondary products and efficient specialization patterns. The term "secondary product," often encountered in a world of joint production, is difficult to define definitively; this study reconsiders the definition. Further, the three-country, three-good model contains a known possibility of multiple efficient specialization patterns (each country specializing in a different production process). We demonstrate that introducing joint production leads to the possibility of price curves intersecting at the boundary where the specialized goods change.

Key Words:
Ricardian model, Joint production, Secondary product, Extreme point, Production possibility frontier

1. Introduction

Items produced secondarily in the course of a production process are called secondary products. In certain cases, however, the secondary products are so valuable that it is difficult to clearly distinguish between primary and secondary.

Secondary products result during joint production in which a single production process yields many goods. Joint production has become indispensable in modern society, primarily in the areas of manufacturing, agriculture, and the environment. A prime example is the use of compost in the livestock industry. The bioethanol beginning to be refined from rice straw and wheat straw is increasingly treated identically to the bioethanol produced from the edible portion of grains. The OECD [10] mentions joint production as an agricultural multifunctionality. In the manufacturing industry as well, as Kainou [7] notes, examples of manufacturing single products are rare; joint production has become vital. He states, for example, that in almost all integrated factories we encounter situations such as the steel industry, which, in addition to steel products, has launched products in three other sectors, including coke for ceramics, stone and clay products, and coal tar products for the chemical industry. Trade in such jointly produced products involves many aspects that currently require theoretical explanation.

Traditionally, many analyses of joint production trade models extend the Heckscher–Ohlin model, with seminal studies including those of Chang et al. [18] and Uekawa [20]. However, empirical studies of trade models incorporating joint production in the Ricardian model, such as Ogawa [14, 16], are relatively recent, after a long gap since the publication of Koopmans' [13] and others' activity analysis methodology.

For the Ricardian model, beginning with Jones [12], researchers have emphasized the conditions that determine efficient specialization patterns indicating which country should produce which good with which production process.[1] The necessary and sufficient conditions for efficient specialization patterns are derived from the Hawkins–Simon theorem. Ogawa [14] argues, however, that with three or more countries and three or more goods, the mere presence of joint production means that (1) the efficient patterns of specialization indicating which country should produce using which production process are not uniquely determined, and (2) the Hawkins–Simon theorem cannot determine the necessary and sufficient conditions for determining efficient specialization patterns.

In the Ricardian trade model incorporating joint production, to uncover efficient specialization patterns, considering consistency with the understanding of the case with no joint production, it is desirable to first address the case in which secondary products can be distinguished, and then attempt to generalize from that basis. The present study thus considers situations where secondary products can be defined. First, we demonstrate that even if we apply Ogawa's [14] definition of secondary products, and the principal diagonal matrix that is a general tool in this field, it is possible that no efficient specialization patterns might exist for individual countries with different primary products. On the basis of that possibility, we present a definition of secondary products that can apply in international trade.

The trade model with joint production has a similar structure to models for trade in intermediate goods. We must also explain efficient specialization patterns in the Ricardian model with trade in intermediate goods. There currently exists no clear understanding here, notwithstanding Amano's [1] groundbreaking paper proposing schematization, Deardorff's [2, 3] attempts to incorporate intermediate goods into a definition of comparative advantage, Higashida's [6] schematic demonstration that multiple efficient specialization patterns in the strong sense could appear even with three countries and three goods, and Shiozawa's [19] findings of the existence of solutions for efficient specialization patterns.

---

[1] For an approach to generalizing the analysis of Jones [12] to the case in which the number of countries and number of goods are different, see Ogawa [17].

Shiozawa [19] demonstrated with great generality the existence of solutions to efficient specialization patterns in both the strong and weak senses of efficiency. In proving efficient specialization patterns that invariably hold in the weak sense of efficiency, he uses Su's [5] Rental-Harmony Theorem. This Theorem originates in combinatorial mathematics, and we can learn from its three conditions that support our understanding of the conditions for the existence of solutions for efficient patterns of specialization. One of these conditions can be interpreted as implying that all countries specialize in the production of different goods (a pricing system exists). Since this condition is satisfied in intermediate goods by merely assuming that the world economy is closed if the number of countries is the same as that of goods (there exists demand for all goods as either intermediate or final goods), Shiozawa [19] does not address this condition. The present study demonstrates that in the nearly-identical joint production model, this condition may not hold. We examine the additional assumptions required to satisfy the condition that the world economy be closed for intermediate goods.

This paper proceeds as follows. Section 2 reviews the model setup. We then demonstrate an example in which, even if we apply both Ogawa's [14] relatively broadly accepted definition of secondary products and the principal diagonal matrix that is a general tool in this field, there exist no efficient patterns of specialization for individual countries with different primary products. Section 3 defines secondary products adapted to the case of intermediate goods, on the basis of which it demonstrates the existence of solutions for efficient patterns of specialization using Su's [5] Rental Harmony Theorem. Section 4 discusses the key to the three-good model, the necessary conditions for Ikema's [9] schema as expanded by Ogawa [14], to encompass joint production. Section 5 presents a two-country case of the principle explaining why the addition of joint production can cause multiple efficient patterns of specialization to appear when there are multiple countries in the three-good model. Section 6 summarizes our findings.

2. Model Setup

Following Ogawa [14], we consider a Ricardo–Graham model with a linear production function involving three countries, three goods, three production processes, and one element (labor), permitting joint production. Let $L^i (> 0)$ be the labor endowment for country i and $L^i_j (\geq 0)$ the labor input for country i and production process j, where $i, j = 1, 2, 3$. The constraint on labor availability can be expressed as

$$L^i_1 + L^i_2 + L^i_3 = L^i.$$

In a world of joint production, it has been common practice since Koopmans's [13] analysis activity to represent the amount that one unit of labor can produce as a production coefficient. Let $a^i_{jk} (\geq 0)$ be the amount of good k that can be produced with one unit of labor using production process j in country i, where $i, j, k = 1,2,3$.[2] The activity for country i's production process j can be written as $(a^i_{j1}, a^i_{j2}, a^i_{j3})^T$.[3] Total production of good k by country i can be written as X^i_k, where $X^i_k = a^i_{1k}L^i_1 + a^i_{2k}L^i_2 + a^i_{3k}L^i_3$. The set W of world production possibilities can be written as[4]

$$W := \left\{ X = (X_1, X_2, X_3)^T \geq 0 \,\middle|\, \begin{array}{l} X_k \leq X^1_k + X^2_k + X^3_k, \quad X^i_k = a^i_{1k}L^i_1 + a^i_{2k}L^i_2 + a^i_{3k}L^i_3, \\ L^i_1 + L^i_2 + L^i_3 = L^i \end{array} \right\},$$ [5]

The elements of W are called production points, and their inclusion in W is called a production possibility. We now use the definition of efficiency in production.

Definition 1.

Production point $X^* \in W$ is efficient only if for production points $X \in W$ where $X \geq X^*$ we have $X = X^*$, and efficient production points are called points on the frontier.

In this study, we distinguish between primary and secondary products, and thus, following Ogawa [14], for each country we consider the primary product from production process k to be good k and others to be secondary products. From that, we may assume that for any $i, j = 1,2,3$, we have $a^i_{jj} > 0$.

Jones [12] addresses the production assignment problem in the n-country, n-good model: efficient production patterns (patterns of specialization) for individual countries specializing one-to-one in producing different goods; in particular, where the $i - i$ assignment, that is, the world production that country i specializes in good i, is an efficient production pattern. He assumed as a precondition the existence of efficient production patterns where each country specializes in production of a different good.[6] In a world with joint production, specialization of production toward a good transforms into specialization of production toward a production process. Ogawa [14] reinterpreted the good for which production is specialized as a primary product, and to distinguish between primary and secondary products assumed that

$$a^i_{kk} > a^i_{jk}. \quad (j \neq k). \tag{1}$$

We demonstrate that under this assumption there exists the case with no production points for efficient production patterns where individual countries specialize in a production process. Let us first define

---

[2] In reality, the difference of each coefficient may be explained as other factors that cannot move, such as the endowment of immobile capital or land.
[3] T indicates transposition.
[4] In this study, the free disposal of goods (with positive value) is permitted.
[5] We represent vector inequality with $\geq, >, \gg$.
[6] The proof of the appropriateness of this assumption was given in more general form when intermediate goods are included by Shiozawa [19].

"pattern of specialization."

Definition 2.

1. For country i to specialize in production process j means that $L^i_j = L^i$, that is, the entire labor force is devoted to production process j. We abbreviate this as specialization.

2. For the world economy to be completely specialized means that each country specializes in one production process, and we call this phenomenon the pattern of specialization.

3. For the world economy to have one-to-one assignment means a pattern of specialization in which each country specializes in a different production process.

4. For the world economy to have $i-i$ assignment means one-to-one assignment of country i in production process i.

If necessary, goods can be assigned names to rewrite an arbitrary one-to-one assignment into the $i-i$ assignment. Thus, to analyze an arbitrary one-to-one assignment, it suffices to analyze an $i-i$ assignment. This capability allows us to present an example of the non-existence of efficient production points for a one-to-one assignment under assumption (1).

Example 1.

Assume that each country has identical production coefficients, with the following activity.

$$\begin{bmatrix} a^i_{11} \\ a^i_{12} \\ a^i_{13} \end{bmatrix} = \begin{bmatrix} 3 \\ 0 \\ 0 \end{bmatrix}, \quad \begin{bmatrix} a^i_{21} \\ a^i_{22} \\ a^i_{23} \end{bmatrix} = \begin{bmatrix} 0 \\ 3 \\ 0 \end{bmatrix}, \quad \begin{bmatrix} a^i_{31} \\ a^i_{32} \\ a^i_{33} \end{bmatrix} = \begin{bmatrix} 2 \\ 2 \\ 5 \end{bmatrix}.$$

Let the labor endowment for all countries be 1.

This example satisfies (1). For any one-to-one assignment, world production point $X = (5,5,5)^T$. If all countries specialize in a third production process, however, world production point $X^* = (6,6,15)^T (\gg X)$. It follows that in this example there are no production points for efficient one-to-one assignment.

This example holds even if assumption (1) is made rigorous using the field's common principal diagonal matrix. Assume, for example, that we replace (1) with the following equation.

$$a^i_{kk} > \sum_{j \neq k} a^i_{jk} \left(\Leftrightarrow |a^i_{kk}| > \sum_{j \neq k} |a^i_{jk}| \right). \tag{2}$$

This equation shows that the technology coefficients for country i take the form of the following principal diagonal matrix:

$$\begin{bmatrix} a^i_{11} & a^i_{21} & a^i_{31} \\ a^i_{12} & a^i_{22} & a^i_{32} \\ a^i_{13} & a^i_{23} & a^i_{33} \end{bmatrix} = \begin{bmatrix} 3 & 0 & 2 \\ 0 & 3 & 2 \\ 0 & 0 & 5 \end{bmatrix}. \tag{3}$$

We further observe that the technology coefficients for $i-i$ assignment also form a principal diagonal matrix:

$$\begin{bmatrix} a^1_{11} & a^2_{21} & a^3_{31} \\ a^1_{12} & a^2_{22} & a^3_{32} \\ a^1_{13} & a^2_{23} & a^3_{33} \end{bmatrix} = \begin{bmatrix} 3 & 0 & 2 \\ 0 & 3 & 2 \\ 0 & 0 & 5 \end{bmatrix}. \tag{4}$$

For this reason, neither (1) nor (2) are defined such that there exists any one-to-one assignment that is an efficient pattern of specialization. It follows that in extending the Ricardo-Graham model to include joint production, we must modify the definition of primary and secondary products. In Section 3, we consider how to define primary and secondary products on the basis of this logic.

3. Defining Primary and Secondary Products

In considering the definition of primary and secondary products, we address the problem of maximizing world output. Given a goods pricing vector $P = (p_1, p_2, p_3)(\gg 0)$, this problem can be expressed as

$$(P1) \quad \max_{L^i_j \geq 0} p_1 \sum_{i,j} a^i_{j1} L^i_j + p_2 \sum_{i,j} a^i_{j2} L^i_j + p_3 \sum_{i,j} a^i_{j3} L^i_j \quad \text{s.t.} \quad L^i_1 + L^i_2 + L^i_3 \leq L^i.$$

The multiplier in this problem reduces wages to $w = (w^1, w^2, w^3)(\gg 0)$. We omit the proof of the following lemma.

Lemma 1.

The following two statements are equivalent for $X \in W$, where $X \gg 0$.

(1) X is efficient and on the frontier.

(2) There exists a positive price system $P(\gg 0)$ for which X maximizes world output.

When considering the definition of primary and secondary products, it is helpful to note the third condition of Su's [5] Rental Harmony Theorem, used in the proof of invariant efficient patterns of specialization, one of the proofs for solutions for efficient patterns of specialization including intermediate goods presented by Shiozawa [19].[7] Su's [5] Rental Harmony Theorem takes the following form.

Fact 1. (Rental Harmony Theorem)

Suppose n housemates in an n-bedroom house seek to decide who gets which room and for what portion of the total rent. Also, suppose that the following conditions hold:

(1) **Good House:** In any partition of the rent, each person finds some room acceptable.

(2) **Miserly Tenants:** Each person always prefers a free room (one that costs no rent) to a non-free room.

(3) **Closed Preference Sets:** A person who prefers a room for a convergent sequence of prices prefers that room at the limiting price.

Then, there exists a partition of the rent such that each person prefers a different room.

We can adapt this model, assuming people as countries, rooms as production processes, and rent as wages. Assuming that wages are uniquely determined by the prices of goods, for a one-to-one assignment, which is an efficient pattern of specialization to exist, it suffices that the following three points be satisfied.

First, for any (positive) wage structure in each country, it specializes in a production process. For this to occur, it suffices that the production coefficient matrix A for an arbitrary one-to-one assignment taking the form of (4) has the following characteristics. For any positive wage vector $w \gg 0$, there exists a wage structure $P \gg 0$ such that $PA = w$. In the linear complementarity problem, this condition is equivalent to A^T being an S matrix[8]. This point is far from obvious and must be assumed. However, recalling the Hawkins–Simon theorem, it is equivalent to considering the range of cases where $X^* \gg 0$ for production points X^* under the $i-i$ assignment in the intermediate goods model. This assumption is not, therefore, a new supposition stemming from the introduction of joint production. From Hawkins and Simon [4], the Hawkins–Simon theorem here refers to the following theorem.

Fact 2. (Hawkins–Simon Theorem)

The following three propositions are equivalent for a non-diagonal, non-positive matrix M.

(1) For any $x \gg 0$, there exists a $v \gg 0$ such that $Mv = x$. (M is an S matrix.)

(2) The leading principle minors of M are all positive.

(3) The principle minors of M are all positive.

---

[7] In Shiozawa [19], this is called a "shared pattern of specialization."
[8] For example, see Chapter 3 of Cottle et al. [11].

In the model incorporating joint production, however, unlike ordinary models and models involving intermediate goods, there are locations where the non-diagonal components are non-positive, meaning that we cannot use the Hawkins–Simon theorem applied by Jones [12].

Next, we check that the third point is satisfied, because the set of price vectors P divided by the production process selected by each country is a closed set.

What changes substantially with the introduction of joint production, therefore, is the second item. This item represents the fact that there exists a price system under which one country no longer selects a production process in which another country specializes; that is, if two or more countries specialize in the same production process, a pricing system change modifies the selection in some form. In the ordinal Ricardo–Graham model, when the number of countries and goods are equal, two or more countries specializing in the same good would cause some good not to be produced. We need to consider only a world in which all goods are necessary. The same holds for the case of intermediate goods; the possibility of a shortage of an intermediate good means this is also not a problem. When joint production enters the picture, however, one production process produces multiple goods, meaning that even if two or more countries specialize in the same production process, all goods may be produced in the world as a whole.

To solve this problem, we consider rewriting the model as an intermediate goods model, while not changing the production process specialization. For all goods in each country, since assumption (1) tells us that the good for which the production process has the highest productivity is the production process with the same name as the good, we subtract the production coefficient for the good with the production process with the second highest productivity. For the foregoing example, we obtain

$$\begin{bmatrix} a_{11}^i - \max_{l \neq 1} a_{l1}^i & a_{21}^i - \max_{l \neq 1} a_{l1}^i & a_{31}^i - \max_{l \neq 1} a_{l1}^i \\ a_{12}^i - \max_{l \neq 2} a_{l2}^i & a_{22}^i - \max_{l \neq 2} a_{l2}^i & a_{32}^i - \max_{l \neq 2} a_{l2}^i \\ a_{13}^i - \max_{l \neq 3} a_{l3}^i & a_{23}^i - \max_{l \neq 3} a_{l3}^i & a_{33}^i - \max_{l \neq 3} a_{l3}^i \end{bmatrix} = \begin{bmatrix} 1 & -2 & 0 \\ -2 & 1 & 0 \\ 0 & 0 & 5 \end{bmatrix}.$$

With this approach, we subtract the same quantity regardless of the production process is selected, so each country's selection is unchanged, with the exception of alternatives where no labor is deployed for a production process. The principal diagonal components are positive, the non-diagonal components non-positive. This example does not satisfy the Hawkins–Simon condition that all minors are positive. However, if all principle minors in this form are positive, no country will select a production process in which no labor is deployed. Thus, we rewrite the production coefficient a_{jk}^i as $a_{jk}^i - \max_{l \neq k} a_{lk}^i$ and instead of (P1) consider the problem of maximizing gross world product as follows:

$$(P2) \quad \max_{L_j^i \geq 0} \sum_k p_k \sum_{i,j} \left(a_{jk}^i - \max_{l \neq k} a_{lk}^i \right) L_j^i \quad \text{s.t.} \quad \sum_j L_j^i \leq L^i.$$

Wages are positive under full employment, and therefore, the following lemma can be directly derived.

Lemma 2.

If the (P2) multiplier $w = (w^1, w^2, w^3)$ satisfies $w \gg 0$, (P2) and (P1) have identical solutions.

It follows that if with these new production coefficients all production coefficient matrices for one-to-one assignments satisfy (or do not satisfy) the Hawkins–Simon condition (i.e., principal minors be uniformly positive), then there exists (does not exist) a pricing system $P(\gg 0)$, under which all countries will specialize in different production processes. As with the case of intermediate goods, considering intentional price adjustments in response to the new production coefficients, the second condition of Su's [5] Rental Harmony Theorem is satisfied. This condition is also a sufficient condition for the first condition.

The foregoing logic can be summarized in the form of Proposition 1, discussed later in this section, allowing us to distinguish between primary and secondary products, for which there are one-to-one assignments that are efficient patterns of specialization. To deal symbolically with arbitrary one-to-one assignments, we first create a third-degree permutation set

$$S_3 := \{\sigma : \{1,2,3\} \to \{1,2,3\} | \sigma \text{ is a bijective function}\}.$$

For an arbitrary one-to-one assignment it suffices to consider patterns of specialization in which country i specializes in production process $\sigma(i)$, where $\sigma \in S_3$. Any one-to-one assignment is characterizable with $\sigma \in S_3$. To discuss Proposition 1, we develop the following definition of primary and secondary products and Assumption 1.

Definition 3.

For each country, the primary product of production process k is good k, with others being secondary products.

Assumption 1.

We make the following three assumptions:
1. For any $\sigma \in S_3$, the principal minors of the non-diagonal non-positive matrix created on the basis of production coefficients for the one-to-one assignment, involving country i specializing in production process $\sigma(i)$ are uniformly positive.

$$\begin{bmatrix} a^1_{\sigma(1)\sigma(1)} - \max_{j \neq \sigma(1)} a^1_{j\sigma(1)} & a^2_{\sigma(2)\sigma(1)} - \max_{j \neq \sigma(1)} a^2_{j\sigma(1)} & a^3_{\sigma(3)\sigma(1)} - \max_{j \neq \sigma(1)} a^3_{j\sigma(1)} \\ a^1_{\sigma(1)\sigma(2)} - \max_{j \neq \sigma(2)} a^1_{j\sigma(2)} & a^2_{\sigma(2)\sigma(2)} - \max_{j \neq \sigma(2)} a^2_{j\sigma(2)} & a^3_{\sigma(3)\sigma(2)} - \max_{j \neq \sigma(2)} a^3_{j\sigma(2)} \\ a^1_{\sigma(1)\sigma(3)} - \max_{j \neq \sigma(3)} a^1_{j\sigma(3)} & a^2_{\sigma(2)\sigma(3)} - \max_{j \neq \sigma(3)} a^2_{j\sigma(3)} & a^3_{\sigma(3)\sigma(3)} - \max_{j \neq \sigma(3)} a^3_{j\sigma(3)} \end{bmatrix}. \quad (5)$$

2. For any $i = 1,2,3$, the principal minors of the following matrix are all positive. (When rewritten for intermediate goods, self-provisioning and self-sufficiency is possible).

$$\begin{bmatrix} a_{11}^i - \max_{l \neq 1} a_{l1}^i & a_{21}^i - \max_{l \neq 1} a_{l1}^i & a_{31}^i - \max_{l \neq 1} a_{l1}^i \\ a_{12}^i - \max_{l \neq 2} a_{l2}^i & a_{22}^i - \max_{l \neq 2} a_{l2}^i & a_{32}^i - \max_{l \neq 2} a_{l2}^i \\ a_{13}^i - \max_{l \neq 3} a_{l3}^i & a_{23}^i - \max_{l \neq 3} a_{l3}^i & a_{33}^i - \max_{l \neq 3} a_{l3}^i \end{bmatrix}, \quad (6)$$

3. When rewriting the problem for intermediate goods, there is always demand for all goods as either intermediate goods or final goods.

The following lemma holds for Assumption 1.2.

Lemma 3.

Under Assumption 1.2, if the problem is constructed such that there are absolutely no changes in each country's selection, whether with joint production or intermediate goods, no selection will be made not to produce, and there will be full employment and positive wages.

Therefore, Proposition 1 can be stated as follows:

Proposition 1.

Under Assumption 1, a production point will invariably exist on the basis of efficient one-to-one assignment.

The proof requires nothing more than applying the three conditions of Su's [5] Rental Harmony Theorem. From Lemmas 2 and 3, not only (P2) but also (P1) holds for these types of efficient patterns of specialization wherein each country specializes in a different production process. We know from Lemma 1 that one-to-one assignments exist that are efficient patterns of specialization. It follows from Proposition 1 that we can define primary and secondary products for a production point that exists on the basis of an efficient one-to-one assignment.

This construction can be extended to allow generalization across countries, goods, and production processes. Let us consider a world where we extend the n-country, n-good model as imagined by Jones [12] to permit joint production, and each country has one production process primarily producing one good. In this case, Assumption 1.3 is the same, but Assumptions 1.1 and 1.2 extend as follows.

Assumption 1.1

For any $\sigma \in S_n$, the principal minors of the non-diagonal non-positive matrix created on the basis of production coefficients for the one-to-one assignment involving country i specializing in production process $\sigma(i)$ are uniformly positive.

$$\begin{bmatrix} a^1_{\sigma(1)\sigma(1)} - \max_{j\neq\sigma(1)} a^1_{j\sigma(1)} & a^2_{\sigma(2)\sigma(1)} - \max_{j\neq\sigma(1)} a^2_{j\sigma(1)} & \cdots & a^n_{\sigma(n)\sigma(1)} - \max_{j\neq\sigma(1)} a^n_{j\sigma(1)} \\ a^1_{\sigma(1)\sigma(2)} - \max_{j\neq\sigma(2)} a^1_{j\sigma(2)} & a^2_{\sigma(2)\sigma(2)} - \max_{j\neq\sigma(2)} a^2_{j\sigma(2)} & \cdots & a^n_{\sigma(n)\sigma(2)} - \max_{j\neq\sigma(2)} a^n_{j\sigma(2)} \\ \vdots & \vdots & \ddots & \vdots \\ a^1_{\sigma(1)\sigma(n)} - \max_{j\neq\sigma(n)} a^1_{j\sigma(n)} & a^2_{\sigma(2)\sigma(n)} - \max_{j\neq\sigma(n)} a^2_{j\sigma(n)} & \cdots & a^n_{\sigma(n)\sigma(n)} - \max_{j\neq\sigma(n)} a^n_{j\sigma(n)} \end{bmatrix}. \quad (5)$$

Here $S_n := \{\sigma : \{1,2,\cdots,n\} \to \{1,2,\cdots,n\} | \sigma \text{ is a bijective function}\}$ is an n-th degree permutation set.

Assumption 1.2

For any $i = 1,2,3$, the principal minors of the following matrix are all positive. (When rewritten for intermediate goods, self-provisioning and self-sufficiency is possible).

$$\begin{bmatrix} a^i_{11} - \max_{l\neq 1} a^i_{l1} & a^i_{21} - \max_{l\neq 1} a^i_{l1} & \cdots & a^i_{n1} - \max_{l\neq 1} a^i_{l1} \\ a^i_{12} - \max_{l\neq 2} a^i_{l2} & a^i_{22} - \max_{l\neq 2} a^i_{l2} & \cdots & a^i_{n2} - \max_{l\neq 2} a^i_{l2} \\ \vdots & \vdots & \ddots & \vdots \\ a^i_{1n} - \max_{l\neq n} a^i_{ln} & a^i_{2n} - \max_{l\neq n} a^i_{ln} & \cdots & a^i_{nn} - \max_{l\neq n} a^i_{ln} \end{bmatrix}, \quad (6)$$

This completes our definition of primary and secondary products.

4. Potential for Use of Price Region Diagrams

In this section, we find conditions for using the schema of Amano [1] and Ikema [9], illustrating the relationship between price and specialization, as used in Ogawa [14], for joint production. This schema could be used for all coefficients with no problem in the absence of joint production, but the inclusion of joint production imposes conditions on the relationship between production coefficients for the schema to take appropriate form. We explain the schema following Ogawa [14]. We assume that each activity for each country is as follows.

Example 2.

$$\begin{bmatrix} a^1_{11} \\ a^1_{12} \\ a^1_{13} \end{bmatrix} = \begin{bmatrix} 3 \\ 0 \\ 0 \end{bmatrix}, \quad \begin{bmatrix} a^1_{21} \\ a^1_{22} \\ a^1_{23} \end{bmatrix} = \begin{bmatrix} 0 \\ 1 \\ 0 \end{bmatrix}, \quad \begin{bmatrix} a^1_{31} \\ a^1_{32} \\ a^1_{33} \end{bmatrix} = \begin{bmatrix} 0 \\ 0 \\ 2 \end{bmatrix}. \quad (7)$$

$$\begin{bmatrix} a_{11}^2 \\ a_{12}^2 \\ a_{13}^2 \end{bmatrix} = \begin{bmatrix} 2 \\ 0 \\ 0 \end{bmatrix}, \begin{bmatrix} a_{21}^2 \\ a_{22}^2 \\ a_{23}^2 \end{bmatrix} = \begin{bmatrix} 0 \\ 4 \\ 0 \end{bmatrix}, \begin{bmatrix} a_{31}^2 \\ a_{32}^2 \\ a_{33}^2 \end{bmatrix} = \begin{bmatrix} 0 \\ 0 \\ 1 \end{bmatrix}. \quad (8)$$

$$\begin{bmatrix} a_{11}^3 \\ a_{12}^3 \\ a_{13}^3 \end{bmatrix} = \begin{bmatrix} 2 \\ 1 \\ 0 \end{bmatrix}, \begin{bmatrix} a_{21}^3 \\ a_{22}^3 \\ a_{23}^3 \end{bmatrix} = \begin{bmatrix} 0 \\ 2 \\ 0 \end{bmatrix}, \begin{bmatrix} a_{31}^3 \\ a_{32}^3 \\ a_{33}^3 \end{bmatrix} = \begin{bmatrix} 0 \\ 0 \\ 2 \end{bmatrix}. \quad (9)$$

This example satisfies Assumptions 1.1 and 1.2. To explain on the basis of this example, the schema of Amano [1] and Ikema [9] takes the following form. For each country, find the region of the price system where specializing in a particular production process maximizes that country's production value. The region of the price system where country i specializing in production process j maximizes that country's production value is represented as follows.

$$\{(p_1, p_2, p_3) > 0 \mid a_{j1}^i p_1 + a_{j2}^i p_2 + a_{j3}^i p_3 > a_{k1}^i p_1 + a_{k2}^i p_2 + a_{k3}^i p_3, \text{ for all } k \neq j\}.$$

Considering this condition, the region of the price system where country 1 completely specializing in production process 1 maximizes country 1's production value is the following.

$$\{(p_1, p_2, p_3) > 0 \mid 3p_1 > p_2, 3p_1 > 2p_3\}.$$

This region is labeled the 1st Production Process in Figure 1. Similarly, the regions of the price system where country 1 specializing in 2nd production process and 3rd production process maximizes country 1's production value are labeled, respectively, the 2nd Production Process and the 3rd Production Process in Figure 1.

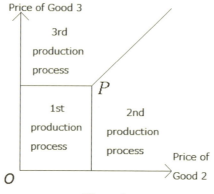

Figure 1

Repeating the exercise for other countries yields Figure 2. In Figure 2, the region of the price system near the origin is the region of specializing in 1st production process, with the regions in the lower right and upper left specializing in 2nd production process and 3rd production process, respectively. Under a pricing system that falls into triangle A in Figure 2, countries 1, 2, and 3 specializing in 1st, 2nd, and 3rd production processes, respectively, maximize each country's gross production value and the grand total, which is gross global production value. The world production points that countries 1, 2, and 3, specializing in 1st, 2nd, and 3rd production processes, respectively, can achieve are therefore on the frontier.

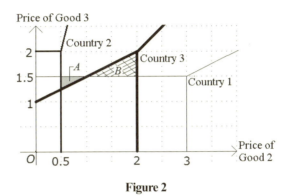

Figure 2

Before we use a figure illustrating prices as coordinates, as in Figure 1, we must review the features of this figure. First, it shows that price regions specializing in the same production process are convex. Now assume that there exist two types of prices, (p_2^A, p_3^A) and (p_2^B, p_3^B), where the marginal productivity measured by price is higher for production process j than for production process k. Including the sign, we can express this condition as

$$\begin{cases} a_{j1}^i + a_{j2}^i p_2^A + a_{j3}^i p_3^A \geq a_{k1}^i + a_{k2}^i p_2^A + a_{k3}^i p_3^A, \\ a_{j1}^i + a_{j2}^i p_2^B + a_{j3}^i p_3^B \geq a_{k1}^i + a_{k2}^i p_2^B + a_{k3}^i p_3^B. \end{cases}$$

Here, for any $0 < t < 1$,

$$a_{j1}^i + a_{j2}^i \{tp_2^A + (1-t)p_2^B\} + a_{j3}^i \{tp_3^A + (1-t)p_3^B\}$$
$$\geq a_{k1}^i + a_{k2}^i \{tp_2^A + (1-t)p_2^B\} + a_{k3}^i \{tp_3^A + (1-t)p_3^B\}$$

is satisfied. It follows that the price region for specializing in the same production process is convex.

Next, (1) is derivable from Assumption 1.1, but using the following from (1)

$$a_{jj}^i > a_{kj}^i, \quad k \neq j$$

allows us to verify the characteristics of the boundary. The boundary shared by the region of country i specializing in 1st production process and 3rd production process is as follows.

$$a_{11}^i + a_{12}^i p_2 + a_{13}^i p_3 = a_{31}^i + a_{32}^i p_2 + a_{33}^i p_3$$
$$\therefore p_3 = \{(a_{12}^i - a_{32}^i)/(a_{33}^i - a_{13}^i)\}p_2 + (a_{11}^i - a_{31}^i)/(a_{33}^i - a_{13}^i)$$

Because $a_{11}^i > a_{31}^i$ and $a_{33}^i > a_{13}^i$, on this boundary when good 2 price $p_2 = 0$, then good 3 price $p_3 > 0$, giving it a positive intercept on the good 3 price axis. A similar analysis demonstrates that on the boundary between the price regions for specializing in 1st production process and 2nd production process, if $p_3 = 0$, then $p_2 > 0$, giving a positive intercept on the good 2 prices axis. By the same token, the boundary between the price regions for specializing in 2nd production process and 3rd production process is

$$a_{21}^i + a_{22}^i p_2 + a_{23}^i p_3 = a_{31}^i + a_{32}^i p_2 + a_{33}^i p_3$$
$$\therefore p_3 = \{(a_{22}^i - a_{32}^i)/(a_{33}^i - a_{23}^i)\}p_2 + (a_{21}^i - a_{31}^i)/(a_{33}^i - a_{23}^i),$$

giving this boundary a positive slope.

In addition, given (1), a price for good 2 much higher than the others yields a specialization in 2nd production process, and a price for good 3 much higher than the others yields a specialization in 3rd production process. In the case that prices for both good 2 and good 3 are very low, the country specializes in 1st production process.

Now, the intersection of the three boundaries of three goods with marginal productivity as measured by value satisfies the following.

$$\begin{cases} a_{11}^i + a_{12}^i p_2 + a_{13}^i p_3 = a_{21}^i + a_{22}^i p_2 + a_{23}^i p_3 \\ a_{11}^i + a_{12}^i p_2 + a_{13}^i p_3 = a_{31}^i + a_{32}^i p_2 + a_{33}^i p_3 \end{cases} \Leftrightarrow \begin{bmatrix} a_{22}^i - a_{12}^i & a_{23}^i - a_{13}^i \\ a_{32}^i - a_{12}^i & a_{33}^i - a_{13}^i \end{bmatrix} \begin{bmatrix} p_2 \\ p_3 \end{bmatrix} = \begin{bmatrix} a_{11}^i - a_{21}^i \\ a_{11}^i - a_{31}^i \end{bmatrix}.$$

If we write this as

$$H := (a_{22}^i - a_{12}^i)(a_{33}^i - a_{13}^i) - (a_{23}^i - a_{13}^i)(a_{32}^i - a_{12}^i),$$

then for consistency with the case of no joint production, $H > 0$ must be satisfied. Using Cramer's rule, this solution may be written as

$$p_2 = \{(a_{11}^i - a_{21}^i)(a_{33}^i - a_{13}^i) - (a_{23}^i - a_{13}^i)(a_{11}^i - a_{31}^i)\}/H,$$
$$p_3 = \{(a_{22}^i - a_{12}^i)(a_{11}^i - a_{31}^i) - (a_{32}^i - a_{12}^i)(a_{11}^i - a_{21}^i)\}/H.$$

Let us consider what determines the sign of this model. We can analyze this condition consistently if this price (point P in Figure 1) is positive, as done by Ikema [9]. The foregoing logic can be summarized in the form of Proposition 2. For this purpose we posit Assumption 2.

Assumption 2.

Assume (10) below.

$$\begin{cases} (a_{22}^i - a_{12}^i)(a_{33}^i - a_{13}^i) > (a_{23}^i - a_{13}^i)(a_{32}^i - a_{12}^i), \\ (a_{11}^i - a_{21}^i)(a_{33}^i - a_{13}^i) > (a_{23}^i - a_{13}^i)(a_{11}^i - a_{31}^i), \\ (a_{22}^i - a_{12}^i)(a_{11}^i - a_{31}^i) > (a_{32}^i - a_{12}^i)(a_{11}^i - a_{21}^i) \end{cases} \quad (10)$$

This assumption holds in the case of no joint production.

Proposition 2.

Given Assumption 2, there exists a pricing system in the first quadrant (point P in Figure 1), where all marginal productivities as measured by value are equal.

Proposition 2 allows us to comfortably use this schema. Given the foregoing logic, the relationship between price and production process specialization can be depicted as in Figure 1. However, Example 1 in Section 2 does not satisfy Assumption 2. Drawing the graph for Example 1, we see, as Figure 3 illustrates, that the pricing system does not fall in the first quadrant.

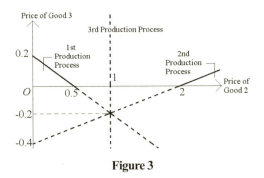

Figure 3

To demonstrate the importance of this schema, let us verify what happens to the correspondence presented by Ogawa [15] in the presence of joint production, specifically its relationship to the efficient facet and frontier from McKenzie [8]. Figure 4 depicts the efficient facet. Ogawa [15] states that the portions corresponding to regions in Figure 2 become production points in Figure 4; thus, we need only to connect the adjacent portions of production points with a line. Points A and B in Figure 1 correspond to regions A and B in Figure 2[9]. On the basis of the shape of Figure 4, we can draw the set of production possibilities in Figure 5. Figure 2 depicts which country specializes in which production process, and Figure 4 depicts an efficient facet of the frontiers. It follows that as with point C in Figure 5, the set of

---

[9] In general, information corresponding to the curve portion would be included in the efficient facet of McKenzie [8], but is not included here because this diagram was derived from the schema of Ikema [9] and can be easily derived by viewing his diagram. Note that this approach cannot reproduce length.

world production possibilities, Figure 4 does not include the point achieved on only the basis of free disposal.

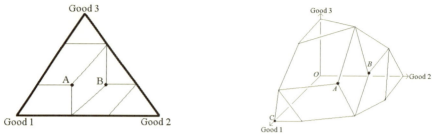

Figure 4 **Figure 5**

The remaining concern is the relationship between Assumptions 1.2 and 2. If Assumption 2 is satisfied when we postulate Assumption 1.2, which would ideally be desirable to extend to general dimensions, then there is no need to state Assumption 2. Regarding this point, Proposition 3 holds.

Proposition 3.

If Assumption 1.2 holds, then Assumption 2 is satisfied.

We provide the proof in two stages as follows.

Proof: We separate (10) into equations (11), (12), and (13) below. We first show (11), and then extend that approach to show (12) and (13).

$$(a_{22}^i - a_{12}^i)(a_{33}^i - a_{13}^i) > (a_{23}^i - a_{13}^i)(a_{32}^i - a_{12}^i), \qquad (11)$$

$$(a_{11}^i - a_{21}^i)(a_{33}^i - a_{13}^i) > (a_{23}^i - a_{13}^i)(a_{11}^i - a_{31}^i), \qquad (12)$$

$$(a_{22}^i - a_{12}^i)(a_{11}^i - a_{31}^i) > (a_{32}^i - a_{12}^i)(a_{11}^i - a_{21}^i). \qquad (13)$$

We assume that the principal minors of (6) are all positive. By the Hawkins–Simon theorem, the leading principal minors and the principal minors are all positive.

Stage 1 We show (11). From the foregoing assumptions,

$$\det \begin{bmatrix} a_{22}^i - \max_{l \neq 2} a_{l2}^i & a_{32}^i - \max_{l \neq 2} a_{l2}^i \\ a_{23}^i - \max_{l \neq 3} a_{l3}^i & a_{33}^i - \max_{l \neq 3} a_{l3}^i \end{bmatrix} \qquad (14)$$
$$= \left(a_{22}^i - \max_{l \neq 2} a_{l2}^i\right)\left(a_{33}^i - \max_{l \neq 3} a_{l3}^i\right) - \left(a_{32}^i - \max_{l \neq 2} a_{l2}^i\right)\left(a_{23}^i - \max_{l \neq 3} a_{l3}^i\right) > 0$$

is satisfied. This condition can be separated into four cases depending on the values of $\max_{l \neq 2} a^i_{l2}$ and $\max_{l \neq 3} a^i_{l3}$.

Case 1: When $\max_{l \neq 2} a^i_{l2} = a^i_{12}$, $\max_{l \neq 3} a^i_{l3} = a^i_{13}$, (11) is immediately satisfied by (14).

Case 2: When $\max_{l \neq 2} a^i_{l2} = a^i_{32}$, $\max_{l \neq 3} a^i_{l3} = a^i_{13}$, first $a^i_{32} \geq a^i_{12}$ is satisfied. Then, from (1) we have

$$(a^i_{22} - a^i_{12})(a^i_{33} - a^i_{13}) - (a^i_{23} - a^i_{13})(a^i_{32} - a^i_{12}) = \det\begin{bmatrix} a^i_{22} - a^i_{12} & a^i_{32} - a^i_{12} \\ a^i_{23} - a^i_{13} & a^i_{33} - a^i_{13} \end{bmatrix}$$

$$= \det\begin{bmatrix} (a^i_{22} - a^i_{32}) + (a^i_{32} - a^i_{12}) & 0 + (a^i_{32} - a^i_{12}) \\ a^i_{23} - a^i_{13} & a^i_{33} - a^i_{13} \end{bmatrix}$$

$$= \det\begin{bmatrix} a^i_{22} - a^i_{32} & 0 \\ a^i_{23} - a^i_{13} & a^i_{33} - a^i_{13} \end{bmatrix} + (a^i_{32} - a^i_{12})\det\begin{bmatrix} 1 & 1 \\ a^i_{23} - a^i_{13} & a^i_{33} - a^i_{13} \end{bmatrix}$$

$$= \det\begin{bmatrix} a^i_{22} - \max_{l \neq 2} a^i_{l2} & a^i_{32} - \max_{l \neq 2} a^i_{l2} \\ a^i_{23} - \max_{l \neq 3} a^i_{l3} & a^i_{33} - \max_{l \neq 3} a^i_{l3} \end{bmatrix} + (a^i_{32} - a^i_{12})(a^i_{33} - a^i_{23}) > 0,$$

and (11) is satisfied.

Case 3: When $\max_{l \neq 2} a^i_{l2} = a^i_{12}$, $\max_{l \neq 3} a^i_{l3} = a^i_{23}$, first $a^i_{23} \geq a^i_{13}$ is satisfied. Similarly, from (1) we have

$$(a^i_{22} - a^i_{12})(a^i_{33} - a^i_{13}) - (a^i_{23} - a^i_{13})(a^i_{32} - a^i_{12}) = \det\begin{bmatrix} a^i_{22} - a^i_{12} & a^i_{32} - a^i_{12} \\ a^i_{23} - a^i_{13} & a^i_{33} - a^i_{13} \end{bmatrix}$$

$$= \det\begin{bmatrix} a^i_{22} - a^i_{12} & a^i_{32} - a^i_{12} \\ 0 + (a^i_{23} - a^i_{13}) & (a^i_{33} - a^i_{23}) + (a^i_{23} - a^i_{13}) \end{bmatrix}$$

$$= \det\begin{bmatrix} a^i_{22} - a^i_{12} & a^i_{32} - a^i_{12} \\ 0 & a^i_{33} - a^i_{23} \end{bmatrix} + (a^i_{23} - a^i_{13})\det\begin{bmatrix} a^i_{22} - a^i_{12} & a^i_{32} - a^i_{12} \\ 1 & 1 \end{bmatrix}$$

$$= \det\begin{bmatrix} a^i_{22} - \max_{l \neq 2} a^i_{l2} & a^i_{32} - \max_{l \neq 2} a^i_{l2} \\ a^i_{23} - \max_{l \neq 3} a^i_{l3} & a^i_{33} - \max_{l \neq 3} a^i_{l3} \end{bmatrix} + (a^i_{23} - a^i_{13})(a^i_{22} - a^i_{32}) > 0,$$

and (11) is satisfied.

Case 4: When $\max_{l \neq 2} a^i_{l2} = a^i_{32} (\geq a^i_{12})$, $\max_{l \neq 3} a^i_{l3} = a^i_{23} (\geq a^i_{13})$. Similarly, from (1) we have

$$(a_{22}^i - a_{12}^i)(a_{33}^i - a_{13}^i) - (a_{23}^i - a_{13}^i)(a_{32}^i - a_{12}^i) = \det\begin{bmatrix} a_{22}^i - a_{12}^i & a_{32}^i - a_{12}^i \\ a_{23}^i - a_{13}^i & a_{33}^i - a_{13}^i \end{bmatrix}$$

$$= \det\begin{bmatrix} a_{22}^i - a_{12}^i & a_{32}^i - a_{12}^i \\ 0 + (a_{23}^i - a_{13}^i) & (a_{33}^i - a_{23}^i) + (a_{23}^i - a_{13}^i) \end{bmatrix}$$

$$= \det\begin{bmatrix} a_{22}^i - a_{12}^i & a_{32}^i - a_{12}^i \\ 0 & a_{33}^i - a_{23}^i \end{bmatrix} + (a_{23}^i - a_{13}^i)\det\begin{bmatrix} a_{22}^i - a_{12}^i & a_{32}^i - a_{12}^i \\ 1 & 1 \end{bmatrix}$$

$$= \det\begin{bmatrix} (a_{22}^i - a_{32}^i) + (a_{32}^i - a_{12}^i) & 0 + (a_{32}^i - a_{12}^i) \\ a_{23}^i - a_{23}^i & a_{33}^i - a_{23}^i \end{bmatrix} + (a_{23}^i - a_{13}^i)(a_{22}^i - a_{32}^i)$$

$$= \det\begin{bmatrix} a_{22}^i - a_{32}^i & 0 \\ a_{23}^i - a_{23}^i & a_{33}^i - a_{23}^i \end{bmatrix} + (a_{32}^i - a_{12}^i)\det\begin{bmatrix} 1 & 1 \\ a_{23}^i - a_{23}^i & a_{33}^i - a_{23}^i \end{bmatrix} + (a_{23}^i - a_{13}^i)(a_{22}^i - a_{32}^i)$$

$$= \det\begin{bmatrix} a_{22}^i - \max_{l \neq 2} a_{l2}^i & a_{32}^i - \max_{l \neq 2} a_{l2}^i \\ a_{23}^i - \max_{l \neq 3} a_{l3}^i & a_{33}^i - \max_{l \neq 3} a_{l3}^i \end{bmatrix} + (a_{32}^i - a_{12}^i)(a_{33}^i - a_{23}^i) + (a_{23}^i - a_{13}^i)(a_{22}^i - a_{32}^i) > 0,$$

and 11 is satisfied. This concludes the demonstration that (11) is satisfied.

Stage 2 We show (12) and (13). Using each determinant,

$$(a_{11}^i - a_{21}^i)(a_{33}^i - a_{13}^i) - (a_{23}^i - a_{13}^i)(a_{11}^i - a_{31}^i) = \det\begin{bmatrix} a_{11}^i - a_{21}^i & a_{31}^i - a_{11}^i \\ a_{13}^i - a_{23}^i & a_{33}^i - a_{13}^i \end{bmatrix} = \det\begin{bmatrix} a_{11}^i - a_{21}^i & a_{31}^i - a_{21}^i \\ a_{13}^i - a_{23}^i & a_{33}^i - a_{23}^i \end{bmatrix},$$

(15)

$$(a_{22}^i - a_{12}^i)(a_{11}^i - a_{31}^i) - (a_{32}^i - a_{12}^i)(a_{11}^i - a_{21}^i) = \det\begin{bmatrix} a_{11}^i - a_{31}^i & a_{21}^i - a_{11}^i \\ a_{12}^i - a_{32}^i & a_{22}^i - a_{12}^i \end{bmatrix} = \det\begin{bmatrix} a_{11}^i - a_{31}^i & a_{21}^i - a_{31}^i \\ a_{12}^i - a_{32}^i & a_{22}^i - a_{32}^i \end{bmatrix},$$

(16)

are satisfied. Now as with (14), from the assumption made earlier

$$\det\begin{bmatrix} a_{11}^i - \max_{l \neq 1} a_{l1}^i & a_{31}^i - \max_{l \neq 1} a_{l1}^i \\ a_{13}^i - \max_{l \neq 3} a_{l3}^i & a_{33}^i - \max_{l \neq 3} a_{l3}^i \end{bmatrix}$$
$$= (a_{11}^i - \max_{l \neq 1} a_{l1}^i)(a_{33}^i - \max_{l \neq 3} a_{l3}^i) - (a_{31}^i - \max_{l \neq 1} a_{l1}^i)(a_{13}^i - \max_{l \neq 3} a_{l3}^i) > 0,$$

(17)

$$\det\begin{bmatrix} a_{11}^i - \max_{l \neq 1} a_{l1}^i & a_{21}^i - \max_{l \neq 1} a_{l1}^i \\ a_{12}^i - \max_{l \neq 2} a_{l2}^i & a_{22}^i - \max_{l \neq 2} a_{l2}^i \end{bmatrix}$$
$$= (a_{11}^i - \max_{l \neq 1} a_{l1}^i)(a_{22}^i - \max_{l \neq 2} a_{l2}^i) - (a_{21}^i - \max_{l \neq 1} a_{l1}^i)(a_{12}^i - \max_{l \neq 2} a_{l2}^i) > 0$$

(18)

are satisfied. Separating this condition into four cases as in the first stage and doing the math, we see that (12) is satisfied by (15) and (17), and (13) by (16) and (18). This concludes the proof that (12) and (13) hold.

From the foregoing logic, (11), (12), and (13) all hold; thus, Assumption 2 is satisfied. **Q.E.D.**

From Proposition 3, we deduce that the only meaningfully necessary condition is Assumption 1. In situations where secondary products can be defined on the basis of Assumption 1, we deduce that the price, at which the value-marginal productivities for each production process are equal, falls in the first quadrant.

5. Principle of Multiple Efficient Patterns of Specialization

Let us now consider the impact of including joint production on our schema. To find the impact in the case of two countries or more, we first examine the two-country case. Ogawa [15] argues that in the absence of joint production, depending on the location of point P in Figure 1, three lines are completely defined. The lines extending leftward never intersect, which is also the case for those extending downward and right upward. Shiozawa [19] and Ogawa [15] assert that the correspondence between the price schema in Amano [1] and frontiers is as follows. Because each country specializes in the region of the schema for each price, the production point becomes an extreme point on the frontier. When regions in the price schema meet at a line, there is one degree of freedom in the price that maximizes both extreme points in gross production value; therefore, the polygonal line connecting the two extreme points appears on the frontier. When regions in the pricing scheme meet at a point, it in practice determines one price that maximizes both extreme points in gross production value. Therefore, both extreme points appear on the frontier as a vertex of the same surface, but the polygonal line connecting the two extreme points does not appear on the frontier. When regions in the pricing scheme do not meet, there exists no price that maximizes both extreme points in gross production value. Thus, there exists a polygonal line between the two extreme points that partitions the frontier.

Because the inclusion of joint production moves the price boundary, the lines extending leftward, may intersect, as is the case for those extending downward and rightward. To examine this in greater detail, consider the correspondence between the price schema mediated by the frontier efficient facet of McKenzie [8] and the frontier. Leaving the details of the approach to Ogawa [15], we now examine what happens when the lines extending downward intersect.

First, Figure 6 depicts a pricing diagram for the two-country, three-good model without joint production. Each country's technology and pricing boundaries are different as represented by the thick and thin lines. Figure 7 depicts a McKenzie [8] efficient facet corresponding to Figure 6. The extreme points corresponding to the regions in the pricing diagram are identified by the same letters. Figure 8 depicts the overall shape of the frontier corresponding to Figure 7, although the precise shape varies depending on the labor endowment.

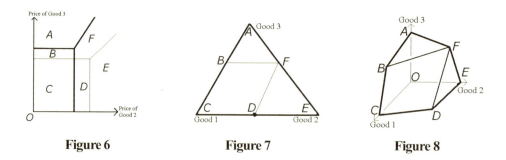

Figure 6 **Figure 7** **Figure 8**

With joint production the slope and intercept of the lines in the pricing diagram may change. Figure 9 depicts a case where under the influence of joint production the situation in Figure 6 changes so that the lines extending downward intersect. The D portion of Figure 6 is separated into *a* and *b* in Figure 9. The thick line represents country 1 and the thin line country 2. In area a, country 1's specialization is in 2nd production process, and country 2's is in 1st production process. In area b, country 1 swaps to specializing in 1st production process and country 2 to specializing in 2nd production process. To move beyond the point at which the price curves intersect in this fashion is to swap the good in which each of the two countries specializes. Figure 10 depicts the McKenzie [8] efficient facet corresponding to Figure 9. The extreme points corresponding to the regions in the pricing figure are indicated with the same letter. Point *a* in Figure 10 does not exist in Figure 7. With the inclusion of joint production, an extreme point in the case of no joint production may separate into two as it does here. As we illustrated the overall frontier shape of Figure 7 in Figure 8, Figure 11 illustrates the overall frontier shape corresponding to Figure 10[10]. The two separated extreme points are on the same plane on the frontier, but no polygonal line on the frontier connects the two extreme points. As with point D in Figure 8 and points *a* and *b* in Figure 9, we shall call the two extreme points separated by the intersection of the corresponding price curves "separated extreme points (on the frontier)." In general, we summarize the preceding discussion in the form of Lemma 3.

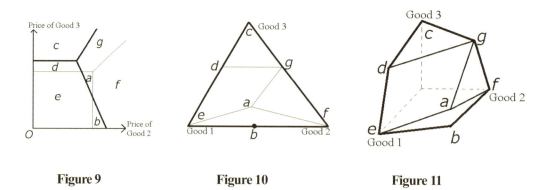

Figure 9 **Figure 10** **Figure 11**

---

[10] Here, the portion shown as a dotted line is not necessarily an axis. We also omit the free disposal portion.

Lemma 3.

With joint production, the price boundary lines at which each country specializes in the same good may intersect. In this case, the price regions separated by the intersection meet at the same points, and the corresponding separated extreme points exists as a vertex on the same plane on the frontier, although no polygonal line on the frontier connects the two extreme points.

The proof follows from the preceding general discussion and is thus omitted. Because two straight lines on the same plane with different slopes intersect at one point, two separated regions meet at only one point between vertical angles. At a price at which the separated extreme points yield the same world output, it is necessary that even if two countries change their production, world output does not change, imposing two conditions on price. Considering the zero-degree homogeneity of price, these two conditions define a single price. For this reason, two extreme points exist on the frontier on the same plane, with no polygonal line on the frontier connecting them.

Using this lemma, we obtain Proposition 4.

Proposition 4.

Consider a two-country, three-good model. For the pricing system (point P), at which one country's value marginal productivities are all identical, let the other country specialize in a production process. In this case, no more than 48 patterns of specialization shapes appear on the price plane.

We observe from Proposition 4 that we can exhaustively draw all 48 shapes (See Appendix). This concludes our reconsideration of the two-country, three-good case to serve as a benchmark for a series of studies.

6. Conclusion

This study analyzed efficient specialization patterns in a three-good Ricardian model with joint production. In a world of joint production, we cannot necessarily distinguish between primary and secondary products. To the extent, however, that "secondary product" is a term commonly used in relationship to joint production, analyzing joint production ideally requires precisely defining the term. In certain cases, however, no production point for an efficient one-to-one assignment exists on the frontier, even if our definition uses the principal diagonal matrices that regularly appear in this field. This study presents a definition for primary and secondary products where a production point for an efficient one-to-one assignment exists by applying the existence criteria for the intermediate goods case. It is impossible to separate primary and secondary products without a precise definition.

Furthermore, unlike the Ikema [9] model, with joint production we cannot indiscriminately use the relationship schema between price and specialization; using it requires the imposition of certain conditions. This study defines these conditions. If the conditions are not met, we obtain unusual results from trying to construct the schema as usual. Regions that should be convex sets may lose their convexity, or no price system, for which the value marginal productivity for all production processes is equal, may exist in the first quadrant. The constraints on how to use such schema have not been closely examined to date for either intermediate goods or joint production.

This study also exhaustively drew all 48 shapes in the two-country, three-good model. In the three-country, three-good model, however, the analysis with scheme is not completed because the classification is complex, considering that 48 shapes exist in the two-country, three-good model. The study presents all 48 shapes in the two-country, three-good model for analysis with schema in the three-country, three-good model.

Acknowledgement

The author gratefully acknowledges Makoto Tawada. This paper was presented in the Japan Society of International Economics (JSIE) Kansai (Kwansei Gakuin University); Research Center in Mathematical Economics (RSME) Kinki (Osaka University); the Japan Society for Mathematical Economics (JSME) (Keio University); and NIESG(Nagoya International Economics Study Group)-IDE/JETRO Joint Workshop in Bangkok (Grande Centre Point Hotel Ratchadamri). The author thanks various members for their useful comments and advice; in particular, Keisaku Higashida (JSIE, Kansai), Jun Iritani (RCME, Kinki), Ken Urai (RCME, Kinki), Toru Maruyama (JSME), and Toshihiro Ichida (NIESG-IDE/JETRO Joint Workshop). This work was supported by JSPS KAKENHI Grant-in-Aid for Young Scientists (B) Number 24730206. The author thanks Crimson Interactive Pvt. Ltd. (Ulatus and Enago) for their assistance in manuscript translation and editing. All remaining errors are the author's.

References

[1] A. Amano, Intermediate goods and the theory of comparative advantage: A two-country, three-commodity case, *Weltwirtschaftliches Archiv*. 96 (1966) 340–345.

[2] A.V. Deardorff, Ricardian Comparative Advantage with Intermediate Inputs, *North Am. J. Econ. Fin.*, 16 (2005a) 16-34.

[3] A.V. Deardorff, How Robust is Comparative Advantage?, *Rev. Int. Econ.* 13 (2005b) 1004-1016.

[4] D. Hawkins and H. A. Simon, Some conditions of macroeconomic stability, *Econometrica*. 17 (1949) 245–248.

[5] F. E. Su, Rental harmony: Sperner's lemma in fair division, *Am. Math. Mon*. 106, (1999) 930–942.

[6] K. Higashida, Intermediate goods and international production specialization patterns: A multi-country multi-good model, *Kokusai Boeki Riron no Tenkai (Development of International Trade Theory)*, 17 (2005) 289–302 [in Japanese].

[7] K. Kainou, Description of the General Energy Statistics, RIETI, (2012) [in Japanese], available at http://www.rieti.go.jp/users/kainou-kazunari/download/index.html, accessed on April 21st, 2013.

[8] L. W. McKenzie, Specialization and efficiency in world production" *Rev. Econ. Stud.* 21 (1954) 165–180.

[9] M. Ikema, Establishing international production patterns of specialization, *Hitotsubashi Ronso*, 110 (1993) 873–894 [in Japanese].

[10] OECD, "Multifunctionality towards an Analytical Framework", OECD, (2001), available at http://www.oecd.org/dataoecd/43/31/1894469.pdf, accessed on April 21st, 2013.

[11] R.W. Cottle, J.-S. Pang, and R.E. Stone, The Linear Complementarity Problem, Siam, (1992).

[12] R. W. Jones, Comparative advantage and the theory of tariffs: A multi-country, multi-commodity model, *Rev. Econ. Stud.* 28 (1961) 161–75.

[13] T.C. Koopmans, Analysis of Production as an Efficient Combination of Activities, Activity Analysis of Production and Allocation (edited by T. C. Koopmans). New York: John Wiley & Sons, Inc., (1951) 33-97.

[14] T. Ogawa, Analysis of patterns of specialization in the Ricardo model with joint production, *Studies in Regional Sciences*. 41 (2011) 331–344 [in Japanese].

[15] T. Ogawa, Classification of the frontier in the three-country, three-good Ricardian model, *Economics Bulletin*, 32 (2012a) 639–647.

[16] T. Ogawa, A consideration of exporting by-products and in a pure exchange economy, *Keizai Kagaku Kenkyu* (Hiroshima Shudo University), 16 (2012b) 27–42 [in Japanese].

[17] T. Ogawa, Application of Jones' inequality to the n-country, m-good Ricardo–Graham model, *Economics Bulletin*. 33 (2013) 379–387.

[18] W.W. Chang, W.J. Ethier, and M.C. Kemp, The theorem of international trade with joint production, *J. Int. Econ.*, 10 (1980) 377-394.

[19] Y. Shiozawa, A new construction of Ricardian trade theory—A many-country, many-commodity case with intermediate goods and choice of production techniques—, *Evolutionary and Institutional Economics Review*. 3 (2007) 141–187.

[20] Y. Uekawa, Some theorem of trade with joint production, *J. Int. Econ.*, 16 (1984) 319-333.

Appendix: Proposition 3 in Section 5

In the actual two-country, three-good model with joint production, when depicting the possible prices and specializations, we obtain the following 48 illustrations without a tie occurring. The sharp lines denote Country 1, and the wide lines Country 2. In the illustrations, each area of specialization patterns is a convex set, with a positive result for each factor of the price under which the marginal value productivity of each production process is equal.

Group A: When the price under which the marginal value productivity of each production process is equal in the second country, the first country specializes in the first production process.

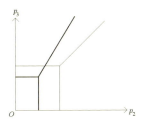

Figure A1

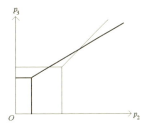

Figure A2

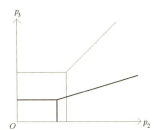

Figure A3

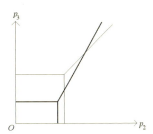

Figure A4

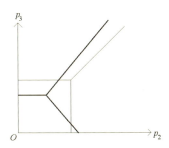

Figure A5

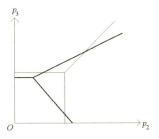

Figure A6

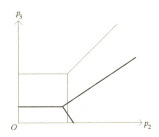

Figure A7

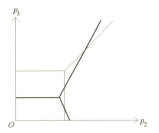

Figure A8

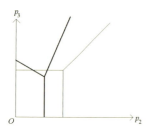

Figure A9

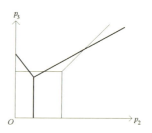

Figure A10

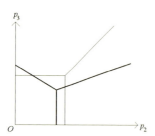

Figure A11

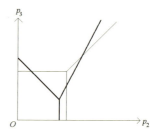

Figure A12

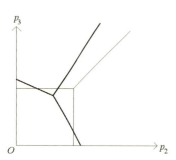

Figure A13

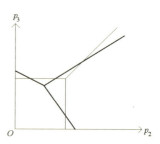

Figure A14

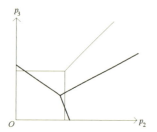

Figure A15

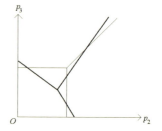

Figure A16

Group B: When the price under which the marginal value productivity of each production process is equal in the second country, the first country specializes in the second production process.

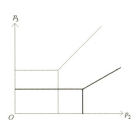

Figure B1

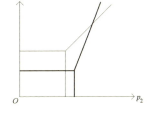

Figure B2

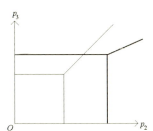

Figure B3

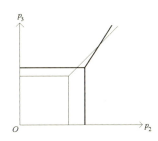

Figure B4

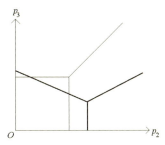

Figure B5

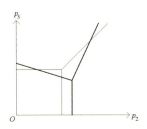

Figure B6

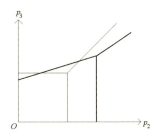

Figure B7

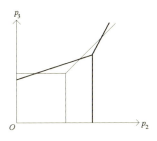

Figure B8

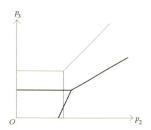

Figure B9

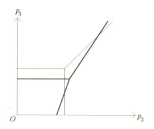

Figure B10

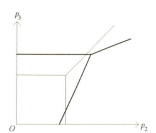

Figure B11

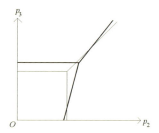

Figure B12

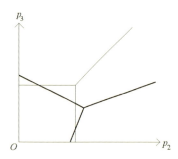

Figure B13

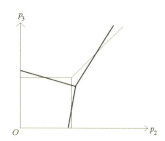

Figure B14

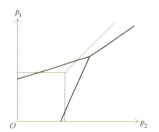

Figure B15

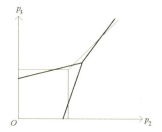

Figure B16

Group C: When the price under which marginal value productivity for each production process is equal in the second country, the first country specializes in the third production process.

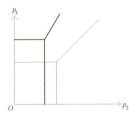

Figure C1

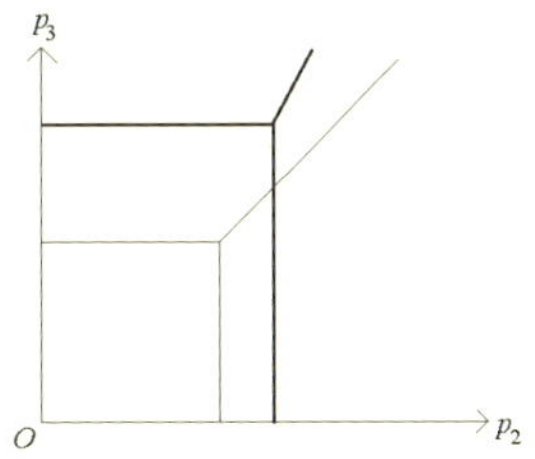

Figure C2

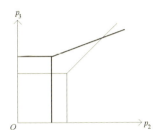

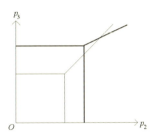

Figure C3

Figure C4

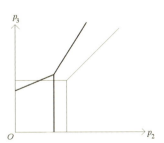

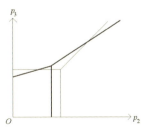

Figure C5

Figure C6

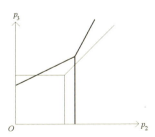

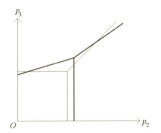

Figure C7

Figure C8

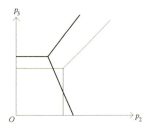

Figure C9

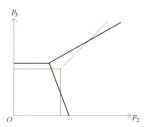

Figure C10

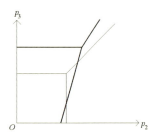

Figure C11

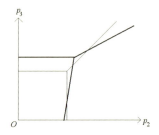

Figure C12

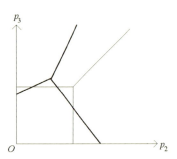

Figure C13

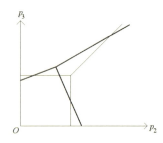

Figure C14

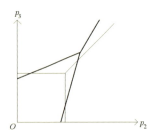

Figure C15

Figure C16

Chapter 3

An Application of Cellular Automata to the Oligopolistic Market

Kouhei Iyori
Faculty of Economic Sciences, Hiroshima Shudo University
1-1 Ozuka-Higashi 1-chome, Asaminami-ku, Hiroshima, JAPAN 731-3195

Abstract

This paper describes a cellular automata model of an oligopolistic market with network externality. When consumers buy a product, they sometimes take their neighbors' choices into consideration. We introduce the effect of consumer decisions into a market model and perform computer simulations under various conditions. The results of simulations show that (1) the final state of the market can be classified into four cases; (2) as neighborhood size increases, the rate of the case where products share the market decreases; and (3) the market requires long periods to reach the final state for a certain neighborhood range.

Key Words:
Cellular automata, Network externality, Oligopolistic market, Computer simulations

1. Introduction

When you buy products, e.g., clothes or digital devices, you may take your neighbors' choices into consideration. Even if you like a product, you may hesitate to purchase it when many of your friends or colleagues use another similar product. However, if your neighbors buy the same products, you may be encouraged to purchase those products as well. In an oligopolistic market, the effect of others' choices (network externality) plays an important role in the diffusion process of products.

We have introduced the effect of consumer choice into a market model using cellular automata [1][5] that consist of regular cells whose states are determined based on their neighbors' states. Each cell represents a consumer, and the state of the cell represents a product that is being used by that consumer. A cell can recognize the states of its neighbors, i.e., other cells located within a particular distance from the cell. The distance represents not only physical distance between consumers but also closeness of a friendship or their interest. They determine their product choices according to their neighbors' states and the cost of the product. If many people use a particular product in a consumer's neighborhood, the consumer is more likely to choose that product.

Our former research [2][3][4] has shown that the cellular automata model generates rich market dynamics. In these studies, we performed simulations with consumer learning, network externality, and costs that change locally, where the neighborhood range is fixed. In this paper, we simplify the model using only network externality and focus on neighborhood size, because the spread of Internet and development of network communities bring expansion of neighborhood and the influence of network externality.

2. Market Model

Assume a closed market with two types of products, wherein consumers buy a new product regularly. Consumers can continue to use the same products they have used or they can change products. A consumer is represented as a cell in a two-dimensional plane. The market model is defined as follows:

[1] There are M^2 consumers in a closed society. There are two types of products in the market, and each consumer can decide whether to purchase only a single product. Each product has an expiry date; therefore, a consumer must buy a new product or buy the same product again at determined periods. A consumer can use only one product in a given period, i.e., two products cannot be used simultaneously.

We designate consumer choice X at period t as follows:

$$\begin{cases} X(m,n,t) = 1 & \text{(if consumer } m \text{ uses product } n \text{ at period } t) \\ X(m,n,t) = 0 & \text{(if consumer } m \text{ does not use a product at period } t) \end{cases} \quad (1)$$

where m is the number of the consumer ($m = (m_1, m_2)$, $1 \leq m_1 \leq M$ and $1 \leq m_2 \leq M$), and n represents the product number ($n = 1$ or 2).

[2] The utility consumer m obtains at period t is as follows:

$$U(m,t) = \max_{n \in (1,2)} X(m,n,t) U(m,n,t) \quad (2)$$

where $U(m,n,t)$ represents consumer m's utility obtained using product n.

$$U(m,n,t) = U_{min} + (U_{max} - U_{min})N(m,n,t) \quad (3)$$

Here, U_{min} and U_{max} are given constants ($0 < U_{min} < U_{max}$). U_{min} represents the basic utility a consumer can obtain from using product n.

[3] The second term in Eq. (3) represents the effect of network externality, which is determined as follows:

$$N(m,n,t) = \frac{\sum_{i \in \Omega(m)} X(i,n,t)}{|\Omega(m)|} \quad (4)$$

Here, $\Omega(m)$ represents the set of consumer m's neighbors, which is expressed as follows:

$$\Omega(m) = \{\text{Consumer } i \mid \text{dis}(i,m) \leq R\} \quad (5)$$

where R is a given constant ($1 < R$), $\text{dis}(i, m)$ is the distance between consumer i and m in the plane, and $|\Omega(m)|$ is the number of consumers within distance R from consumer m. We refer to these consumers as consumer m's "neighbors." In our market model, we assume that neighbors are not those who live in a neighborhood but are those who share the same interest, and they frequently exchange information about products. A consumer does not care about the choices of consumers that are outside of their neighborhood, i.e., a consumer's choice is affected by a local collection of information rather than global information.

[4] The consumer cost of using a product is given as follows:

$$C(m,t) = X(m,n,t)P_1 + X(m,n,t)P_2 \quad (6)$$

where P_n represents the cost of using product n. In this paper, we assume cost is a constant.

[5] At time t, consumer m calculates the following;

$$V(m,n,t) = U(m,t) - C(m,t) \quad (7)$$

for each product, chooses a product that maximizes $V(m,n,t)$, or does not purchase either product when $\max(V(m,n,t)) < 0$. If two products give the same positive value, the consumer chooses one product randomly.

3. Simulations

Here, we show some results of computer simulations for the following parameter values: $M = 100$, $U_{min} = 0.2$, $U_{max} = 1.0$ for all consumers and products, and $P_1 = P_2 = 0.25$. We examine various values of R (neighborhood range), i.e., $R = 1, 2, 3, 4, 5$, and 20. The market is represented as a two-dimensional panel, and each edge of the panel is virtually connected with the edge on the opposite side (i.e., a torus).

The initial users of products 1 and 2 are located randomly in the market, and we define the number of initial users of product n as $I_n(0)$. In the following figures, the black cells represent the users of product 1, the gray cells represent the users of product 2, and the white cells represent consumers who use neither product.

3.1 Typical Cases of Final States

Here, we show typical samples of the final states of simulations. We can classify the final states of the market into four cases according to the number of users that use a given product.

Case 1: Product 1 monopolizes the market

Figure 1 shows the simulation results for $R = 4$, $I_1(0) = 700$, and $I_2(0) = 500$. The entire market is represented as a square, and there are 10,000 cells (consumers) in the market. The leftmost image in Figure 1 is the initial state of the market, and the rightmost image is the final state. The two middle figures show the progress of the simulation. In this case, the number of users of products 1 and 2 gradually increased initially; however, the users of the latter product decreased and eventually disappeared. As can be seen, the market becomes monopolized by product 1.

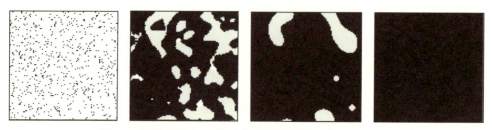

Figure 1. Case 1–product 1 monopolizes the market

Case 2: Product 2 monopolizes the market

Figure 2 shows the results for $R = 4$, $I_1(0) = 500$, and $I_2(0) = 700$. In contrast to Case 1, product 2 monopolizes the market in this case. This reversal of the final state results from very small differences in the initial states, e.g., when $I_1(0) = 525$ and $I_2(0) = 500$, product 1 monopolizes the market; however, when $I_1(0) = 500$ and $I_2(0) = 525$, product 2 monopolizes the market. The difference between these two cases is 50 users, i.e., only 0.5% of all consumers.

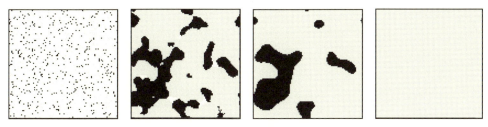

Figure 2. Case 2–product 2 monopolizes the market

Case 3: Two products share the market

Figure 3 shows the results for $R = 4$, $I_1(0) = 500$, and $I_2(0) = 500$. When the difference between the initial users of the two products is sufficiently small, both products 1 and 2 can obtain sufficient users to survive in the market. In addition, users of each product create large clusters with consumers who use the same product, and no consumer changes their product in the long run; i.e., two products share the market in Case 3.

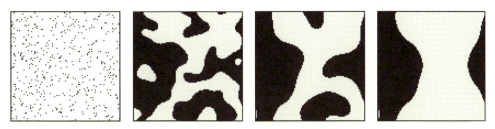

Figure 3. Case 3–two products share the market

Case 4: No product survives in the market

Figure 4 shows the results for $R = 4$, $I_1(0) = 80$, and $I_2(0) = 80$. If both products cannot obtain sufficient users in the initial state, they lose users immediately, and no product survives in the market. In our simulations, it is difficult to survive if the number of initial users is less than approximately 100 (1% of all consumers) when initial users are located randomly.

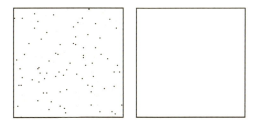

Figure 4. Case 4–no product survives in the market

The final state of the market depends on both the number of initial users and the neighborhood range R. When R is small, a consumer recognizes only a small local area. Therefore, if the users of one product make a small group in the market, they can obtain sufficient utility to continue using the same product from network externality. However, if R is large, consumers see a wide area around them, and their utilities are defined by the results of many consumer choices. Then, consumer choices will be common to many consumers, and the final state of the market will converge to large clusters. We examine the effects of neighborhood size in the next section.

3.2 Results with Various R

In a market with network externality, the number of neighbors affects the diffusion process of products and the final state of the market. When consumers recognize a small area as their neighborhood, one product may not require many users to survive in the market; however, if they can see a wide area of the market, it is difficult for a product that has fewer users than the other product to survive. In this section, we examine various ranges for the neighborhood R, as well as the effects of the number of neighbors over time.

Case 3 (R = 1, 2, 3, and 20)

Here, we focus on Case 3 with various neighborhood ranges because the final states in Case 0, 1, and 2 are common. Figure 5 shows the simulation results for $I_1(0) = 500$, $I_2(0) = 500$, and $R = 1, 2, 3$, and 20 (results for $R = 4$ are shown in Figure 3). The initial number of users and their locations are equal for all conditions; however, the final distributions differ significantly. These markets converge to Case 3; however, when R is small, users of the same product form small clusters in the market. As R becomes larger, the cluster grows larger and rectilinearly. For $R = 1$, we observe many small clusters; however, there are only two clusters for $R = 3$ and $R = 20$. For $R = 20$, the cluster resembles a rectangle.

The diffusion process of products for $R = 20$ is also noteworthy. In this case, many of the initial users stop using products at least once because they do not have sufficient users in their neighborhood; however, they do finally choose a product. When R is large, it is difficult to obtain sufficient users in the wide area initially. However, once consumers who use a product form a cluster in the market, they can diffuse rapidly and widely.

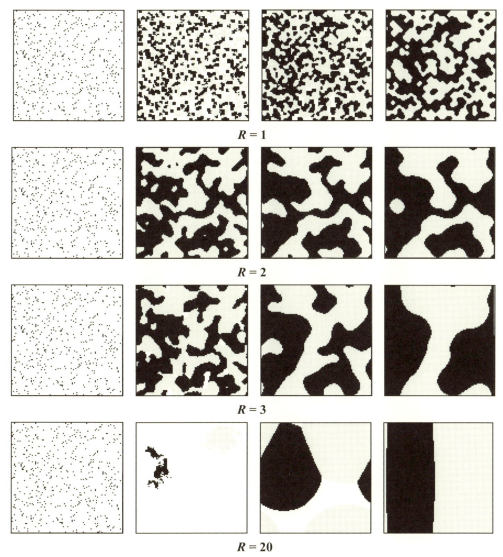

Figure 5. Case 3 ($R = 1, 2, 3,$ and 20)

Initial users and final states

Here, we examine the relationship between the initial number of users and the final state of the market for various R values. Figures 6–10 show the final states of the market with various initial conditions where $R = 1, 2, 3, 4,$ and 20. As can be seen in Figure 6, most combinations of initial users lead to Case 3 when the neighborhood range is small. This indicates that, if a consumer recognizes a small area as their neighborhood, both products are more likely to survive in the market. However, from Figures 7 to 9, it can be seen that the rate of Case 3 rapidly decreases if R becomes large. When the neighborhood is large, consumers often form large clusters with users of the same product, and these clusters sometimes surround smaller clusters of the other products' users. Therefore, it is difficult for both products to survive to the final market state when R is large. When R is greater than 4, the rate of Case 3 is mostly stable at approximately 5% (Figure 11).

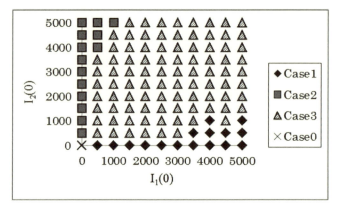

Figure 6. Final market state ($R = 1$)

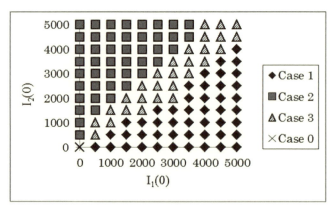

Figure 7. Final market state ($R = 2$)

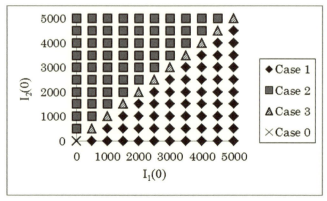

Figure 8. Final market state ($R = 3$)

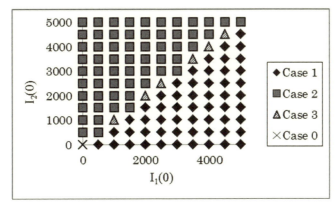

Figure 9. Final state ($R = 4$)

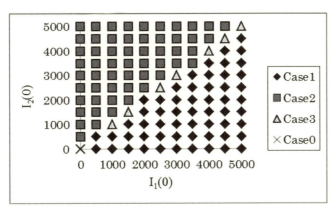

Figure 10. Final market state ($R = 20$)

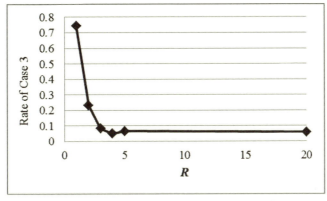

Figure 11. Rate of Case 3 with various R

Neighborhood size also affects the time required to reach the final state of the market. Figure 12 shows the average number of periods the market requires to converge to a stable state. In the case in which two products share the market (i.e., Case 3), the average periods required to converge change drastically. Initially, the average time to obtain stability increases as the neighborhood range increases; however, this decreases sharply when R is greater than 3. When R is small, the users of a product form small clusters, and they are satisfied with their product in a small community. If R is greater, users of a product must compete with users of the other product, and sometimes they continue to use the same product and sometimes they change products. Consequently, more time is required to reach a stable market state. Then, if the size of a neighborhood is sufficiently large, they can judge the relative merits of the products in the initial simulation stage, and the market stabilizes in less time.

When the market is monopolized by one product, the average periods required to reach convergence change slightly if R becomes large. For Cases 1 and 2, all consumers use the same product in the final stages. In these cases, users of a product form large clusters in the market, and this leads to greater effect on other consumers. When many users use a single product, the effects of network externality are increased; thus, the product diffuses rapidly in the market.

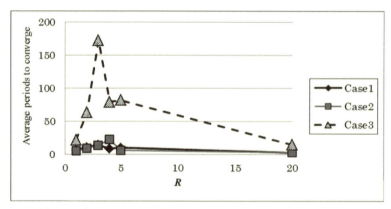

Figure 12. Average periods required to reach convergence

4. Discussion

We examined the diffusion process in an oligopolistic market with network externality. If two products exist in the market, the final (stable) state of the market can be classified by four patterns. We found that neighborhood size, R, has significant effect on the diffusion process and the final state, particularly for a case in which two products share the market.

First, the final distribution of users of a product changes drastically according to neighborhood size. If R is small, consumers form small groups or communities, and the market stabilizes with small clusters (Figure 5; $R = 1$). In other words, when consumers communicate with a limited number of other customers, different products are more likely to survive in local and small communities. In addition, if R is small, the probability of Case 3 (i.e., both products survive) increases. As can be seen in Figures 6–11, two products can survive in the market with 74% probability for $R = 1$. However, if R is large, consumers are affected by the many users around them, and it is difficult to maintain local characteristics. Thus, the group of users becomes large, and the product with fewer users is eliminated in most cases. As can be seen in Figure 11, the rate of Case 3 is approximately 5% when R is greater than 3. Most consumers are absorbed into larger groups for a given product; thus, the product monopolizes the market in the final state.

Second, neighborhood range changes the average time required to reach a stable state significantly, particularly in Case 3. As can be seen in Figure 12, the average periods required to converge increases drastically for $R = 3$; however, this decreases when R becomes large. When consumers communicate with only small communities, they can determine a product choice quickly. Similarly, when consumers are included in a large community, they can determine choices quickly by following the decision of the group majority.

These results correspond to the diffusion processes of particular products in the real world. With the development of Internet communities, we can obtain information from many sources. Communication through network tools, websites, or social networking services sometimes produces explosive spread of a product. On the other hand, it is difficult for various products to survive in a networked society because major products absorb other products' users into their community.

5. Conclusion

We have described an application of a cellular automata model to an oligopolistic market. We introduced the effects of network externality on consumer choices, and we have examined various initial user and neighborhood size values. The results of computer simulations show the following:

(1) The final state of the market can be classified into four cases.
(2) If neighborhood size is large, the rate of the case where two products share the market is smaller. When neighborhood size is small, products are more likely to survive in small and local communities.
(3) Neighborhood size also has significant effect on the time required to reach the final state, particularly for a case where two products share the market. When the neighborhood range is very small or sufficiently large, consumers can determine product choice quickly. However, when neighborhood size is within a certain range, the market requires significant time to reach convergence.

The development of communication tools makes our "neighborhood" larger, and we sometimes observe explosive diffusion or decline of products. We hope that our market model will contribute to better understanding of consumer decisions in a networked society.

References

[1] Epstein, J.M. and Axtell, R., Growing Artificial Society; Social Science From the Bottom Up, Brooking Institution Press (1996)
[2] Oda, S.H., Miura, K. and Ueda, K., "The application of cellular automata to network externality in consumer's theory: a generalisation of life game", Artificial Life Five in Langton, C.G., and Shimohara, K. (ed). MIT Press, pp. 473-480 (1997)
[3] Oda, S.H., Iyori, K., Miura, K. and Ueda, K., "The application of cellular automata to the consumer's theory: simulating a duopolistic market", Simulated Evolution and Learning, B. McKay, B., Yao, X., Newton, C. S., Kim, J-H., and Furuhashi, T. (eds.), Springer Verlag, pp. 454-461 (1999)
[4] Oda, S.H., Iyori, K., Miura, K. and Ueda, K., "The Application of Cellular Automata to the Theory of Consumers' Learning and Behavioral Interdependence", Complex Systems 98, Complexity International vol.6 (1999)
[5] Wolfram, S., Cellular Automata and Complexity, Addison-Wesley Publishing (1994)

Chapter 4

Development of a Multi-Country Multi-Sectoral Model in International Dollars

Takashi Yano* and Hiroyuki Kosaka**
* Faculty of Economic Sciences, Hiroshima Shudo University
1-1 Ozuka-Higashi 1-chome, Asaminami-ku, Hiroshima, JAPAN 731-3195
** Faculty of Policy Management, Keio University
5322 Endo, Fujisawa, JAPAN 252-0882

Abstract

The purpose of this chapter is to develop a multi-country multi-sectoral model and to demonstrate its application. Regarding the model, the following features are included: 1) the model is constructed by using multi-period international input-output tables in constant prices and international dollars, 2) most parameters of the model are econometrically estimated, 3) the monopoly model is incorporated, 4) input coefficient varies over time, 5) sectoral price and output are simultaneously determined. As an application, the effects of tariff reduction between Japan and the United States on the Asia-Pacific region are quantified. Based on the results, the United States would have positive impact while Japan's findings would be negative with respect to output. The main cause of Japan's output decline is the shift in demand from domestic products to U.S. products due to improved U.S. price competitiveness in Japan's market.

Key Words:
Multi-country multi-sectoral model, International input-output table, Monopoly, Trade liberalization

1. Introduction

Resulting from economic deregulation and development of information technology, trade and investment at the firm level have been growing rapidly. This shows that, in addition to macro analysis, a more detailed level approach is required for analyzing a contemporary global economy.

Recently, a multi-country multi-sectoral model is often employed for global economic analysis. In particular, a computable general equilibrium (CGE) model is widely applied (e.g., the Michigan model [7], the GTAP model [8], the G-Cubed model [23]). A CGE model is supply-oriented and has rigorous microeconomic foundation. However, this model does not have statistical foundation since the parameters are usually calibrated by single-period data.[1]

What we see from the Asian economic development is fast growth in production capability led by foreign direct investment. This evidence shows that major economic powers in a global economy suffer from demand shortage rather than supply shortage caused by limited amount of capital stock. That is, demand rather than supply determines the output level. Therefore, a demand-oriented model can describe a better picture of the structure of a global economy than a supply-oriented model.

As for demand-oriented modeling, two approaches have been applied. One is the INFORUM approach [1] [31].[2] In this approach, an input-output model with a macroeconometric model is constructed per country. Linking these domestic systems by trade at the commodity level establishes the INFORUM system. In general, classifications of an input-output table and trade data are not consistent. In addition, sector classification of an input-output table also differs among countries. Hence, this approach may have a problem with data consistency. The other is international input-output modeling [21] [29] [34]. This approach develops an international input-output model following the structure of an international input-output table. Differed from the INFORUM approach, data classification consistency is held. However, this approach works only if the table is available. Similar to a CGE model, an international input-output model also lacks statistical foundation.

From the review of existing models, we can see that a global model is preferred to be demand-oriented with econometrically estimated parameters, microeconomic foundation and classification consistency. This chapter constructs a multi-country multi-sectoral model which satisfies these attributes.

With respect to the use of international input-output tables, our modeling approach is close to international input-output modeling yet several novel features are incorporated in ours. The first feature is data and econometric estimation of parameters.[3] Since a multi-sectoral model is generally constructed by using a single-period input-output table, the parameters are calibrated, not estimated. By contrast, we convert multi-period international input-output tables in current prices to international input-output tables in constant prices and international dollars. With these tables, we estimate parameters econometrically by applying a panel data model. The second feature is the introduction of imperfect competition; specifically referring to monopoly. This allows us to determine sectoral price by monopoly behavior, which differs from the traditional input-output approach. The last feature is the formulation of household behavior. Household consumption is derived from utility maximization, employing the household block in Ballard et al. [3] as the benchmark model.

This chapter also demonstrates an in-sample simulation on trade liberalization between Japan and the United States as an application of the model. Concerning outcomes on Japan and the United States, we find that sectoral prices for both Japan and the United States decline in exception to the agricultural sector of the United States. Additionally, outputs in all sectors of the United States increase whereas those of Japan decrease.

---

[1] An exception is McKibbin and Wilcoxen [23]. They built a multi-country CGE model by econometrically estimating parameters.
[2] INFORUM stands for Interindustry Forecasting at the University of Maryland.
[3] Uno [31] also estimates parameters by econometric techniques; however, his estimation is based on single-country input-output tables, not international input-output tables.

The remainder of this chapter consists of four sections. Sections 2 and 3 illustrate theoretical and empirical structures of the model, respectively. Section 4 presents an application of the model. Finally, section 5 provides conclusions.

2. Theoretical Structure of the Model

The model is based on international input-output tables in constant prices and international dollars. Differed from a traditional input-output model, output and price by country and sector are determined simultaneously. Additionally, sectoral price is determined by monopoly pricing, not by adding up cost factors. In the following explanation, we assume that there R countries and each country has N sectors.

2.1 Sectoral Output

From the identity with respect to demand, sectoral output equals the summation of intermediate and final demands as:

$$XXR_{i,t}^{h} = \sum_{k=1}^{R}\sum_{j=1}^{N} XR_{ij,t}^{hk} + \sum_{k=1}^{R} CPR_{i,t}^{hk} + \sum_{k=1}^{R} CGR_{i,t}^{hk} + \sum_{k=1}^{R} IR_{i,t}^{hk} + \sum_{k=1}^{R} IVR_{i,t}^{hk} \\ + EXR_{i,t}^{h} + QXR_{i,t}^{h} \quad (1)$$

where $XXR_{i,t}^{h}$ is output in constant prices in sector i of country h at time t, $XR_{ij,t}^{hk}$ is intermediate goods in constant prices delivered from sector i of country h to sector j of country k at time t, $CPR_{i,t}^{hk}$ is household consumption in constant prices delivered from sector i of country h to country k at time t, $CGR_{i,t}^{hk}$ is government consumption in constant prices delivered from sector i of country h to country k at time t, $IR_{i,t}^{hk}$ is fixed investment in constant prices delivered from sector i of country h to country k at time t, $IVR_{i,t}^{hk}$ is inventories in constant prices delivered from sector i of country h to country k at time t, $EXR_{i,t}^{h}$ is export in constant prices from sector i of country h to the rest of the world (ROW) at time t, and $QXR_{i,t}^{h}$ is statistical discrepancy in constant prices in sector i of country h at time t.

2.2 Household Behavior

Household behavior of the model principally follows that of Ballard et al. [3].[4] This behavior employs

---

[4] Although Ballard et al. [3] explain labor supply by household utility maximization, its determination is omitted in the model. Instead, sectoral employment is determined by producer behavior.

the two-stage utility maximization. A representative household determines current consumption and savings in the first stage while the household allocates current consumption into consumption by sector in the second stage. Following the Armington approach [2], consumption by sector is further distributed with respect to source country.

2.2.1 Consumption-Savings Decision

In order to determine current consumption and savings, a representative household of country k solves the following utility maximization problem as:

$$\max_{CPR_t^k, CRF_t^k} U^k\left(CPR_t^k, CRF_t^k\right) = \left[\alpha^{k\,1/\sigma^k} CPR_t^{k\,(\sigma^k-1)/\sigma^k} + \left(1-\alpha^k\right)^{1/\sigma^k} CRF_t^{k\,(\sigma^k-1)/\sigma^k}\right]^{\sigma^k/(\sigma^k-1)} \quad (2)$$

subject to

$$YI_t^k = PCP_t^k CPR_t^k + PS_t^k SR_t^k \quad (3)$$

where U^k is a constant elasticity of substitution (CES) utility function of the household in country k, CPR_t^k is current consumption in constant prices of country k at time t, CRF_t^k is future consumption in constant prices of country k at time t, α^k is distribution parameter of country k, σ^k is the elasticity of substitution between CPR_t^k and CRF_t^k, YI_t^k is income in current prices of country k at time t, PCP_t^k is the price for CPR_t^k, PS_t^k is the price for SR_t^k, and SR_t^k is savings of country k at time t. Current consumption is a composite of consumption by sector, which is written in the following Cobb-Douglas form as:

$$CPR_t^k = \prod_{i=1}^{N} CPR_{i,t}^{k\,\lambda_{CP_i}^k} \quad (4)$$

where $\sum_{i=1}^{N} \lambda_{CP_i}^k = 1$ and $0 < \lambda_{CP_i}^k < 1$.

The representative household purchases capital goods through savings. Firms borrow the capital goods and pay returns to the household. The household's expected return per unit of savings can be written as $PK_t^{Dk} \zeta^k$, where PK_t^{Dk} and ζ^k are the price at time t and unit service of capital goods in country k, respectively. The household purchases future goods by the return of savings. We assume that the price for future goods is identical to the price for the current consumption of country k: i.e., PCP_t^k. Hence, we have the following relationship between nominal savings and future consumption of country k as:

$$PS_t^k SR_t^k = PF_t^k CRF_t^k \tag{5}$$

where $PF_t^k = \left(PS_t^k PCP_t^k\right)/\left(PK_t^{Dk}\zeta^k\right)$. Same as Ballard et al. [3], the price for savings is defined as:

$$PS_t^k = \sum_{i=1}^{N} P_{i,t}^k \left(\frac{XXR_{i,t}^k}{\sum_{l=1}^{N} XXR_{l,t}^k} \right) \tag{6}$$

where $P_{i,t}^k$ is the price in sector i of country k at time t. Using this relationship, the constraint of the utility maximization problem is rewritten as:

$$YI_t^k = PCP_t^k CPR_t^k + PF_t^k CRF_t^k \tag{7}$$

Manipulating the first-order conditions for the utility maximization problem yields the optimal current and future consumptions of country k as:

$$CPR_t^k = \frac{\alpha^k YI_t^k}{PCP_t^{k\sigma^k} \Theta_t^k} \tag{8}$$

$$CRF_t^k = \frac{(1-\alpha^k) YI_t^k}{PF_t^{k\sigma^k} \Theta_t^k} \tag{9}$$

where $\Theta_t^k = \alpha^k PCP_t^{k^{1-\sigma^k}} + (1-\alpha^k) PF_t^{k^{1-\sigma^k}}$. The optimal savings of country k can be obtained by substituting equation (9) into equation (5) as:

$$SR_t^k = \frac{(1-\alpha^k) YI_t^k}{PS_t^k PF_t^{k^{\sigma^k-1}} \Theta_t^k} \tag{10}$$

2.2.2 Determination of Consumption by Sector

For the determination of sectoral consumption of country k, the household of the corresponding country solves the following problem:

$$\max_{CPR_{i,t}^k} CPR_t^k = \prod_{i=1}^{N} CPR_{i,t}^{k \, \lambda_{CP_i}^k} \qquad (11)$$

subject to

$$YI_t^k - PS_t^k SR_t^k = \sum_{i=1}^{N} PCP_{i,t}^k CPR_{i,t}^k \qquad (12)$$

where $PCP_{i,t}^k$ is the price for $CPR_{i,t}^k$. Solving this optimization problem yields the optimal consumption in sector i of country k as:

$$CPR_{i,t}^k = \frac{\lambda_{CP_i}^k}{PCP_{i,t}^k} \left(YI_t^k - PS_t^k SR_t^k \right) \qquad (13)$$

Substituting equation (13) into the corresponding objective function gives the price for CPR_t^k. This substitution yields the following equation as:

$$YI_t^k - PS_t^k SR_t^k = CPR_t^k \prod_{i=1}^{N} \left(\frac{PCP_{i,t}^k}{\lambda_{CP_i}^k} \right)^{\lambda_{CP_i}^k} \qquad (14)$$

Since $YI_t^k - PS_t^k SR_t^k = PCP_t^k CPR_t^k$,

$$PCP_t^k = \prod_{i=1}^{N} \left(\frac{PCP_{i,t}^k}{\lambda_{CP_i}^k} \right)^{\lambda_{CP_i}^k} \qquad (15)$$

Additionally, $PCP_{i,t}^k$ is explained as follows:

$$PCP_{i,t}^k = \sum_{h=1}^{R} P_{i,t}^h \left(\frac{CPR_{i,t}^{hk}}{\sum_{q=1}^{R} CPR_{i,t}^{qk}} \right) \qquad (16)$$

2.2.3 Determination of Consumption by Sector and Country

The optimal consumption by sector is allocated with respect to source country by the Armington approach [2]. The expression for the allocation is written as:[5]

$$\frac{CPR_{i,t}^{hk}}{CPR_{i,t}^k} = \left(\frac{P_{i,t}^h}{\sum_{q=1}^{R} f_{CP_{i,t}}^{qk} P_{i,t}^q} \right)^{-s_{CP_i}^{hk}} \left(\frac{YIR_t^k}{YIR_{2000}^k} \right)^{\vartheta_i^k} \qquad (17)$$

where $f_{CP_{i,t}}^{hk}$ is the share of household consumption in constant prices of country k delivered from sector i of country h at time t, $s_{CP_i}^{hk}$ is the elasticity of substitution regarding household consumption in constant prices of country k delivered from sector i of country h, YIR_t^k is household income in constant prices of country k at time t, YIR_{2000}^k is household income in constant prices of country k in the base year 2000, and ϑ_i^k is the income elasticity of goods i in country k.

2.2.4 Determination of Household Income

Household income of country k is simply explained by wages of the corresponding country as:

$$YI_t^k = YI^k \left(\sum_{j=1}^{N} w_{j,t}^k L_{j,t}^k \right) \qquad (18)$$

where $w_{j,t}^k$ and $L_{j,t}^k$ are the wage rate and employment in sector j of country k at time t, respectively.

The deflator for household income of country k is determined by the weighted average of the sectoral price (i.e., the price for savings in the model) of the corresponding country as:

$$PYI_t^k = PYI^k \left(PS_t^k \right) \qquad (19)$$

---

[5] A similar income variable is employed in Ichioka [11].

2.3 The Other Demand Components

The other final demand components (government consumption, investment, inventories) and export to the ROW are exogenously given in the model. In addition, statistical discrepancy is also exogenous.

2.4 Producer Behavior

In this study, we assume that goods market is described by the monopoly theory. Thus, sectoral price equals marginal cost multiplied by the mark-up factor of the corresponding sector.

For simplicity, we also assume that the firm produces goods by using intermediate inputs plus labor (i.e., capital stock is omitted) and possess a slightly modified version of a generalized Ozaki unit cost function with factor limitationality [24]. The cost function is written as:

$$UC_{j,t}^k = \sum_{i=1}^{N} a_{ij}^k \left(XXR_{j,t}^k\right)^{b_{ij}^k} PA_{ij,t}^k \exp\left(b_{Tij}^k T\right) + a_{Lj}^k w_{j,t}^k \tag{20}$$

where $UC_{j,t}^k$ is the unit cost in sector j of country k at time t, $PA_{ij,t}^k$ is the price for $XR_{ij,t}^k \left(= \sum_{h=1}^{R} XR_{ij,t}^{hk}\right)$, T is time trend, a_{Lj}^k is employment coefficient in sector j of country k, a_{ij}^k, b_{ij}^k, and b_{Tij}^k are parameters. Particularly, the parameter b_{ij}^k represents the degree of scale economies in sector j of country k with respect to input i. Applying the Shephard's lemma, we obtain the optimal unit derived demand as:

$$\frac{\partial UC_{j,t}^k}{\partial PA_{ij,t}^k} = \frac{XR_{ij,t}^k}{XXR_{j,t}^k} = a_{ij}^k \left(XXR_{j,t}^k\right)^{b_{ij}^k} \exp\left(b_{Tij}^k T\right) \tag{21}$$

$$\frac{\partial UC_{j,t}^k}{\partial w_{j,t}^k} = \frac{L_{j,t}^k}{XXR_{j,t}^k} = a_{Lj}^k \tag{22}$$

Similar to the formulation of consumption by sector and country, intermediate input by sector and country is determined by the Armington approach [2] as:

$$\frac{X_{ij,t}^{hk}}{X_{ij,t}^k} = \left[\frac{\left(1+\tau_{i,t}^k\right) P_{i,t}^h}{PA_{ij,t}^k}\right]^{-s_{ij}^{hk}} \tag{23}$$

where $\tau_{i,t}^k$ is the tariff rate in sector i of country k at time t.

Development of a Multi-Country Multi-Sectoral Model in International Dollars   67

Manipulating partial derivative of equation (20) with respect to output, we obtain the marginal cost as:

$$MC_{j,t}^k = \sum_{i=1}^{N} a_{ij}^k \left(b_{ij}^k + 1\right)\left(XXR_{j,t}^k\right)^{b_{ij}^k} PA_{ij,t}^k \exp\left(b_{Tij}^k T\right) + a_{Lj}^k w_{j,t}^k \qquad (24)$$

where $MC_{j,t}^k$ is the marginal cost in sector j of country k at time t. Hence, the sectoral monopoly price can be written as:

$$P_{j,t}^k = \frac{\varepsilon_j^k}{\varepsilon_j^k - 1}\left[\sum_{i=1}^{N} a_{ij}^k \left(b_{ij}^k + 1\right)\left(XXR_{j,t}^k\right)^{b_{ij}^k} PA_{ij,t}^k \exp\left(b_{Tij}^k T\right) + a_{Lj}^k w_{j,t}^k\right] \qquad (25)$$

where ε_j^k is the elasticity of demand for goods j of country k. The price for $XR_{ij,t}^k$, $PA_{ij,t}^k$, is simply expressed as:

$$PA_{ij,t}^k = \sum_{h=1}^{R} \left(1 + \tau_{i,t}^k\right) P_{i,t}^h \left(\frac{XR_{ij,t}^{hk}}{XR_{ij,t}^k}\right) \qquad (26)$$

2.5 Sectoral Wage Rate

Adding labor productivity to the wage rate equation in McKibbin and Nguyen [22, p. 47], we explain the sectoral wage rate as follows:

$$w_{j,t+1}^k = w_{j,t}^k \left(\frac{EPC_{t+1}^k}{EPC_t^k}\right)^{\beta^k} \left(\frac{EPC_t^k}{EPC_{t-1}^k}\right)^{1-\beta^k} \left(\frac{L_{j,t}^k}{L_j^{k*}}\right)^{\gamma^k} \left(\frac{XXR_{j,t}^k}{L_{j,t}^k}\right)^{\xi_j^k} \qquad (27)$$

where EPC_t^k is the expected consumer price of country k at time t, L_j^{k*} is full employment in sector j of country k, β^k and γ^k are parameters of country k, and ξ_j^k is the parameter on sectoral labor productivity for sector j of country k.[6] Due to unavailability of data on full employment at the sector level, equation (27) is further modified as:

---

[6] Assuming perfect mobile labor among sectors, McKibbin and Nguyen [22] explain the wage rate at the macro level. In contrast, without their assumption on labor mobility, we formulate the sectoral wage rate by incorporating the labor market factor at the sector level instead of at the macro level.

$$w_{j,t}^k = \left(EPC_t^k\right)^{\beta^k} \left(\frac{XXR_{j,t}^k}{L_{j,t}^k}\right)^{\xi_j^k} \tag{28}$$

3. Empirical Structure of the Model

3.1 Data

The parameters of the model is estimated or calibrated by using the Asian International Input-Output Tables 1985, 1990, 1995, and 2000 which covers the ten economies (Indonesia, Malaysia, the Philippines, Singapore, Thailand, China, Taiwan, South Korea, Japan, and the United States) [12] [13] [14] [15] [16].[7] Since these input-output tables are evaluated in current prices, conversion to the tables in constant prices and international dollars is required. To do this, we use nominal and real gross domestic product (GDP) by industry in national currencies.[8] To begin, we compile the six-sector version of the input-output tables and the GDP data, since their original sector classifications differ from each other. The unified sector classification is provided in Table 1.[9] Following, we compute the GDP deflators by industry (base year = 2000) in U.S. dollars for the ten economies.[10] Multiplying these deflators for sectoral GDP by the corresponding country's purchasing power parity (PPP) per its exchange rate gives the relative price deflators.[11] These relative deflators for GDP by industry correspond to those for value added in our international input-output framework. Omitting international freight and insurance, imports from Hong Kong, the European Union (EU), and the rest of the world (ROW), and duties for simplicity, we have the following identity on the relative deflator for value added as:

$$PVA_{j,t}^k = \frac{XXV_{j,t}^k - \sum_{h=1}^{R}\sum_{i=1}^{N} XV_{ij,t}^{hk}}{\left(XXV_{j,t}^k / P_{j,t}^k\right) - \sum_{h=1}^{R}\sum_{i=1}^{N} \left(XV_{ij,t}^{hk} / P_{i,t}^h\right)} \tag{29}$$

where $PVA_{j,t}^k$ is the deflator for value added in sector j of country k at time t, $XXV_{j,t}^k$ is nominal output in sector j of country k at time t, and $XV_{ij,t}^{hk}$ is nominal intermediate input delivered from sector i of country h to sector j of country k. Manipulating this identity yields:

---

[7] The layout of the Asian International Input-Output Table is available at http://www.ide.go.jp/English/Publish/Books/Io/index.html.
[8] The GDP data are taken from the United Nations (UN). The UN data are downloadable from the United Nations' National Accounts Main Aggregates (http://data.un.org).
[9] Although inconsistency of industrial coverage for the fifth and sixth sectors between the UN data and the input-output tables occurs, the inconsistency was ignored in the computation of sectoral price.
[10] The deflator for the mining and utilities sector of China cannot be computed due to missing data. Therefore, this study employs the GDP deflator as its proxy.
[11] Due to data limitation, the PPP over GDP is used instead of that by sector. The PPP data are taken from the Penn World Table Version 6.2 [9] while data for the exchange rate come from the International Monetary Fund's International Financial Statistics and the Central Bank of the Republic of China. Taiwan's exchange rate data are available online at http://www.cbc.gov.tw/mp2.html.

$$P_{j,t}^k = \frac{XXV_{j,t}^k}{\sum_{h=1}^{R}\sum_{i=1}^{N}(XV_{ij,t}^{hk}/P_{i,t}^h) + [(XXV_{j,t}^k - \sum_{h=1}^{R}\sum_{i=1}^{N}XV_{ij,t}^{hk})/PVA_{j,t}^k]} \quad (30)$$

Table 1. Sector Classification

	6 Sectors		UN 7 Sectors		AIIO 24 Sectors
1	Agriculture, livestock, forestry, and fishery	1	Agriculture, hunting, forestry, and fishery	1	Paddy
				2	Other agricultural products
				3	Livestock
				4	Forestry
				5	Fishery
2	Mining and utilities	2	Mining, quarrying, and utilities (less manufacturing)	6	Crude petroleum and natural gas
				7	Other mining
				20	Electricity, gas, and water supply
3	Manufacturing	3	Manufacturing	8	Food, beverage, and tobacco
				9	Textile, leather, and the products thereof
				10	Timber and wooden products
				11	Pulp, paper, and printing
				12	Chemical products
				13	Petroleum and petro products
				14	Rubber products
				15	Non-metallic mineral products
				16	Metal products
				17	Machinery
				18	Transport equipment
				19	Other manufacturing products
4	Construction	4	Construction	21	Construction
5	Trade and transport	5	Trade, restaurants and hotels	22	Trade and transport
		6	Transport and communication		
6	Service	7	Other activities	23	Services
				24	Public administration

Note: This table is tabulated following the Institute of Developing Economies-Japan External Trade Organization [16]. AIIO stands for Asian International Input-Output.

Solving a system of $R \times N$ equations, a collection of equation (30) over j and k, gives the relative sectoral price for our model. Applying the double deflation method with the resultant relative sectoral price, we can convert the Asian International Input-Output Tables in current prices to the Asian International Input-Output Tables in constant prices and international dollars.[12]

The Institute of Developing Economies-Japan External Trade Organization [15] [16] provides employment matrices in only the year 2000 for the ten economies. Therefore, the sectoral employment coefficient, a_{Lj}^k, is fixed at the figures in the year 2000. This coefficient is applied for the computation of sectoral employment and wage rate in the other years (1985, 1990, and 1995).

3.2 Computation of Household Income and Savings

From the definition of savings, household income of country k at time t is computed as $\sum_{j=1}^{N} WAGE_{j,t}^{k} - \sum_{h=1}^{R} \sum_{i=1}^{N} CP_{i,t}^{hk}$. Yet, wages in an international input-output table only covers those of employees. Income of the other workers (e.g., self-employed and workers in the agricultural sector) is included in the operating surplus. In this study, the consumption function in Klein Model I is utilized to estimate income [20]. Simplifying his formulation, we employ the following consumption function:

$$\sum_{h=1}^{R} \sum_{i=1}^{N} CP_{i,t}^{hk} = c(1)^k \left(\frac{\sum_{j=1}^{N} WAGE_{j,t}^{k}}{PCP_t^k} \right) + c(2)^k \left(\frac{\sum_{j=1}^{N} YC_{j,t}^{k}}{PCP_t^k} \right) \quad (31)$$

where $YC_{j,t}^{k}$ is operating surplus in sector j of country k at time t. Rearranging equation (31), we obtain:

$$\sum_{h=1}^{R} \sum_{i=1}^{N} CP_{i,t}^{hk} = c(1)^k \frac{\left[\sum_{j=1}^{N} WAGE_{j,t}^{k} + \left\{ c(2)^k / c(1)^k \right\} \sum_{j=1}^{N} YC_{j,t}^{k} \right]}{PCP_t^k} \quad (32)$$

Nominal income of country k at time t can be expressed as:

$$YI_t^k = \sum_{j=1}^{N} WAGE_{j,t}^{k} + \frac{c(2)^k}{c(1)^k} \sum_{j=1}^{N} YC_{j,t}^{k} \quad (33)$$

Savings are computed by subtracting the total consumption from nominal income.

Equation (31) is estimated by using pooled data of the ten economies for the years 1985, 1990, 1995,

---

[12] The use of the relative price for compiling international input-output tables in constant prices is proposed in Shimizu and Ikeda [28].

and 2000. In this estimation, the White heteroscedasticity-consistent standard errors are applied. To maintain the degree of freedom, we assume that the parameter $c(1)^k$ is common among the ten economies; i.e., $c(1)^k = c(1)$.

3.3 Calibration of Parameters of the CES Utility Function

The parameters of the CES utility function are calibrated by an approach in Ichioka [11, pp. 153-155]. To begin, PF_t^k must be defined. $PI_t^k r_t^k$ is used as a proxy for $PK_t^{Dk} \zeta^k$ where PI_t^k and r_t^k are the investment deflator and the long-term interest rate of country k at time t, respectively. PI_t^k is explained by PS_t^k while r_t^k is given in this model.[13]

The parameter σ^k is calibrated by using the elasticity of savings with respect to the real rate of return which is defined as $rs_t^k = PK_t^{Dk} \zeta^k / PS_t^k$.[14] Same as Ballard et al. [3], the value of 0.4 in Boskin [4] is employed for the saving elasticity of the United States. Concerning the saving elasticities of the other economies (in exception to Indonesia, China, and South Korea), we compute them by multiplying the U.S. saving elasticity (0.4) by the ratio of the corresponding economy's value to the U.S. value in Ogaki et al. [25].[15] As for the countries not shown in Ogaki et al. [25] (Indonesia, China, South Korea), the saving elasticity of low income countries is applied to Indonesia and China whereas that of upper-middle income countries is applied to South Korea. This income classification follows the World Bank [33], on which Ogaki et al. [25] is also based.

3.4 Estimation Results of Selected Variables

Parameter estimation is carried out by employing panel data methods because each variable of an economy has only four observations. The sectoral wage rate equation is estimated by economy whereas the rest of the stochastic equations are by sector. In the estimation, the unobservable individual effects represent sector or economy-specific factors. Thus, these specific factors have potential correlations with explanatory variables. With this consideration, the fixed-effect model is employed. For estimation, the method of least squares is applied to all stochastic equations.

---

[13] Data for the long-term interest rate come from the International Monetary Fund's International Financial Statistics and the Central Bank of the Republic of China. Taiwan's interest rate data are available online at http://www.cbc.gov.tw/mp2.html.

[14] Calibration procedure of the parameter α^k in Ichioka [11] is identical to that in Ballard et al. [3]. Concerning the parameter σ^k, however, the calibration procedure of Ichioka [11] differs from that of Ballard et al. [3]. To begin, Ichioka [11] assumes that the only factor which changes rs_t^k is ζ^k. This assumption enables us to derive the saving elasticity of country k analytically. Solving the derived equation of the saving elasticity for the parameter σ^k, we obtain its expression.

[15] The saving elasticities in Ogaki et al. [25] are not directly applied since they compute the saving elasticities by employing a simple endogenous growth model with parameters estimated from data of low and middle income countries.

Table 2. Estimation Results for Equation (34)

Sector	Estimate	S. E.	p-value	Adj. R^2
1	0.624	0.117	0.000	0.954
2	−0.075	0.035	0.042	0.475
3	0.577	0.301	0.065	0.789
4	N.A.	N.A.	N.A.	N.A.
5	0.260	0.182	0.164	0.735
6	−1.404	0.403	0.002	0.800

Note: Economy-specific control is suppressed. N.A. is not available. The number of observations is 40 for each sector. S. E. is standard error. Adj. R^2 is adjusted R-squared.

3.4.1 Consumption Share by Sector: Equation (13)

The parameter $\lambda_{CP_i}^k$ is normally fixed and calibrated by using data in the base year. However, it varies over time. Therefore, we endogenize it after calibrating by using data in the years of 1985, 1990, 1995, and 2000. Specifically, the parameter $\lambda_{CP_i,t}^k$ is explained as follows:

$$\lambda_{CP_i,t}^k = c(3)_i^k + c(4)_i \left(\frac{1}{EDR_t^k}\right) \tag{34}$$

where EDR_t^k is the ratio of population aged over 65 to the total population in country k at time t.[16] Table 2 illustrates estimation results for the parameter $c(4)_i$ of equation (34). Due to the shortage in the number of (non-zero) observations, we cannot estimate equation (34) for the construction sector. Since a reciprocal model is employed, negative coefficient implies that the consumption share of the corresponding sector rises in parallel to the ratio of elderly people. Among six sectors, the estimated coefficients for the mining and utilities sector and service sector are negative.

3.4.2 Intermediate Demand by Sector: Equation (21)

Regarding coefficients on output and time trend, we assume that they are common among the ten economies. The estimated equation is rewritten by taking logarithms as:

---

[16] Population data are taken from the World Bank's World Development Indicators and the Statistical Yearbook of the Republic of China.

$$\ln\left(\frac{XR_{ij,t}^k}{XXR_{j,t}^k}\right) = \ln c(5)_{ij}^k + c(6)_{ij} \ln\left(XXR_{j,t}^k\right) + c(7)_{ij} T \tag{21'}$$

The White heteroscedasticity-consistent standard errors are applied for the estimation of this equation. Table 3 demonstrates estimation results for the agricultural sector (i.e., $i = 1, 2, \ldots, 6; j = 1$). In equation (21'), $c(6)_{ij} < 0$ and $c(7)_{ij} < 0$ indicate economies of scale and the corresponding input-saving technical change, respectively. According to the results, the agricultural sector exhibits economies of scale with respect to every input. We find no technical change on input from the manufacturing sector. The agricultural sector has technical progress on input from the own sector whereas technical retrogression on inputs from the mining and utilities sector, the construction sector, the trade and transportation sector as well as the service sector.

Table 3. Estimation Results for Equation (21')

Parameter	Estimate	S. E.	p-value	Adj. R^2
$c(6)_{11}$	0.176	0.032	0.000	0.921
$c(7)_{11}$	−0.009	0.003	0.005	
$c(6)_{21}$	0.616	0.229	0.015	0.971
$c(7)_{21}$	0.024	0.007	0.002	
$c(6)_{31}$	0.428	0.048	0.000	0.924
$c(7)_{31}$	-	-	-	
$c(6)_{41}$	−1.916	0.402	0.000	0.763
$c(7)_{41}$	0.044	0.011	0.001	
$c(6)_{51}$	−0.448	0.183	0.021	0.838
$c(7)_{51}$	0.021	0.005	0.000	
$c(6)_{61}$	−0.157	0.132	0.246	0.892
$c(7)_{61}$	0.014	0.004	0.001	

Note: A dummy variable (1 for 2000; 0 otherwise) in estimation for the mining and utilities sector as well as economy-specific control are suppressed. Hyphen denotes dropped variables. The number of observations is 40 for each estimation. S. E. is standard error. Adj. R^2 is adjusted R-squared.

Table 4. Estimation Results for Equation (25')

Parameter	Indonesia	Malaysia	Philippines	Singapore	Thailand	China	Taiwan	South Korea	Japan	United States	Adj. R^2
$c(8)_1$	2.899	1.014	1.851	1.336	2.059	1.030	1.128	2.062	1.799	1.344	0.996
	-0.190	-0.033	-0.091	-0.030	-0.085	-0.070	-0.023	-0.04	-0.019	-0.019	
	[0.000]	[0.000]	[0.000]	[0.000]	[0.000]	[0.000]	[0.000]	[0.000]	[0.000]	[0.000]	
$c(8)_2$	2.588	1.038	1.647	1.963	1.387	1.196	1.439	1.537	1.519	1.435	0.942
	-0.698	-0.147	-0.288	-0.137	-0.211	-0.247	-0.100	-0.122	-0.062	-0.072	
	[0.001]	[0.000]	[0.000]	[0.000]	[0.000]	[0.000]	[0.000]	[0.000]	[0.000]	[0.000]	
$c(8)_3$	1.697	1.160	1.909	1.306	1.559	1.337	1.242	1.298	1.195	1.223	0.994
	-0.109	-0.042	-0.105	-0.031	-0.072	-0.085	-0.027	-0.028	-0.014	-0.020	
	[0.000]	[0.000]	[0.000]	[0.000]	[0.000]	[0.000]	[0.000]	[0.000]	[0.000]	[0.000]	
$c(8)_4$	1.385	1.143	1.651	1.306	1.512	1.222	1.177	1.201	1.139	1.099	0.992
	-0.099	-0.044	-0.098	-0.028	-0.074	-0.085	-0.027	-0.029	-0.014	-0.021	
	[0.000]	[0.000]	[0.000]	[0.000]	[0.000]	[0.000]	[0.000]	[0.000]	[0.000]	[0.000]	
$c(8)_5$	2.534	1.05	2.115	1.589	2.310	1.543	1.371	1.777	1.227	1.263	0.989
	-0.232	-0.058	-0.193	-0.051	-0.177	-0.189	-0.049	-0.056	-0.021	-0.031	
	[0.000]	[0.000]	[0.000]	[0.000]	[0.000]	[0.000]	[0.000]	[0.000]	[0.000]	[0.000]	
$c(8)_6$	1.420	0.967	1.470	1.313	1.398	1.207	1.384	1.283	1.306	1.147	0.996
	-0.081	-0.029	-0.089	-0.026	-0.059	-0.120	-0.029	-0.029	-0.014	-0.021	
	[0.000]	[0.000]	[0.000]	[0.000]	[0.000]	[0.000]	[0.000]	[0.000]	[0.000]	[0.000]	

Note: Estimates on dummy variable are suppressed. The number of observations is 40 for each estimation. Adj. R^2 is adjusted R-squared. Standard errors and p-values are in parentheses and brackets, respectively.

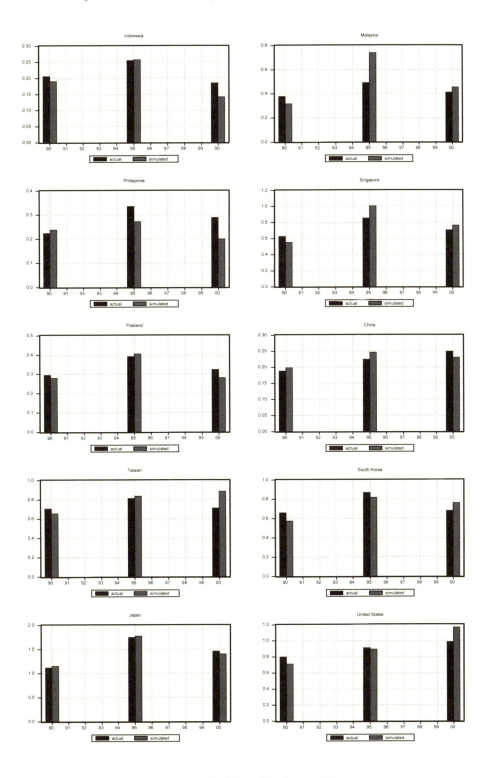

Figure 1. Final Test of the Average Price

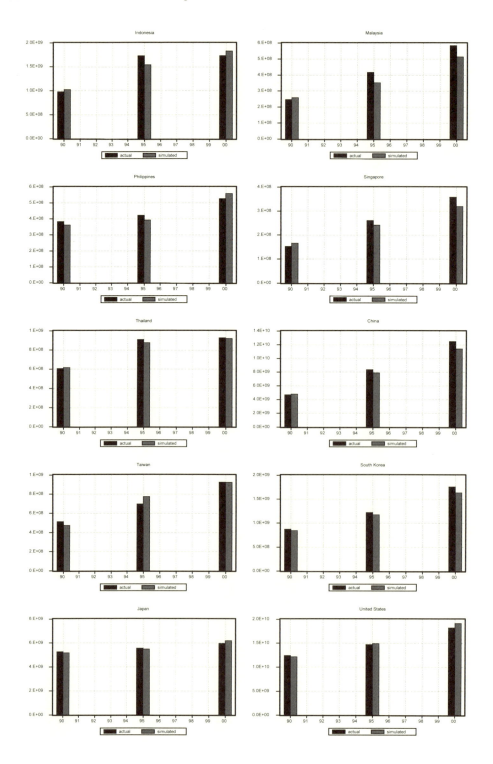

Figure 2. Final Test of the Aggregate Output

3.4.3 Sectoral Price: Equation (25)

The estimated equation of the sectoral price is expressed as:

$$P_{j,t}^k = c(8)_j^k MC_{j,t}^k + c(9)_j^k D00 \tag{25'}$$

where $D00$ is a dummy variable (1 for 2000; 0 otherwise). Table 4 demonstrates estimation results for the parameter $c(8)_j^k$ of equation (25'). In exception to the service sector of Malaysia, substantial markup factors are found.

3.5 Final Test

The final test was performed from 1990 to 2000. The test results for the weighted average of sectoral prices and the aggregate output are demonstrated in Figures 1 and 2, respectively.[17] Although the error for price of Malaysia in 1995 is relatively large, we conclude that the overall results are sufficient.

4. Application

Recently, bilateral or regional free trade agreements (FTAs) have become popular. The Association of Southeast Asian Nations (ASEAN) has formed the ASEAN Free Trade Area since 1993. The United States, Canada, and Mexico initiated the North American Free Trade Area in 1994. The economic partnership agreement between Japan and Singapore has been effective since 2002. The FTA between the United States and South Korea was concluded in 2007 and became effective in 2012. Currently, the Trans-Pacific Partnership (TPP) is under negotiation. Following the interests in FTAs, many studies have quantified the effects of FTAs by employing a general equilibrium framework. Some examples for analysis on FTAs in the Asia-Pacific region are Tsutsumi and Kiyota [30], Brown et al. [5] [6], Kawasaki [18], Urata and Kiyota [32], Kawai and Zhai [17], Kitwiwattanachai et al. [19], and Petri et al. [26] [27].

Table 5. Tariff Rates of Japan and the United States in the Year 2000 (%)

Sector	Japan	United States
1	6.886	0.899
2	7.842	0.275
3	8.716	0.982
4	5.705	1.618
5	1.176	0.534
6	6.623	0.818

---

[17] The unit of Figure 2 is U.S.$ 1,000.

Concerning trade agreement, increasing attention is drawn to the TPP. Since Japan and the United States are major countries among the TPP candidate nations, we analyze the effects of trade liberalization between Japan and the United States as an application of the model developed in this chapter. Specifically, we completely remove the tariff rates between Japan and the United States in the year 2000.

To begin, the tariff rates of Japan and the United States in the year 2000 are shown in Table 5. Using the Asian International Input-Output Tables, the tariff rates are computed as duties and import sales tax divided by the total import. For all sectors, Japan levies heavier tariff rates than the United States.

Table 6 presents percent deviations of sectoral price, output, and household utility from the baseline. The sectoral prices of Japan and the United States would decline in exception to the agricultural sector of the United States.[18] The sectoral prices for Malaysia and Singapore would decline whereas that for China would rise. Regarding the other economies, changes in the sectoral prices would differ. These dispersive changes would come from trade and production structures. As for sectoral output, the United States would have positive impact whereas the other nine economies would have negative ones. Household utility of the United States and Singapore would be improved while that of the other eight economies would fall.

An interesting outcome of this simulation is the decrease in output for Japan, which differs from Tsutsumi and Kiyota [30]. Table 7 demonstrates decomposition of output changes into contributions of changes in intermediate and final demands. According to Table 7, output changes result from changes in intermediate demand rather than final demand. We further decompose changes in intermediate demand for Japanese products in terms of destination economies. Table 8 shows the results and indicates that intermediate demand for Japanese products would substantially decrease in the home market (over 100%) while it would increase in the other markets (excluding the agricultural sector of South Korea).[19] Consider the case of the manufacturing sector as an example. Table 9 illustrates percent deviations of price competitiveness for Japan and the United States in the Japanese and U.S. market from the baseline.[20] In the Japanese market, price competitiveness of Japan is slightly deteriorated while that of the United States is greatly improved (over 5% in exception to the trade and transportation sector). By contrast, price competitiveness of Japan is somewhat improved (less than 2%) while that of the United States falls in the U.S. market. The difference between U.S. price competitiveness change in the Japanese market and vice versa reflects the difference in the tariff rates between the two countries. Consequently, demand shift from Japanese products to U.S. products in the home market due to significant changes in price competitiveness becomes a dominant factor to the decrease in output for Japan.

---

[18] Sectoral price is affected by the corresponding sector's output, the average input price, and wage rate. The signs of these three factors and ascendancy of one of the three over the other two rely on industrial and trade structures as well as trade balance of an economy. As a result of tariff reduction between Japan and the United States, demand for U.S. products would increase while that for domestic products would decrease in the market of Japan, the reverse occurring in the U.S. market. Depending on the magnitude of demand changes, sectoral output change possesses either positive or negative impact on sectoral price change. The signs of change in the composite input price and the sectoral wage rate are theoretically unclear. In the United States, the positive output change effect would be dominant in price change of the agricultural sector while it would be trivial compared to the other negative factor(s) in the rest of the six sectors. As for Japan, the negative output change effect would be critical to the fall of sectoral price.

[19] Since intermediate demands for the Japanese products decline, positive values in Table 8 indicate decreases in the corresponding markets.

[20] Price competitiveness in sector i of country h at time t is defined as $\left(1+\tau_{i,t}^{k}\right)P_{i,t}^{h}/PA_{ij,t}^{k}$.

Table 6. Percent Deviations of Sectoral Price, Output, and Household Utility from the Baseline

Sector	Indonesia	Malaysia	Philippines	Singapore	Thailand	China	Taiwan	South Korea	Japan	United States
Price										
1	0.009	-0.021	0.002	-0.065	0.000	0.001	-0.002	0.001	-0.298	0.014
2	-0.013	-0.022	-0.004	-0.009	0.004	0.003	-0.001	0.006	-0.207	-0.011
3	0.022	-0.011	0.009	-0.041	0.003	0.002	-0.009	-0.001	-0.314	-0.034
4	0.008	-0.005	0.006	-0.019	-0.002	0.002	0.000	0.002	-0.164	-0.032
5	0.010	-0.004	0.006	-0.008	0.002	0.002	0.002	0.004	-0.131	-0.025
6	0.008	-0.010	0.001	-0.011	-0.001	0.002	0.001	0.003	-0.160	-0.024
Output										
1	-0.014	-0.022	-0.018	0.031	-0.010	-0.005	-0.018	-0.013	-0.167	0.105
2	-0.070	-0.038	-0.023	-0.009	-0.010	-0.006	-0.011	-0.007	-0.045	0.058
3	-0.040	-0.024	-0.025	-0.013	-0.028	-0.010	-0.030	-0.027	-0.028	0.069
4	-0.001	-0.001	-0.001	0.000	0.000	0.000	-0.001	0.000	-0.007	0.008
5	-0.027	-0.013	-0.024	-0.005	-0.011	-0.008	-0.012	-0.009	-0.130	0.073
6	-0.015	-0.008	-0.010	-0.006	-0.007	-0.003	-0.010	-0.007	-0.054	0.049
Utility	-0.022	-0.002	-0.027	0.000	-0.011	-0.006	-0.013	-0.010	-0.011	0.089

Table 7. Contributions of Changes in Intermediate and Final Demands to Output Change (%)

	Sector					
	1	2	3	4	5	6
Indonesia						
Intermediate demand	52.894	98.850	70.339	100.000	71.447	42.867
Final demand	47.106	1.150	29.661	0.000	28.553	57.133
Malaysia						
Intermediate demand	98.647	98.558	92.438	100.000	87.465	79.705
Final demand	1.353	1.442	7.562	0.000	12.535	20.295
Philippines						
Intermediate demand	68.683	85.937	64.968	100.000	64.891	43.914
Final demand	31.317	14.063	35.032	0.000	35.109	56.086
Singapore						
Intermediate demand	54.860	66.939	100.775	100.000	68.435	68.699
Final demand	45.140	33.061	−0.775	0.000	31.565	31.301
Thailand						
Intermediate demand	88.738	79.450	77.156	100.000	61.663	46.949
Final demand	11.262	20.550	22.844	0.000	38.337	53.051
China						
Intermediate demand	57.908	93.468	69.442	100.000	84.249	60.481
Final demand	42.092	6.532	30.558	0.000	15.751	39.519
Taiwan						
Intermediate demand	73.306	70.248	83.857	100.000	56.352	54.566
Final demand	26.694	29.752	16.143	0.000	43.648	45.434
South Korea						
Intermediate demand	85.334	71.734	82.701	100.000	64.166	57.266
Final demand	14.666	28.266	17.299	0.000	35.834	42.734
Japan						
Intermediate demand	116.125	99.726	218.160	100.000	77.714	68.979
Final demand	−16.125	0.274	−118.160	0.000	22.286	31.021
United States						
Intermediate demand	99.868	76.805	80.295	100.000	67.569	55.425
Final demand	0.132	23.195	19.705	0.000	32.431	44.575

Table 8. Economy-Specific Contribution to Changes in Intermediate Demand for the Products of Japan (%)

Sector	Indonesia	Malaysia	Philippines	Singapore	Thailand	China	Taiwan	South Korea	Japan	United States
1	−0.001	−0.016	−0.043	−0.006	−0.005	−0.023	−0.032	0.002	102.609	−2.484
2	−0.012	−0.005	−0.014	−0.002	−0.008	−0.028	−0.018	−0.070	100.181	−0.025
3	−0.390	−1.511	−0.287	−0.243	−1.406	−3.797	−2.931	−4.615	167.681	−52.501
4	0.000	0.000	0.000	0.000	0.000	0.000	0.000	0.000	100.000	0.000
5	−0.007	−0.016	−0.011	−0.007	−0.016	−0.017	−0.109	−0.066	101.595	−1.346
6	0.000	0.011	0.000	0.000	0.000	0.000	0.000	0.000	100.070	−0.081

Table 9. Percent Deviations of Price Competitiveness for Japan and the United States from the Baseline: Manufacturing Sector

	In the Japanese market		In the U.S. market	
Sector	Japan	United States	Japan	United States
1	0.044	−6.138	−1.160	0.008
2	0.046	−6.968	−0.531	0.023
3	0.140	−7.630	−1.228	0.023
4	0.021	−5.111	−1.861	0.007
5	0.015	−0.871	−0.795	0.016
6	0.070	−5.882	−1.072	0.017

Due to its fast growing popularity, no country can disregard FTAs. However, these results show that FTAs would not always provide profits to the participating countries. FTAs generally reduce price levels of all countries which are engaged in the FTAs. Thus, it might be required for a member country of a FTA to make domestic policies to reduce international price differentials concurrently in order to acquire gains from the FTA. Regarding the FTA between Japan and the United States, it is imperative for Japan to make such policies.

5. Conclusions

This paper constructs another variety of multi-country multi-sectoral models by using international input-output tables in constant prices and international dollars. In contrast to typical models, most parameters of the model are econometrically estimated and the monopoly framework is employed. Estimation of the monopoly price equation principally yields positive markups, which show suitability on the incorporation of monopoly. Applying the model, we analyze the effects of trade liberalization between Japan and the United States on the Asia-Pacific region. From the results, the United States might have an output increase while Japan might have a decrease. The main cause of Japan's output decline is the shift in demand from domestic products to U.S. products due to improved U.S. price competitiveness in Japan's market.

Due to its small number of sectors, the model is relatively compact and easy to operate. However, a model with more detailed sectors is required in order to thoroughly analyze policy issues. Constructing a model which are based on more detailed sectors is crucial for further analysis. Additionally, recent financial deregulations strengthen the interdependence of countries with respect to investment. In fact, foreign direct investment is one of the major factors for Asia's high economic growth. Incorporation of a consistent mechanism to explain household savings and investment by sector and country is also one of the topics for our future research.

References

[1] Almon, C., "The INFORUM Approach to Interindustry Modeling," *Economic Systems Research*, Vol. 3, No.1, pp. 1-7 (1991).

[2] Armington, P. S., "A Theory of Demand for Products Distinguished by Place of Production," *IMF Staff Papers*, Vol. 16, No. 1, pp. 159-178 (1969).

[3] Ballard, C. L., Fullerton, D., Shoven, J. B. and Whalley, J., *A General Equilibrium Model for Tax Policy Evaluation*, Chicago, Ill: University of Chicago Press (1985).

[4] Boskin, M. J., "Taxation, Saving, and the Rate of Interest," *Journal of Political Economy*, Vol. 86, No. 2, Part 2, pp. S3-S27 (1978).

[5] Brown, D. K., Deardorff, A.V. and Stern, R. M., "Multilateral, Regional and Bilateral Trade-Policy Options for the United States and Japan," *World Economy*, Vol. 26, No. 6, pp. 803-828 (2003).

[6] Brown, D. K., Kiyota, K. and Stern, R. M., "Computational Analysis of the Menu of US-Japan Trade Policies," *World Economy*, Vol. 29, No. 6, pp. 805-855 (2006).

[7] Deardorff, A. V. and Stern, R. M., *The Michigan Model of World Production and Trade*, Cambridge, Mass.: MIT Press (1986).

[8] Hertel, T. W. (ed.), *Global Trade Analysis: Modeling and Applications*, Cambridge, UK: Cambridge University Press (1997).

[9] Heston, A., Summers, R. and Aten, B., *Penn World Table Version 6.2*, Center for International Comparisons of Production, Income and Prices at the University of Pennsylvania (2006).

[10] Hickman, B. G. and Lau, L. J., "Elasticities of Substitution and Export Demands in a World Trade Model," *European Economic Review*, Vol. 4, No. 4, pp. 347-380 (1973).

[11] Ichioka, O., *Applied General Equilibrium Analysis*, Tokyo: Yuhikaku (1991). (in Japanese)

[12] Institute of Developing Economies, *Asian International Input-Output Table 1985*, Tokyo: Institute of Developing Economies (1993).

[13] Institute of Developing Economies, *Asian International Input-Output Table 1990*, Tokyo: Institute of Developing Economies (1998).

[14] Institute of Developing Economies, *Asian International Input-Output Table 1995*, Tokyo: Institute of Developing Economies (2001).

[15] Institute of Developing Economies-Japan External Trade Organization, *Asian International Input-Output Table 2000: Volume 1. Explanatory Notes*, Chiba: Institute of Developing Economies-Japan External Trade Organization (2006a).

[16] Institute of Developing Economies-Japan External Trade Organization, *Asian International Input-Output Table 2000: Volume 2. Data*, Chiba: Institute of Developing Economies-Japan External Trade Organization (2006b).

[17] Kawai, M., and Zhai, F., "China-Japan-United States Integration amid Global Rebalancing: A Computable General Equilibrium Analysis," *Journal of Asian Economics*, Vol. 20, No. 6, pp. 688-699 (2009).

[18] Kawasaki, K., "The Impact of Free Trade Agreements in Asia," RIETI Discussion Paper Series No. 03-E-018, Tokyo: Research Institute of Economy, Trade and Industry (2003).

[19] Kitwiwattanachai, A., Nelson, D. and Reed, G., "Quantitative Impacts of Alternative East Asia Free Trade Areas: A Computable General Equilibrium (CGE) Assessment," *Journal of Policy Modeling*, Vol. 32, No. 2, pp. 286-301 (2010).

[20] Klein, L. R., *Economic Fluctuations in the United States 1921-1941*, New York: John Wiley & Sons (1950).

[21] Kosaka, H., *Model Analysis on Global System*, Tokyo: Yuhikaku (1994). (in Japanese)

[22] McKibbin, W. J. and Nguyen, J., "Modeling Global Demographic Change: Results for Japan," Working Papers in International Economics No. 3.04, Sydney: Lowy Institute for International Policy (2004).

[23] McKibbin, W. J. and Wilcoxen, P. J., "The Theoretical and Empirical Structure of the G-Cubed Model," *Economic Modelling*, Vol. 16, No. 1, pp. 123-148 (1999).

[24] Nakamura, S., "A Nonhomothetic Generalized Leontief Cost Function Based on Pooled Data," *Review of Economics and Statistics*, Vol. 72, No. 4, pp. 649-656 (1990).

[25] Ogaki, M., Ostry, J. D. and Reinhart, C. M., "Saving Behavior in Low- and Middle-Income Developing Countries: A Comparison," *IMF Staff Papers*, Vol. 43, No. 1, pp. 38-71 (1996).

[26] Petri, P. A., Plummer, M. G. and Zhai, F., "ASEAN Economic Community: A General Equilibrium Analysis," *Asian Economic Journal*, Vol. 26, No. 2, pp. 93-118 (2012a).

[27] Petri, P. A., Plummer, M. G. and Zhai, F., *The Trans-Pacific Partnership and Asia-Pacific Integration: A Quantitative Assessment*, Washington, D.C.: Peterson Institute for International Economics (2012b).

[28] Shimizu, M. and Ikeda, A., "Compilation of International Input-Output Tables in Constant Prices and Its Problems: Price Linkage of the 1985 and 1990 International Input-Output Tables," KEO Discussion Paper No. 43, Tokyo: Keio Economic Observatory, Keio University (1996). (in Japanese)

[29] Torii, Y., Shim, S.-J. and Akiyama, Y., "Effects of Tariff Reductions on Trade in the Asia-Pacific Region," in Millar, R. E., Polenske, K. R. and Rose, A. Z. (eds.), *Frontiers in Input-Output Analysis*, New York: Oxford University Press, pp. 165-179 (1989).

[30] Tsutsumi, M. and Kiyota, K., "The Effects of Free Trade Agreement throughout Japan: A CGE Approach," Discussion Paper No. 74, Tokyo: Japan Center for Economic Research (2002). (in Japanese)

[31] Uno, K. (ed.), *Economy-Energy-Environment Simulation: Beyond the Kyoto Protocol*, Dordrecht: Kluwer Academic Publishers (2002).

[32] Urata, S. and Kiyota, K., "The Impacts of an East Asian Free Trade Agreement on Foreign Trade in

East Asia," in Ito, T. and Rose, A. K. (eds.), *International Trade in East Asia*, Chicago, Ill: University of Chicago Press, pp. 217-252 (2006).

[33] World Bank, *Adjustment in Africa: Reforms, Results, and the Road Ahead*, New York: Oxford University Press (1994).

[34] Yano, T. and Kosaka, H., "Trade Patterns and Exchange Rate Regimes: Testing the Asian Currency Basket Using an International Input-Output System," *Developing Economies*, Vol. 41, No. 1, pp. 3-36 (2003).

Chapter 5

Stochastic Inventory Model with Time-Varying Demand

*Michinori Sakaguchi and Masanori Kodama**
Faculty of Economic Sciences, Hiroshima Shudo University,
1-1 Ozuka-Higasi 1-chome, Asaminami-ku, Hiroshima, JAPAN 739-3195
*Honorary Professor of Kyushu University and Hiroshima Shudo University

Abstract

Stochastic inventory models with salvaged opportunities at the beginning of each period are constructed in order to research the inventory system with style goods. These inventory models are equipping the notion of demand changes with time in the period. The demand distribution is assumed to be a general continuous distribution. It is attempted to get the way to reduce the expectation of the total inventory cost analytically by differentiating the object function.

We state precisely the optimal policies in the inventory model of single period. There are two threshold levels which are founded by solving equations, and using them the object function would take the minimal value at there.

Key Words:
Inventory problem, Probabilistic model, Dynamic programming, Demand distribution

1. Introduction

For investigating the inventory with a style good type of products, a newsvendor model with two salvage opportunities are developed by Cheaitou A. [1], in which there are the usual quantity ordered at the beginning of the horizontal, the usual quantity salvaged at the end of the horizontal and a new quantity salvaged at the beginning of the horizontal. This model is constructed by taking account of the supply chain. First the optimal policy of the single period model is shown in terms of threshold levels, and next he proceeds to a two-period production planning and inventory control model.

On the other hand the probabilistic and dynamic inventory problems under different situations have been studied in [2] and [3], namely whether demand is subject to a continuous distribution or a discrete distribution and whether demand of each period is stable or not. All demands of each period are assumed to be subject to the same kind of the distribution and an optimal policy of the model with multi-period is reseached. In these models a method to obtain an economic order quantity is presented. This method is attempted to be useful in an inventory model with a varying continuous demand in [3]. The method as above is also generalized to the case demand is decreasing from period to period.

In this paper we attempt to integrate Cheaitou's work to our one, because he does not consider the change of demand with passage of time. There are some situations such that the demand of one period occurs with constant rate or demand at the first half of single period is larger than one at the latter half of the period. The optimal policy is influenced by these conditions. A minor change of inventory model is done for the reason of finding the optimization. We refer fundamental facts of inventory problems to [4].

2. Preparation

Though our inventory models are one of single period or of two-period, we prepare third period in order to conclude several matters.

2.1 Notation

Let us introduce some notation:

- i = order of period ($i = 1, 2, 3$).
- t = length of single period.
- h_i = holding cost per unit per period i ($i = 1, 2$).
- t_1 = time when the inventory level is zero.
- p_i = penalty cost per unit per period i ($i = 1, 2$).
- c_i = purchasing cost per unit at period i ($i = 1, 2, 3$).
- d_i = salvage value per unit at the beginning of the period i ($i = 1, 2, 3$).

2.2 Assumption 1

It is assumed the followings about the constants. The salvage value is less than the purchasing cost at period i,

$$0 < d_i < c_i \quad (i = 1, 2, 3). \tag{1}$$

The purchasing cost is less than the penalty cost at period i,

$$c_i < p_i \quad (i = 1, 2). \tag{2}$$

The salvage value is decreasing as time passes,

$$d_3 < d_2 < d_1. \tag{3}$$

It is necessary to avoid the situation that a factory purchases the items only for the purpose of salvaging them at next period,

$$d_{i+1} < c_i + h_i \quad (i = 1, 2). \tag{4}$$

A factory should not purchase any product at first period in order to dispose it at the end of second period,

$$d_3 < c_1 + h_1 + h_2. \tag{5}$$

Without the following assumption there is no purchase at second period by buying them only at first period,

$$c_2 < c_1 + h_1. \tag{6}$$

2.3 Variables

The variables in this model are shown:

- x_i = initial inventory level at the beginning of the period i ($i = 1, 2, 3$).
- y_i = regular ordered quantity at the beginning of the period i ($i = 1, 2, 3$).
- s_i = quantity salvaged at the beginning of the period i ($i = 1, 2, 3$).
- b_i = quantity of demand in the period i ($i = 1, 2$).
- T = time ($0 \leq T \leq 2t$).

z_i = initial inventory level after the regular order is placed, $z_i = x_i + y_i$ i ($i = 1, 2, 3$).

2.4 Assumption 2

It is assumed the followings about the variables. Assume that the salvage at the beginning is carried before the regular order is placed, that is,

$$0 \leq s_1 \leq x_1^+. \tag{7}$$

Since the regular ordered quantity y_i is non–negative,

$$z_i \geq x_i \quad (i = 1, 2, 3). \tag{8}$$

Because the quantity salvaged at the end of the period is less than or equal the inventory level at the end of the period, it is obtained that

$$0 \leq s_{i+1} \leq (z_i - s_i - b_i)^+ \quad (i = 1, 2). \tag{9}$$

2.5 Functions

The demand is subject to a continuous distribution. We let the functions be as follows:

- $\varphi_i(b_i)$ = probabilistic density function of the variable b_i ($i = 1, 2$).
- m_i = mean of the probabilistic density function $\varphi_i(b_i)$ ($i = 1, 2$)
- $g(x)$ = increasing and differential function on $[0, 1]$ such that $g(0) = 0$ and $g(1) = 1$.
- $G(y) = \int_0^y g(x)dx$ ($0 \leq y \leq 1$).
- $I_1(z_i, s_i, b_i)$ = average of the holding inventory quantity in the period i ($i = 1, 2$).
- $I_2(z_i, s_i, b_i)$ = average of the shortage quantity in the period i ($i = 1, 2$).

3. Inventory Model of Single Period

The single period inventory problem with two disposal opportunities is considered in which model there are two chances to sale the excess at a salvage value. These are carried out at the beginning of the period and at the end of the period. The regular order is placed at the beginning of single period. It is studied that the type of demand occurrence in the period changes the optimal policy. For example the demand of one period occurs with constant rate, or the demand at the first half of single period is larger than one at the latter half of the period.

The expected total cost function would be minimized under some constraints

3.1 Demand

Assume that quantity of demand from the beginning of the period through the time $T(0 \leq T \leq t)$ is just $g(T/t)b_1$. Since $g(1)=1$, it is reconfirmed that the amount of demand in the period is b_1. Moreover the inventory level at time $T(0 \leq T \leq t)$ comes

$$z_1 - s_1 - g(T/t)b_1. \tag{10}$$

Two functions $I_1(z_1, s_1, b_1)$ and $I_2(z_1, s_1, b_1)$ could be evaluated in [5] (confer pp.135-138).

$$I_1(z_1, s_1, b_1) = \begin{cases} 0, & \text{if } z_1 - s_1 \leq 0 \\ \frac{1}{t}\int_0^t (z_1 - s_1 - g(T/t)b_1)dT = z_1 - s_1 - G(1)b_1, \\ & \text{if } z_1 - s_1 \geq 0 \text{ and } 0 \leq b_1 \leq z_1 - s_1 \\ \frac{1}{t}\int_0^{t_1} (z_1 - s_1 - g(T/t)b_1)dT = \\ (z_1 - s_1)g^{-1}((z_1 - s_1)/b_1) - b_1 G(g^{-1}((z_1 - s_1)/b_1)), \\ & \text{if } z_1 - s_1 \geq 0 \text{ and } z_1 - s_1 \leq b_1, \end{cases} \tag{11}$$

$$I_2(z_1, s_1, b_1) = \begin{cases} \frac{1}{t}\int_0^t (g(T/t)b_1 - z_1 - s_1)dT = G(1)b_1 - z_1, & \text{if } z_1 - s_1 \leq 0 \\ 0, & \text{if } z_1 - s_1 \geq 0 \text{ and } 0 \leq b_1 \leq z_1 - s_1, \\ \frac{1}{t}\int_{t_1}^t (g(T/t)b_1 - z_1 - s_1)dT = [G(1) - G(g^{-1}((z_1 - s_1)/b_1))]b_1 \\ -(z_1 - s_1)[1 - g^{-1}((z_1 - s_1)/b_1)] - (z_1 - s_1)[1 - g^{-1}((z_1 - s_1)/b_1)] \\ & \text{if } z_1 - s_1 \geq 0 \text{ and } z_1 - s_1 \leq b_1. \end{cases} \tag{12}$$

3.2 Objective Function

The optimal inventory level is based on the minimization of expected inventory cost which includes the purchasing cost, the benefits of salvage revenue at the beginning of single period and at the end of the period, the holding cost and the shortage cost.

It is assumed that stock replenishment occurs instantaneously without setup cost. Then the total inventory cost is

$$c_1(z_1 - x_1) - d_1 s_1 + h_1 I_1(z_1, s_1, b_1) + p_1 I_2(z, s_1, b_1) - d_2 s_2 + c_2 y_2. \tag{13}$$

The expected total cost function $\Pi(x_1, z_1, y_2, s_1, s_2)$ is

$$\Pi(x_1, z_1, y_2, s_1, s_2) = c_1(z_1 - x_1) - d_1 s_1 + h_1 \int_0^\infty I_1(z_1, s_1, b_1)\varphi_1(b_1)db_1 \\ + p_1 \int_0^\infty I_2(z_1, s_1, b_1)\varphi_1(b_1)db_1 - d_2 s_2 + c_2 y_2. \tag{14}$$

Therefore we obtain by the equations (11) and (12) that if $z_1 - s_1 \geq 0$, then

$$\Pi(x_1, z_1, y_2, s_1, s_2) = c_1(z_1 - x_1) - d_1 s_1 + h_1 \left(\int_0^{z_1 - s_1} (z_1 - s_1 - G(1)b_1) \varphi_1(b_1) db_1 \right.$$
$$+ \int_{z_1 - s_1}^{\infty} \left((z_1 - s_1) g^{-1}((z_1 - s_1)/b_1) - b_1 G(g^{-1}((z_1 - s_1)/b_1)) \right) \varphi_1(b_1) db_1 \right) \quad (15)$$
$$+ p_1 \int_{z_1 - s_1}^{\infty} \left\{ [G(1) - G(g^{-1}((z_1 - s_1)/b_1))]b_1 - (z_1 - s_1)[1 - g^{-1}((z_1 - s_1)/b_1)] \right\} \varphi_1(b_1) db_1$$
$$+ c_2 y_2 - d_2 s_2$$

and if $z_1 - s_1 < 0$, then

$$\Pi(x_1, z_1, y_2, s_1, s_2) = c_1(z_1 - x_1) - d_1 s_1 + p_1 \int_0^{\infty} (G(1)b_1 - z_1) \varphi_1(b_1) db_1 + c_2 y_2 - d_2 s_2 \quad (16)$$
$$= (c_1 - p_1) z_1 - c_1 x_1 - d_1 s_1 + p_1 G(1) m_1 + c_2 y_2 - d_2 s_2.$$

Now considering the variable x_1 a given constant value, the problem is to find the value $z_1^*, y_2^*, s_1^*, s_2^*$ such that the function $\Pi(x_1, z_1, y_2, s_1, s_2)$ has a minimum value under constrains (7), (8) and (9).

3.3 Reduction of Single Period Problem

The partial derivatives in the case can be calculated as follows: In the case $z_1 - s_1 \geq 0$ we have

$$\frac{\partial \Pi}{\partial z_1} = c_1 - p_1 + (h_1 + p_1) \left\{ \int_0^{z_1 - s_1} \varphi_1(b_1) db_1 + \int_{z_1 - s_1}^{\infty} g^{-1}((z_1 - s_1)/b_1) \varphi_1(b_1) db_1 \right\}$$
$$\frac{\partial \Pi}{\partial s_1} = p_1 - d_1 - (h_1 + p_1) \left\{ \int_0^{z_1 - s_1} \varphi_1(b_1) db_1 + \int_{z_1 - s_1}^{\infty} g^{-1}((z_1 - s_1)/b_1) \varphi_1(b_1) db_1 \right\} \quad (17)$$
$$\frac{\partial \Pi}{\partial y_2} = c_2, \quad \frac{\partial \Pi}{\partial s_1} = -d_2.$$

In the case where $z_1 - s_1 < 0$ the partial derivatives of the function $\Pi(x_1, z_1, y_2, s_1, s_2)$ are

$$\frac{\partial \Pi}{\partial z_1} = c_1 - p_1, \quad \frac{\partial \Pi}{\partial s_1} = -d_1, \quad \frac{\partial \Pi}{\partial y_2} = c_2, \quad \frac{\partial \Pi}{\partial s_1} = -d_2. \quad (18)$$

The function $\Pi(x_1, z_1, y_2, s_1, s_2)$ is a convex function on the entire region with respect to z_1, y_2, s_1, s_2 since the Hessian matrix $\nabla^2 \Pi(z_1, y_2, s_1, s_2)$ is semi–definite positive. In fact if $z_1 - s_1 \geq 0$, then

$$\nabla^2\Pi(x_1,z_1,y_2,s_1,s_2) = \begin{bmatrix} \Pi_{z_1z_1} & \Pi_{z_1y_2} & \Pi_{z_1s_1} & \Pi_{z_1s_2} \\ \Pi_{y_2z_1} & \Pi_{y_2y_2} & \Pi_{y_2s_1} & \Pi_{y_2s_2} \\ \Pi_{s_1z_1} & \Pi_{s_1y_2} & \Pi_{s_1s_1} & \Pi_{s_1s_2} \\ \Pi_{s_2z_1} & \Pi_{s_2y_2} & \Pi_{s_2s_1} & \Pi_{s_2s_2} \end{bmatrix} \quad (19)$$

$$= (h_1 + p_1)\int_{z_1-s_1}^{\infty} \frac{\varphi_1(b_1)}{b_1 dg/dx((z_1-s_1)/b_1)} db_1 \begin{bmatrix} 1 & 0 & -1 & 0 \\ 0 & 0 & 0 & 0 \\ -1 & 0 & 1 & 0 \\ 0 & 0 & 0 & 0 \end{bmatrix}$$

Therefore for every $\mathbf{v}^T = (v_1, v_2, v_3, v_4)$ in $\mathbf{R}^4$, it is shown that

$$\mathbf{v}^T \nabla^2\Pi(x_1,z_1,s_1,s_2)\mathbf{v} = (h_1+p_1)\int_{z_1-s_1}^{\infty} \frac{\varphi_1(b_1)}{b_1 dg/dx((z_1-s_1)/b_1)} db_1 (v_1-v_3)^2 \geq 0 \quad (20)$$

Because the Hessian matrix $\nabla^2\Pi(z_1, y_2, s_1, s_2)$ is a zero matrix in case $z_1 - s_1 < 0$, the function $\Pi(x_1, z_1, y_2, s_1, s_2)$ is also a convex function.

On the other hand, by the fact that

$$\frac{\partial \Pi}{\partial y_2} = c_2, \quad \frac{\partial \Pi}{\partial s_2} = -d_2 \text{ and } c_2 > 0, \quad (21)$$

there is no solution of the equation $\nabla \Pi = 0$.

In the equations (15) and (16) the only term which relates to the variable s_2 is $-d_2 s_2$. Since $d_2 > 0$, then the function $\Pi(x_1, z_1, y_2, s_1, s_2)$ has a smaller value as the value of s_2 is larger. It leads us that if $z_1 - s_1 \geq 0$, then

$$s_2^* = (z_1 - s_1 - b_1)^+ \quad (22)$$

considering constrains (9). However it contains the probabilistic variable b_1, we will use the expectation of $(z_1 - s_1 - b_1)^+$ instead of it, that is

$$s_2 = \int_0^{z_1-s_1} (z_1 - s_1 - b_1)\varphi_1(b_1) db_1 \quad (23)$$

It is enough to purchase the shortage quantity during the first period at the beginning of the second period. Thus

$$y_2^* = (b_1 + s_1 - z_1)^+ \quad (24)$$

and by the similar reason we set

$$y_2 = \int_{z_1-s_1}^{\infty} (b_1 + s_1 - z_1)\varphi_1(b_1) db_1. \quad (25)$$

Substituting (23) and (25) to the equation (15) it is obtained that if $z_1 - s_1 \geq 0$, then

$$\Pi(x_1, z_1, s_1) = c_1(z_1 - x_1) - d_1 s_1 + h_1 \left(\int_0^{z_1 - s_1} (z_1 - s_1 - G(1)b_1) \varphi_1(b_1) db_1 \right.$$
$$+ \int_{z_1 - s_1}^{\infty} \left((z_1 - s_1) g^{-1}((z_1 - s_1)/b_1) - b_1 G(g^{-1}((z_1 - s_1)/b_1)) \right) \varphi_1(b_1) db_1 \right)$$
$$+ p_1 \int_{z_1 - s_1}^{\infty} \left\{ \left[G(1) - G(g^{-1}((z_1 - s_1)/b_1)) \right] b_1 - (z_1 - s_1) \left[1 - g^{-1}((z_1 - s_1)/b_1) \right] \right\} \varphi_1(b_1) db_1 \quad (26)$$
$$+ c_2 \int_{z_1 - s_1}^{\infty} (b_1 + s_1 - z_1) \varphi_1(b_1) db_1 - d_2 \int_0^{z_1 - s_1} (z_1 - s_1 - b_1) \varphi_1(b_1) db_1.$$

Next we observe in the case $z_1 - s_1 < 0$. It is seen by the similar reason that

$$s_2^* = 0 \quad y_2^* = (b_1 + s_1 - z_1)^+ \quad \text{for all } b_1 \geq 0 \quad (27)$$

and so we put

$$s_2 = 0 \quad \text{and} \quad y_2 = \int_0^{\infty} (b_1 + s_1 - z_1) \varphi_1(b_1) db_1. \quad (28)$$

It follows from (16) that

$$\Pi(x_1, z_1, s_1) = (c_1 - p_1) z_1 - c_1 x_1 - d_1 s_1 \\ + p_1 G(1) m_1 + c_2 \int_0^{\infty} (b_1 + s_1 - z_1) \varphi_1(b_1) db_1. \quad (29)$$

It is reduced to minimize the function $\Pi(x_1, z_1, s_1)$ with respect to variables z_1, s_1 under constrains (7) and (8) ($i = 1$). If we could find the desired numbers z_1^*, s_1^*, then

$$s_2^* = \int_0^{z_1^* - s_1^*} (z_1^* - s_1^* - b_1) \varphi_1(b_1) db_1, \\ y_2^* = \int_{z_1^* - s_1^*}^{\infty} (b_1 + s_1^* - z_1^*) \varphi_1(b_1) db_1 \quad (30)$$

or

$$s_2^* = 0, \quad y_2^* = \int_0^{\infty} (b_1 + s_1 - z_1) \varphi_1(b_1) db_1. \quad (31)$$

3.4 Analysis of Single Period Problem

It is also proved that the function $\Pi(x_1, z_1, s_1)$ is convex with respect to variable z_1, s_1. Let the function $w(z)$ for $z \geq 0$ be

$$w(z) = \int_0^z \varphi_1(b_1) db_1 + \frac{h_1 + p_1}{h_1 + p_1 + c_2 - d_2} \int_z^{\infty} g^{-1}\left(\frac{z}{b_1}\right) \varphi_1(b_1) db_1. \quad (32)$$

If $z_1 - s_1 \geq 0$, then we have

$$\frac{\partial \Pi}{\partial z_1}(x_1, z_1, s_1) = c_1 - p_1 - c_2 + (h_1 + p_1 + c_2 - d_2) w(z_1 - s_1), \\ \frac{\partial \Pi}{\partial s_1}(x_1, z_1, s_1) = p_1 - d_1 + c_2 - (h_1 + p_1 + c_2 - d_2) w(z_1 - s_1). \quad (33)$$

If $z_1 - s_1 < 0$, then it is obtained that

$$\frac{\partial \Pi}{\partial z_1}(x_1, z_1, s_1) = c_1 - p_1,$$
$$\frac{\partial \Pi}{\partial s_1}(x_1, z_1, s_1) = c_2 - d_2. \qquad (34)$$

In the case $z_1 - s_1 \geq 0$, the Hessian matrix $\nabla^2 \Pi(x_1, z_1, s_1)$ is calculated as follows:

$$\nabla^2 \Pi(x_1, z_1, s_1) = \begin{bmatrix} \Pi_{z_1 z_1} & \Pi_{z_1 s_1} \\ \Pi_{s_1 z_1} & \Pi_{s_1 s_1} \end{bmatrix} = \left\{ (c_2 - d_2)\varphi_1(z_1 - s_1) \right.$$
$$\left. + (h_1 + p_1) \int_{z-s_1}^{\infty} \frac{\varphi_1(b_1)}{b_1 dg/dx((z_1 - s_1)/b_1)} db_1 \right\} \begin{bmatrix} 1 & -1 \\ -1 & 1 \end{bmatrix} \qquad (35)$$

By the assumptions on the inequality (1) and the function $g(x)$, it is shown that

$$(c_2 - d_2)\varphi_1(z_1 - s_1) + (h_1 + p_1)\int_{z-s_1}^{\infty} \frac{\varphi_1(b_1)}{b_1 dg/dx((z_1 - s_1)/b_1)} db_1 \geq 0. \qquad (36)$$

Therefore the Hessian matrix $\nabla^2 \Pi(x_1, z_1, s_1)$ is semi–definite positive, and hence it is proved that the function $\Pi(x_1, z_1, s_1)$ is convex with respect to variable z_1, s_1.

In the case $z_1 - s_1 < 0$, the Hessian matrix $\nabla^2 \Pi(x_1, z_1, s_1)$ is

$$\nabla^2 \Pi(x_1, z_1, s_1) = \begin{bmatrix} \Pi_{z_1 z_1} & \Pi_{z_1 s_1} \\ \Pi_{s_1 z_1} & \Pi_{s_1 s_1} \end{bmatrix} = \begin{bmatrix} 0 & 0 \\ 0 & 0 \end{bmatrix} \qquad (37)$$

and the function $\Pi(x_1, z_1, s_1)$ is convex with respect to variable z_1, s_1. In particular this property gives us that for any point (a, b)

$$\Pi(x_1, z_1, s_1) \geq \Pi(x_1, a, b) + \frac{\partial \Pi}{\partial z_1}(x_1, a, b)(z_1 - a) + \frac{\partial \Pi}{\partial s_1}(x_1, a, b)(s_1 - b). \qquad (38)$$

The problem of single period is to find the minimal value of the function $\Pi(x_1, z_1, s_1)$ under the restrictions.

Now we study an optimal policy by the similar method of [1](pp.35-37). First find two threshold levels Y_1^* and Y_2^* by the following lemma.

3.4.1 Lemma *Assume the probabilistic density function $\varphi_1(b)$ is continuous on the interval $[0, \infty)$. Then the followings are hold.*

(1) *If* $w(x_1) \leq \dfrac{p_1 + c_2 - c_1}{h_1 + p_1 + c_2 - d_2}$, *then there exists a number Y_1^* such that $x_1 \leq Y_1^*$ and*

$$w(Y_1^*) = \frac{p_1 + c_2 - c_1}{h_1 + p_1 + c_2 - d_2}.$$

(2) *If* $\dfrac{p_1 + c_2 - d_1}{h_1 + p_1 + c_2 - d_2} \leq w(x_1)$, *then there exists a number Y_2^* such that $0 \leq Y_2^* \leq x_1$*

and

$$w(x_1 - Y_2^*) = \frac{p_1 + c_2 - d_1}{h_1 + p_1 + c_2 - d_2}.$$

In fact there exist the numbers Y_1^* and Y_2^*. First the function $w(z)$ is increasing because of the inequality

$$\frac{dw}{dz}(z) = \frac{c_2 - d_2}{h_1 + p_1 + c_2 - d_2} \varphi_1(z) + \frac{h_1 + p_1}{h_1 + p_1 + c_2 - d_2} \int_z^\infty \frac{\varphi_1(b_1)}{b_1 dg/dx(z/b_1)} db_1 \geq 0. \quad (39)$$

Next it is clear that $w(0) = 0$, and it is seen that $\lim_{z \to \infty} w(z) = 1$ by using the relations $0 \leq g^{-1}(z/b_1) \leq 1$ and so

$$0 \leq \int_z^\infty g^{-1}(z/b_1) \varphi_1(b_1) db_1 \leq \int_z^\infty \varphi_1(b_1) db_1. \quad (40)$$

Finally by the condition (2) $c_1 < p_1$, it is obtained $p_1 + c_2 - c_1 \geq 0$. It follows from assumption (4) $d_2 \leq c_1 + h_1$ that $p_1 + c_2 - c_1 \leq h_1 + p_1 + c_2 - d_2$. Thus we know that

$$0 \leq \frac{p_1 + c_2 - c_1}{h_1 + p_1 + c_2 - d_2} \leq 1. \quad (41)$$

By these arguments it is proved that the number Y_1^* exists.

With respect to Y_2^* it is necessary to have

$$0 \leq \frac{p_1 + c_2 - d_1}{h_1 + p_1 + c_2 - d_2} \leq 1. \quad (42)$$

These inequalities are shown as follows. The condition (2) $d_1 \leq p_1$ leads us to $p_1 + c_2 - d_1 \geq 0$, and condition (3) $d_2 \leq d_1$ yields $d_2 \leq h_1 + d_1$, and so $p_1 + c_2 - d_1 \leq h_1 + p_1 + c_2 - d_2$. Therefore we get the inequalities (42) and it shows the existence of u^* such that

$$0 \leq u^* \leq x_1 \quad \text{and} \quad w(u^*) = \frac{p_1 + c_2 - d_1}{h_1 + p_1 + c_2 - d_2}.$$

Put $Y_2^* = x_1 - u^*$. Then it implies $0 \leq Y_2^* \leq x_1$ and $w(x_1 - Y_2^*) = \frac{p_1 + c_2 - d_1}{h_1 + p_1 + c_2 - d_2}$. It is completed to prove our lemma.

It is also shown by the condition (1) $d_1 < c_1$ that

$$\frac{p_1 + c_2 - c_1}{h_1 + p_1 + c_2 - d_2} < \frac{p_1 + c_2 - d_1}{h_1 + p_1 + c_2 - d_2}. \quad (43)$$

This implies the inequality

$$Y_1^* \leq Y_2^* - x_1. \quad (44)$$

3.4.2 Problem

Let the domain D be

$$D = \{(z_1, s_1) \mid x_1 \leq z_1 \quad \text{and} \quad 0 \leq s_1 \leq x_1^+\} \quad (45)$$

Then the problem of single period is to find the minimal value of the function $\Pi(x_1, z_1, s_1)$ under the domain D. It is necessary to notice the fact that if $x_1 \geq 0$ and $(z_1, s_1) \in D$, then $z_1 - s_1 \geq 0$. Now optimal policies are stated as follows.

3.4.3 Optimal Policies

Assume $x_1 \geq 0$. Then we have *optimal policies*.

(1) If $w(x_1) \leq \dfrac{p_1 + c_2 - c_1}{h_1 + p_1 + c_2 - d_2}$, then $z_1^* = Y_1^*$ and $s_1^* = 0$, and therefore $y_1^* = Y_1^* - x_1$.

(2) If $\dfrac{p_1 + c_2 - c_1}{h_1 + p_1 + c_2 - d_2} \leq w(x_1) \leq \dfrac{p_1 + c_2 - d_1}{h_1 + p_1 + c_2 - d_2}$, then $z_1^* = x_1$ and $s_1^* = 0$, thus $y_1^* = 0$.

(3) If $\dfrac{p_1 + c_2 - d_1}{h_1 + p_1 + c_2 - d_2} \leq w(x_1)$, then $z_1^* = x_1$ and $s_1^* = Y_2^*$, and so $y_1^* = 0$.

We will show these statements. There exist Y_1^* and Y_2^* by Lemma. In the case (1) the partial derivatives of $\Pi(x_1, z_1, s_1)$ is not negative at the point $(Y_1^*, 0)$, because we have by (1), (33) and Lemma that

$$\frac{\partial \Pi}{\partial z_1}(x_1, Y_1^*, 0) = c_1 - p_1 - c_2 + (h_1 + p_1 + c_2 - d_2)w(Y_1^*)$$
$$= c_1 - p_1 - c_2 + (p_1 + c_2 - c_1) = 0,$$
$$\frac{\partial \Pi}{\partial s_1}(x_1, Y_1^*, 0) = p_1 - d_1 + c_2 - (h_1 + p_1 + c_2 - d_2)w(Y_1^*)$$
$$= p_1 - d_1 + c_2 - (p_1 + c_2 - c_1) = c_1 - d_1 > 0.$$

(46)

Thus it follows from the inequality (38) that

$$\Pi(x_1, z_1, s_1) \geq \Pi(x_1, Y_1^*, 0) + \frac{\partial \Pi}{\partial z_1}(x_1, Y_1^*, 0)(z_1 - Y_1^*) + \frac{\partial \Pi}{\partial s_1}(x_1, Y_1^*, 0)s_1$$
$$= \Pi(x_1, Y_1^*, 0) + \frac{\partial \Pi}{\partial s_1}(x_1, Y_1^*, 0)s_1 \geq \Pi(x_1, Y_1^*, 0)$$

(47)

for all (z_1, s_1) in the domain D. Since the point $(Y_1^*, 0)$ belongs to D, it is proved that $z_1^* = Y_1^*$ and $s_1^* = 0$, thus $y_1^* = Y_1^* - x_1$.

In the case (2) by the assumptions we know that
$$p_1 + c_2 - c_1 \leq (h_1 + p_1 + c_2 - d_2)w(x_1) \leq p_1 + c_2 - d_1,$$
(48)
and hence the partial derivatives at the point $(x_1, 0)$ are calculated as

$$\frac{\partial \Pi}{\partial z_1}(x_1, x_1, 0) = c_1 - p_1 - c_2 + (h_1 + p_1 + c_2 - d_2)w(x_1)$$
$$\geq c_1 - p_1 - c_2 + (p_1 + c_2 - c_1) = 0,$$
$$\frac{\partial \Pi}{\partial s_1}(x_1, x_1, 0) = p_1 - d_1 + c_2 - (h_1 + p_1 + c_2 - d_2)w(x_1)$$
$$\geq p_1 - d_1 + c_2 - (p_1 + c_2 - d_1) = 0.$$

(49)

By the inequality (38) it is shown

$$\Pi(x_1,z_1,s_1) \geq \Pi(x_1,x_1,0) + \frac{\partial \Pi}{\partial z_1}(x_1,x_1,0)(z_1 - x_1) + \frac{\partial \Pi}{\partial s_1}(x_1,x_1,0)s_1 \geq \Pi(x_1,x_1,0) \quad (50)$$

for all (z_1, s_1) in the domain D. It implies $z_1^* = x_1$ and $s_1^* = 0$, thus $y_1^* = 0$ for $(x_1, 0) \in D$.

In the case (3) we discuss the values of the partial derivatives at the point (x_1, Y_2^*) in the domain D. The condition (3) indicates

$$p_1 + c_2 - d_1 \leq (h_1 + p_1 + c_2 - d_2)w(x_1 - Y_2^*), \quad (51)$$

which leads us by (33) and Lemma to

$$\begin{aligned}
\frac{\partial \Pi}{\partial z_1}(x_1, x_1, Y_2^*) &= c_1 - p_1 - c_2 + (h_1 + p_1 + c_2 - d_2)w(x_1 - Y_2^*) \\
&= c_1 - p_1 - c_2 + (p_1 + c_2 - d_1) = c_1 - d_1 > 0, \\
\frac{\partial \Pi}{\partial s_1}(x_1, x_1, Y_2^*) &= p_1 - d_1 + c_2 - (h_1 + p_1 + c_2 - d_2)w(x_1 - Y_2^*) \\
&= p_1 - d_1 + c_2 - (p_1 + c_2 - d_1) = 0.
\end{aligned} \quad (52)$$

Therefore it is shown that $(x_1, Y_2^*) \in D$ and

$$\begin{aligned}
\Pi(x_1,z_1,s_1) &\geq \Pi(x_1,x_1,Y_2^*) + \frac{\partial \Pi}{\partial z_1}(x_1,x_1,Y_2^*)(z_1 - x_1) + \frac{\partial \Pi}{\partial s_1}(x_1,x_1,Y_2^*)(s_1 - Y_2^*) \\
&\geq \Pi(x_1,x_1,Y_2^*) + \frac{\partial \Pi}{\partial z_1}(x_1,x_1,Y_2^*)(z_1 - x_1) \geq \Pi(x_1,x_1,Y_2^*)
\end{aligned} \quad (53)$$

for all (z_1, s_1) in the domain D. Therefore we see that $z_1^* = x_1$ and $s_1^* = Y_2^*$, and so $y_1^* = 0$.

4. Numerical Illustration

It is shown some numerical illustrations of inventory models giving a special function $g(x)$ and a peculiar probabilistic density function $\varphi_1(b_1)$. The optimal policies are follow from the discussion as above.

4.1 Distribution of Demand

We deal with two distributions of demand, a truncated normal distribution $N[\mu, \sigma^2]$ at zero value and an exponential distribution.

4.1.1 Truncated Normal Distribution

Let $v(x)$ be the probabilistic density function of a normal random variable with parameters μ and σ. Let $F(x)$ be its distribution function. Then the probabilistic density function of a truncated normal distribution at zero value is given by

$$f(b_1) = \begin{cases} 0 & \text{if} \quad b_1 < 0, \\ \dfrac{1}{1-F(0)} v(b_1) & \text{if} \quad b_1 \geq 0. \end{cases} \tag{54}$$

4.1.2 Exponential Distribution

Assume that demand in a period is distributed with an exponential distribution, and that its mean is $1/\lambda$. It is well known that the probabilistic density function of the exponential random variable is

$$f(b_1) = \begin{cases} 0 & \text{if} \quad b_1 < 0, \\ \lambda e^{-\lambda b_1} & \text{if} \quad b_1 \geq 0. \end{cases} \tag{55}$$

4.2 Pattern of Demand

It will be shown the optimal policy in the three cases $g(x) = x$, $g(x) = x^2$ and $g(x) = \sqrt{x}$ that indicates the demand pattern in a period. In case $g(x) = x$, the inventory level l at time T comes

$$l = z_1 - s_1 - g(T/t)b_1 = z_1 - s_1 - (b_1/t)T \tag{56}$$

as a function of variable T. This function is a line.

In case $g(x) = x^2$, the inventory level l at time T gains

$$l = z_1 - s_1 - g(T/t)b_1 = z_1 - s_1 - (b_1/t^2)T^2. \tag{57}$$

This function is a parabola.

In case $g(x) = \sqrt{x}$, the inventory level l at time T becomes

$$l = z_1 - s_1 - g(T/t)b_1 = z_1 - s_1 - (b_1/\sqrt{t})\sqrt{T}. \tag{58}$$

This function is also a parabola.

4.3 Example

Let constants be

$$p_1 = 100, \quad c_1 = 50, \quad c_2 = 40, \quad d_1 = 30, \quad d_2 = 20, \quad h_1 = 5.$$

For the sake of getting the values Y_1^* and Y_2^*, the following constants are required:

$$\frac{h_1 + p_1}{h_1 + p_1 + c_2 - d_2} = 0.84, \quad \frac{p_1 + c_2 - c_1}{h_1 + p_1 + c_2 - d_2} = 0.72, \quad \frac{p_1 + c_2 - d_1}{h_1 + p_1 + c_2 - d_2} = 0.88. \tag{59}$$

The function $w(z)$ is written by

$$w(z) = \int_0^z \varphi_1(b_1) db_1 + 0.84 \int_z^\infty g^{-1}\left(\frac{z}{b_1}\right) \varphi_1(b_1) db_1. \tag{60}$$

Now we could obtain the values of Y_1^* and Y_2^* by the equations

$$w(Y_1^*) = 0.72 \quad \text{and} \quad w(x_1 - Y_2^*) = 0.88. \tag{61}$$

4.3.1 Demand with a Truncated Normal Distribution

In the case demand in a period is a random variable with truncated normal distribution of $N[1000, 400^2]$. Then we have the following table in which there are approximate values of Y_1^* and Y_2^*.

Table 1. Truncated Normal Distribution

	Y_1^*	$x_1 - Y_2^*$
$g(x) = x$	812	1121
$g(x) = x^2$	655	1032
$g(x) = \sqrt{x}$	942	1209

From the values of Y_1^* and Y_2^*, the optimal policies are obtained. For example in the case $g(x) = x$ these are:

Table 2. Optimal Policies in case $g(x) = x$

$w(x_1) \leq 0.72$		$0.72 \leq w(x_1) \leq 0.88$		$0.88 \leq w(x_1)$	
s_1^*	y_1^*	s_1^*	y_1^*	s_1^*	y_1^*
0	$812 - x_1$	0	0	1121	0

4.3.2 Demand with an Exponential Distribution

In the case the distribution of demand in a period is an exponential distribution with mean Then we have the following.

Table 3. Exponential Distribution

	Y_1^*	$x_1 - Y_2^*$
$g(x) = x$	692	1330
$g(x) = x^2$	483	1083
$g(x) = \sqrt{x}$	889	1573

5. Model of Two-Period

5.1 Object Function

In 2-period inventory system there are three costs which are the cost in the first period, one in the second period and the cost of settling demand. Sum them and evaluate its expectation. Then an objective function is obtained as follows.

$$\Pi(x_1, z_1, z_2, y_3, s_1, s_2, s_3)$$
$$= c_1(z_1 - x_1) - d_1 s_1 + h_1 \int_0^\infty I_1(z_1, s_1, b_1) \varphi_1(b_1) db_1$$
$$+ p_1 \int_0^\infty I_2(z_1, s_1, b_1) \varphi_1(b_1) db_1 + c_2(z_2 - x_2) - d_2 s_2 \qquad (62)$$
$$+ h_2 \int_0^\infty I_2(z_2, s_2, b_2) \varphi_2(b_2) db_2 + p_2 \int_0^\infty I_2(z_2, s_2, b_2) \varphi_2(b_2) db_2$$
$$+ c_3 \int_{z_2 - s_2}^\infty (b_2 + s_2 - z_2) \varphi_2(b_2) db_2 - d_3 \int_{z_2 - s_2}^\infty (z_2 - b_2 - s_2) \varphi_2(b_2) db$$

We consider that the variable x_1 is a given constant value. Then it is a problem to find numbers $z_1^*, z_2^*, y_3^*, s_1^*, s_2^*, s_3^*$ such that the function $\Pi(x_1, z_1, z_2, y_3, s_1, s_2, s_3)$ has the minimal value under the conditions:

$$\begin{aligned} z_1 \geq x_1, \ z_2 \geq x_2, \ y_3 \geq 0, \\ 0 \leq s_1 \leq x_1^+, \ 0 \leq s_2 \leq x_2^+, \ 0 \leq s_3 \leq x_3^+. \end{aligned} \qquad (63)$$

5.2 Decomposition of the Object Function

We decompose this problem into two subprograms. The expected cost function $\Pi_2(x_2, z_2, s_2)$ of the problem with only second period is

$$\Pi_2(x_2, z_2, s_2)$$
$$= c_2(z_2 - x_2) - d_2 s_2 + h_2 \int_0^\infty I_2(z_2, s_2, b_2) \varphi_2(b_2) db_2 + p_2 \int_0^\infty I_2(z_2, s_2, b_2) \varphi_2(b_2) db_2 \qquad (64)$$
$$+ c_3 \int_{z_2 - s_2}^\infty (b_2 + s_2 - z_2) \varphi_2(b_2) db_2 - d_3 \int_0^{z_2 - s_2} (z_2 - b_2 - s_2) \varphi_2(b_2) db_2.$$

Since this inventory problem with the second period is considered as a problem of single period, the optimal policy is given at the paragraph 3.4.3.

Next the expected cost function $\Pi_1(x_1, z_1, s_1)$ in the first period is

$$\Pi_1(x_1, z_1, s_1) = c_1(z_1 - x_1) - d_1 s_1 \qquad (65)$$
$$+ h_1 \int_0^\infty I_1(z_1, s_1, b_1) \varphi_1(b_1) db_1 + p_1 \int_0^\infty I_2(z_1, s_1, b_1) \varphi_1(b_1) db.$$

By the relation $x_2 = x_1 - s_1 + y_1 - b_1 = z_1 - s_1 - b_1$, if the total quantity of demand in first period is b_1, then the value of the initial inventory level at second period is decided. It follows from the dynamic programming theory that

$$\Pi(x_1, z_1, z_2, y_3, s_1, s_2, s_3) = \Pi_1(x_1, z_1, s_1) + E_{D_1}\{\Pi_2^*(x_2, z_2^*(x_2), s_2^*(x_2))\} \qquad (66)$$

Finally this suggests that the solutions will be got to solve twice the problem of single period. That is,

$$\Pi^*(x_1) = \max_{z_1, s_1}\{\Pi(x_1, z_1, s_1)\} = \max_{z_1, s_1}\{\Pi_1(x_1, z_1, S_1) + E_{D_1}\{\Pi_2^*(x_2, z_2^*(x_2), s_2^*(x_2))\}\} \qquad (67)$$

under $z_1 \geq x_1$ and $0 \leq s_1 \leq x_1^+$.

We are going to study the solution of this problem in next chance.

References

[1] Cheaitou, A., Production Planning and Inventory Control, Stochastic Optimization Models for Short Life-Cycle, Lap Lambert Academic Publishing, (2010).

[2] Kodama, M., "Probabilistic single period inventory model with partial returns and additional orders", Computers Industrial Engineering, Vol.29, pp.455-459, (1995).

[3] Sakaguchi, M., Kodama, M., "On the Probabilistic Inventory Models with Time-Varying Demand", System Sciences for Economics and Informatics, Kyushu University Press, (2007).

[4] Silver, A. E., Pyke, F. D., Peterson, R., Inventory Management and Production Planning and Scheduling, third edition, John Wiley and Sons, (1998).

[5] Kodama, M., "The Foundation of Production and Inventory System", Kyushu University Press (In Japanese), (1996).

Chapter 6

A Study on Adaptive Parameter Control for Interactive Differential Evolution Using Pairwise Comparison

Setsuko Sakai* and Tetsuyuki Takahama**
*Faculty of Commercial Sciences, Hiroshima Shudo University
1-1 Ozuka-Higashi 1-chome, Asaminami-ku, Hiroshima, JAPAN 731-3195
**Graduate School of Information Sciences, Hiroshima City University
4-1 Ozuka-Higashi 3-chome, Asaminami-ku, Hiroshima, JAPAN 731-3194

Abstract

A key issue in interactive evolutionary computation is to reduce fatigue of a user when the user evaluates candidate solutions. In a pairwise comparison, the user compares two solutions at a time and judges which is superior or inferior. It is thought that the fatigue can be reduced by using the pairwise comparison, compared with usual comparisons where all solutions are compared at a time. In this study, interactive differential evolution (interactive DE, IDE) using the pairwise comparison is improved to realize efficient search by introducing adaptive parameter control into IDE. One of the most successful studies on the adaptive parameter control in DE is JADE. In JADE, two parameter values for DE are generated according to a probability density function which is learned by the parameter values in success cases. There are two problems to introduce the parameter control of JADE into IDE. Sufficient number of function evaluations required for the parameter control is not provided in order to avoid the fatigue. The mutation strategy "current-to-pbest" cannot be adopted in IDE because only the order relation between a parent and its child is provided in pairwise comparison. In this chapter, we study an effective parameter control when the number of function evaluations is limited and "current-to-pbest" strategy is not adopted.

Key Words:
Interactive differential evolution, Adaptive parameter control, Interactive evolutionary computation, Pairwise comparison

1. Introduction

Optimization problems, where objective functions are minimized under given constraints, are very important and frequently appear in the real world. The objective functions are usually defined by mathematical formulas or outputs of simulations. However, there exist some problems where the objective functions are defined by human preference. For example, since a favorite picture or a favorite music is different from person to person, it is necessary for the person to evaluate pictures or pieces of music which are generated in optimization process. Also, since a favorite combination of colors and styles for clothes is different from person to person and is changed day by day, it is necessary for the person to evaluate the combinations.

In order to deal with the human preference, interactive evolutionary computation (IEC) has been studied where the objective values are given by interaction between a person and a system based on evolutionary computation (EC). EC is an optimization method which models biological evolution and is a population-based stochastic search method where an optimal solution is searched using multiple candidate solutions, or individuals. In IEC, generating candidate solutions and evaluating the solutions by a human are repeated: Plural solutions generated by EC is presented to a user, the user evaluates the solutions, and new solutions are generated by EC using the evaluation values. For example, in the human evaluation, pictures or images created by combinations of colors and styles are presented to the user. The user compares pictures or images and evaluates them.

However, it is harder work than expected to compare plural individuals and to give evaluation values to all individuals. Therefore, it has been the biggest problem in IEC to reduce human fatigue. In order to reduce the fatigue, there are following methods [1, 2]:

(A) Reducing fatigue in evaluation by using rough measure for evaluation:

For example, it is difficult for a user to distinguish between 50 point and 51 point on a scale of a hundred. The user will feel unsure for selecting a proper score and the feeling brings a mental burden to the user. On the other hand, if a rough measure like five-grade evaluation is adopted, the evaluation can be done with confidence and it is thought that the fatigue is reduced. In addition, there exists a pairwise comparison or a paired comparison method where user compares two solutions at a time and judges which is superior or inferior. The evaluation becomes easier than evaluation using other comparisons.

However, the rough measure decreases the amount of information obtained from a user and it might increases the number of evaluations to obtain a satisfactory solution.

Also, for example, when plural images are shown to a user, if similar images are arranged in the neighborhood, the comparison of images will become easier compared with images being arranged at random.

(B) Reducing the number of function evaluations:

In IEC, it is important to realize sufficient evolution using a small number of individuals in a small number of generations when the fatigue is taken into consideration. Thus, it is necessary to develop efficient EC using a limited number of individuals.

Also, there exist researches where user's preference is learned from already obtained evaluation values and the learned preference model is used to estimate values of evaluation function and reduce the number of function evaluations by the user.

In this study, Interactive Differential Evolution (IDE) [2, 3] using the pairwise comparison and adaptive parameter control is proposed. It is thought that the problem (A) can be solved by using the pairwise comparison and the problem (B) can be solved by realizing efficient search by introducing adaptive parameter control into IDE.

One of the most successful studies on the adaptive parameter control in DE is JADE. In JADE, two parameter values for DE are generated according to a probability density function which is learned by the parameter values in success cases, where the child is better than the parent. There are two problems when the parameter control of JADE is introduced into IDE. Sufficient number of function evaluations required for the parameter control is not provided in order to avoid the fatigue. The mutation strategy "current-to-pbest", which realizes efficient search around near best solutions using total order among all solutions, cannot be adopted in IDE because only the order relation between a parent and its child is provided in pairwise comparison.

In this study, we propose an improved effective parameter control when the number of function evaluations is limited and "current-to-pbest" strategy is not adopted. The advantage of the proposed method is shown by solving some benchmark functions and by comparing the results with those by standard IDEs.

In Section 2, related works are briefly reviewed. DE is explained in Section 3. In Section 4, JADE is explained and IDE with parameter control of JADE is proposed. In Section 5, experimental results on benchmark problems are shown. Finally, conclusions are described in Section 6.

2. Related Works

Evolutionary algorithms (EAs) are optimization algorithms inspired by biological evolution and include Genetic Algorithm (GA), Evolution Strategy (ES), Differential Evolution (DE) [4, 5] and so on. EAs are population-based stochastic optimization algorithms. EAs have been proved to be powerful function optimization algorithms and outperform conventional optimization algorithms for various problems including discontinuous, non-differential, multimodal, noisy problems, and multi-objective problems. EAs can be easily implemented and have been successfully applied to various fields including science and engineering.

In order to improve the efficiency, many researchers have been studying on controlling the parameters and the strategies in EAs. The methods of the control can be classified into some categories. For example, following methods are proposed in DE [6].

(1) selection-based control: Strategies and parameter values are selected regardless of current search state. CoDE(composite DE) [7] generates three trial vectors using three strategies with randomly selected parameter values from parameter candidate sets and the best trial vector will head to the survivor selection.

(2) observation-based control: The current search state is observed, proper parameter values are inferred according to the observation, and parameters and/or strategies are dynamically controlled. FADE(Fuzzy Adaptive DE) [8] observes the movement of search points and the change of function values between successive generations, and controls F and CR. DESFC(DE with Speciation and Fuzzy Clustering) [9] adopts fuzzy clustering, observes partition entropy of search points, and controls CR and the mutation strategies between the rand and the species-best strategy. In some researches, landscape modality of objective function is observed to decide current landscape of the function is unimodal or multimodal. The modality is detected by checking the changes of objective values in sampling points which is generated along a line connecting the centroid of individuals and the best individual. LMDE(DE with detecting Landscape Modality) [6] controls F and LMDEa(DE with Landscape Modality detection and an diversity Archive) [10] controls F, CR and crossover operations based on the landscape modality.

(3) success-based control: It is recognized as a success case when a better search point than

the parent is generated. The parameters and/or strategies are adjusted so that the values in the success cases are frequently used. It is thought that the self-adaptation, where parameters are contained in individuals and are evolved by applying evolutionary operators to the parameters, is included in this category. DESAP(Differential Evolution with Self-Adapting Populations) [11] controls F, CR and population size self-adaptively. SaDE(Self-adaptive DE) [12] controls the selection probability of the mutation strategies according to the success rates and controls the mean value of CR for each strategy according to the mean value in success case. jDE(self-adaptive DE algorithm) [13] controls F and CR self-adaptively. JADE(adaptive DE with optional external archive) [14] and MDE_pBX(modified DE with p-best crossover) [15] control the mean and power mean values of F and CR according to the mean values in success cases.

In the category (1), useful knowledge to improve the search efficiency is ignored. In the category (2), it is difficult to select proper type of observation which is independent of the optimization problem and its scale. In the category (3), when a new good search point is found near the parent, parameters are adjusted to the direction of convergence. In problems with ridge landscape or multimodal landscape, where good search points exist in small region, parameters are tuned for small success and big success will be missed. Thus, search process would be trapped at a local optimal solution. In JADE, as for a mean value of F a weighted mean value by the value of F is used to generate larger F than a usual mean value and it is succeeded to reduce the problem of the convergence.

In this study, we introduce the parameter control of JADE in the category (3) to IDE.

3. Optimization by Differential Evolution

3.1 Optimization Problems

In this study, the following optimization problem with lower bound and upper bound constraints will be discussed.

$$\begin{aligned} &\text{minimize} \quad f(\boldsymbol{x}) \\ &\text{subject to} \quad l_i \leq x_i \leq u_i, \ i = 1, \ldots, D, \end{aligned} \tag{1}$$

where $\boldsymbol{x} = (x_1, x_2, \cdots, x_D)$ is a D dimensional vector and $f(\boldsymbol{x})$ is an objective function. The function f is a nonlinear real-valued function. Values l_i and u_i are the lower bound and the upper bound of x_i, respectively. Let the search space in which every point satisfies the lower and upper bound constraints be denoted by $\mathcal{S}$.

3.2 Differential Evolution

DE is a stochastic direct search method using a population or multiple search points. In DE, initial individuals are randomly generated within given search space and form an initial population. Each individual contains D genes as decision variables. At each generation or iteration, all individuals are selected as parents. Each parent is processed as follows: The mutation operation begins by choosing several individuals from the population except for the parent in the processing. The first individual is a base vector. All subsequent individuals are paired to create difference vectors. The difference vectors are scaled by a scaling factor F and added to the base vector. The resulting vector, or a mutant vector, is then recombined with the parent. The probability of recombination at an element is controlled by a crossover rate CR. This crossover operation produces a trial vector. Finally, for survivor selection, the trial vector is accepted for the next generation if the trial vector is better than the parent.

There are some variants of DE that have been proposed. The variants are classified using the notation DE/*base*/*num*/*cross* such as DE/rand/1/bin and DE/rand/1/exp. "*base*" specifies a way of selecting an individual that will form the base vector. For example, DE/rand selects an individual for the base vector at random from the population. DE/best selects the best individual in the population. "*num*" specifies the number of difference vectors used to perturb the base vector. In case of DE/rand/1, for example, for each parent x^i, three individuals x^{r1}, x^{r2} and x^{r3} are chosen randomly from the population without overlapping x^i and each other. A new vector, or a mutant vector m is generated by the base vector x^{r1} and the difference vector $x^{r2} - x^{r3}$, where F is the scaling factor.

$$m = x^{r1} + F(x^{r2} - x^{r3}) \quad (2)$$

"*cross*" specifies the type of crossover that is used to create a child. For example, 'bin' indicates that the crossover is controlled by the binomial crossover using a constant crossover rate, and 'exp' indicates that the crossover is controlled by a kind of two-point crossover using exponentially decreasing the crossover rate. Fig. 1 shows the binomial and exponential crossover. A new child x^{child} is generated from the parent x^i and the mutant vector m, where CR is a crossover rate.

```
binomial crossover DE/·/·/bin
   j_rand=randint(1,D);
   for(k=1; k ≤ D; k++) {
      if(k == j_rand || u(0,1) < CR) x_k^child=m_k;
      else x_k^child=x_k^i;
   }
exponential crossover DE/·/·/exp
   k=1; j=randint(1,D);
   do {
      x_j^child=m_j;
      k=k+1; j=(j+1)%D;
   } while(k ≤ D && u(0,1) < CR);
   while(k ≤ D) {
      x_j^child=x_j^i;
      k=k+1; j=(j+1)%D;
   }
```

Figure 1. Binomial and exponential crossover operation, where randint(1,D) generates an integer randomly from $[1, D]$ and $u(l, r)$ is a uniform random number generator in $[l, r]$.

3.3 The Algorithm of Differential Evolution

The algorithm of DE is as follows:

Step1 Initialization of a population. Initial N individuals $P = \{x^i | i = 1, 2, \cdots, N\}$ are generated randomly in search space and form an initial population.

Step2 Termination condition. If the number of function evaluations exceeds the maximum number of evaluation $FE_{\max}$, the algorithm is terminated.

Step3 DE operations. Each individual x^i is selected as a target vector (parent). If all individuals are selected, go to Step4. A mutant vector m is generated according to Eq. (2). A trial vector (child) is generated from the parent x^i and the mutant vector m using a crossover operation shown in Fig. 1. Pairwise comparison between the parent and the child is performed and if the child is better than the parent, or the DE operation is succeeded, the child survives. Otherwise the parent survives. In IDE, the pairwise comparison is performed by a user or a human. Go back to Step3 and the next individual is selected as a parent.

Step4 Survivor selection. The population P is formed by the survivors. Go back to Step2.

Fig. 2 shows a pseudo-code of DE/rand/1.

```
DE/rand/1()
{
// Initialize a population
 P=N individuals generated randomly in S;
 FE=N;
 for(t=1; FE ≤ FE_max; t++) {
  for(i=1; i ≤ N; i++) {
// DE operation
    x^r1=Randomly selected from P(r1 ≠ i);
    x^r2=Randomly selected from P(r2 ∉ {i,r1});
    x^r3=Randomly selected from P(r3 ∉ {i,r1,r2});
    m=x^r1+F(x^r2 − x^r3);
    x^child=trial vector is generated from x^i and m by a crossover operation;
// Survivor selection
    if(f(x^child) < f(x^i))  z^i=x^child;
    else                      z^i=x^i;
    FE=FE+1;
  }
  P={z^i, i = 1,2,···,N};
 }
}
```

Figure 2. The pseudo-code of DE, FE is the number of function evaluations.

4. JADE

4.1 Original Algorithm

In JADE, the mean value of the scaling factor μ_F and the mean value of the crossover rate μ_{CR} are learned to define two probability density functions, where initial values are $\mu_F=\mu_{CR}=0.5$. The scaling factor F_i and the crossover rate CR_i for each individual x^i are independently generated according to the following equations:

$$F_i \sim C(\mu_F, \sigma_F) \quad (3)$$
$$CR_i \sim N(\mu_{CR}, \sigma_{CR}^2) \quad (4)$$

where $C(\mu_F, \sigma_F)$ is Cauchy distribution with a location parameter μ_F and a scale parameter $\sigma_F=0.1$, and $N(\mu_{CR}, \sigma_{CR}^2)$ is normal distribution of a mean μ_{CR} and a standard deviation $\sigma_{CR}=0.1$. CR_i is truncated to $[0, 1]$ and F_i is truncated to be 1 if $F_i \geq 1$ or regenerated if $F_i \leq 0$. The location μ_F and the mean μ_{CR} are updated as follows:

$$\mu_F = (1-c)\mu_F + cS_{F2}/S_F \quad (5)$$
$$\mu_{CR} = (1-c)\mu_{CR} + cS_{CR}/S_N \quad (6)$$

where S_N is the number of success cases, S_F, S_{F^2} and S_{CR} are the sum of F, F^2 and CR in success cases, respectively. A constant c is a weight of update in (0,1] and the recommended value is 0.1.

JADE adopts a strategy called "current-to-pbest" where an intermediate point between a target vector and a randomly selected point from top individuals is used as a base vector. A mutation vector is generated as follows:

$$\bm{m} = \bm{x}^i + F_i(\bm{x}^{pbest} - \bm{x}^i) + F_i(\bm{x}^{r1} - \bm{x}^{r2}) \qquad (7)$$

where $\bm{x}^{pbest}$ is a randomly selected individual from the top $100p\%$ individuals and the recommended value is 0.05.

It is shown that JADE with an archive, which consists of inferior solutions, can attain good performance. The archive A is initiated to be empty. After each generation, the parent solutions that defeated by the trial vectors in the survivor selection are added to the archive. If the archive size exceeds a threshold N_A, some solutions are randomly removed from the archive to keep the archive size constant. In this case, $\bm{x}^{r2}$ is selected from the union $P \cup A$ where P is the current population.

Fig. 3 shows the pseudo-code of JADE/current-to-pbest/1/bin with an archive.

4.2 Proposed Algorithm

In IEC with pairwise comparison, the best individuals used in JADE/current-to-pbest cannot be identified because the objective values of individuals are not given. In this study, three mutation strategies that can be used with pairwise comparison are adopted as follows:

- rand:

$$\bm{m} = \bm{x}^{r1} + F_i(\bm{x}^{r2} - \bm{x}^{r3}) \qquad (8)$$

where $r1$ and $r2$ are random integers in $[1, N]$ and are different with each other and from the target vector $\bm{x}^i$. $\bm{x}^{r3}$ is randomly selected from $P \cup A$ and is different from $\bm{x}^{r1}$, $\bm{x}^{r2}$ and $\bm{x}^i$.

- current-to:

$$\bm{m} = \bm{x}^i + F_i(\bm{x}^{r2} - \bm{x}^{r3}) \qquad (9)$$

where $r2$ is a random integer in $[1, N]$ and is different from the target vector $\bm{x}^i$. $\bm{x}^{r3}$ is randomly selected from $P \cup A$ and is different from $\bm{x}^{r2}$ and $\bm{x}^i$.

- current-to-rand:

$$\bm{m} = \bm{x}^i + F_i(\bm{x}^{r1} - \bm{x}^i) + F_i(\bm{x}^{r2} - \bm{x}^{r3}) \qquad (10)$$

where $r1$ and $r2$ are random integers in $[1, N]$ and are different with each other and from the target vector $\bm{x}^i$. $\bm{x}^{r3}$ is randomly selected from $P \cup A$ and is different from $\bm{x}^{r1}$, $\bm{x}^{r2}$ and $\bm{x}^i$.

The algorithm of modified JADE can be described as follows:

Step0 Parameter setup.

The mean value of scaling factor $\mu_F = 0.5$ and the mean value of crossover rate $\mu_{CR} = 0.5$. The standard deviations $\sigma_F = 0.1$ and $\sigma_{CR} = 0.1$. An archive A is initialized as an empty set.

```
JADE/current-to-pbest/1/bin()
{
  μ_F=μ_CR=0.5; σ_F = σ_CR=0.1; A=∅;
// Initialize a population
  P=N individuals generated randomly in S;
  FE=N;
  for(t=1; FE ≤ FE_max; t++) {
    SC=∅;
    for(i=1; i ≤ N; i++) {
      do {
        F_i=μ_F + C(0,σ_F);
      } while(F_i ≤ 0);
      if(F_i > 1) F_i = 1;
      CR_i=μ_CR + N(0,σ_CR);
      if(CR_i < 0) CR_i=0;
      else if(CR_i > 1) CR_i=1;
      x^pbest=Randomly selected from top 100p% in P;
      x^r1=Randomly selected from P(r1 ∉ {i});
      x^r2=Randomly selected from P ∪ A(r2 ∉ {i,r1});
      m=x^i+F_i(x^pbest − x^i)+F_i(x^r1 − x^r2);
      x^child=trial vector is generated from x^i and m by binomial crossover;
      FE=FE+1;
// Survivor selection
      if(f(x^child) < f(x^i)) {
        z^i=x^child;
        SC=SC ∪ {(F_i,CR_i)}; // success cases are stored
        if(|A| == N_A) a randomly selected element in A is removed.
        A=A ∪ {x^i};
      }
      else z^i=x^i;
    }
    P={z^i, i=1,2,⋯,N};
    if(|SC| > 0) {
      μ_F=(1 − c)μ_F + c∑_{F_i∈SC} F_i^2/∑_{F_i∈SC} F_i;
      μ_CR=(1 − c)μ_CR + c∑_{CR_i∈SC} CR_i/|SC|;
    }
  }
}
```

Figure 3. The pseudo-code of JADE/current-to-pbest with an archive where N_A is archive size

Step1 Initialization of the individuals.

t=0. Initial N individuals $P = \{x^i | i = 1, 2, \cdots, N\}$ are generated randomly in search space S and form an initial population.

Step2 New generation.

t=t+1. The list of success cases SC is made empty.

Step3 Termination condition.

If the number of function evaluations exceeds the maximum number of evaluations FE_{max}, the algorithm is terminated.

Step4 DE operation with adaptive parameters.

The following DE operation is applied to all individuals in the current population P: The scaling factor F_i is generated according to Cauchy distribution with location μ_F and scale σ_F. The crossover rate CR_i is generated according to normal distribution with mean μ_{CR} and standard deviation σ_{CR}. rand/1/bin, current-to/1/bin or current-to-rand/1/bin operation with F_i and CR_i is executed and a new child x^{child} is generated. If the new one is better than the parent, then the operation is treated as a success case, the child becomes a survivor and the parent is added to the archive A. If the archive size $|A|$ exceeds a threshold N_A, a randomly selected element in A is removed. In the success case, the successful combination of parameter values (F_i, CR_i) is added to success cases SC. Otherwise, the parent x^i becomes a survivor.

After the DE operation is applied to all individuals, the population is replaced with survivors.

Step5 Update of adaptive parameters.

The mean of the scaling factor μ_F and the mean of crossover rate μ_{CR} are updated using SC. Go back to Step2.

5. Numerical Experiments

5.1 Test Problems

In this section, benchmark problems including sphere function (f_1), Rosenbrock function (f_2), ill-scaled Rosenbrock function (f_3) and Rastrigin function (f_4) are solved. These functions have various surfaces such as unimodal surface in f_1, ridge structure in f_2 and f_3, and multimodal bumpy surfaces. The function definitions and their search spaces, where D is the dimension of the decision vector, are as follows:

- f_1: Sphere function

$$f(\boldsymbol{x}) = \sum_{i=1}^{D} x_i^2, \quad -5.12 \leq x_i \leq 5.12 \tag{11}$$

This function is a unimodal function and has the minimum value 0 at $(0, 0, \cdots, 0)$.

- f_2: Rosenbrock function

$$f(\boldsymbol{x}) = \sum_{i=2}^{D} \{100(x_1 - x_i^2)^2 + (x_i - 1)^2\}, \tag{12}$$

$$-2.048 \leq x_i \leq 2.048$$

This function is a unimodal function with steep surface and has the minimum value 0 at $(1, 1, \cdots, 1)$.

- f_3: ill-scaled Rosenbrock function

$$f(\boldsymbol{x}) = \sum_{i=2}^{D} \{100(x_1 - (ix_i)^2)^2 + (ix_i - 1)^2\}, \tag{13}$$

$$-2.048/i \leq x_i \leq 2.048/i$$

This function is a unimodal and ill-scaled function with steep surface and has the minimum value 0 at $(1, \frac{1}{2}, \cdots, \frac{1}{D})$.

- f_4: Rastrigin function

$$f(\boldsymbol{x}) = 10D + \sum_{i=1}^{D} \{x_i^2 - 10\cos(2\pi x_i)\}, \tag{14}$$

$$-5.12 \leq x_i \leq 5.12$$

This function is a multimodal function with bumpy surface and has the minimum value 0 at $(0, 0, \cdots, 0)$.

Figure 4, 5 and 6 show the graphs of three functions f_1, f_2 and f_4 in the case of $D = 2$.

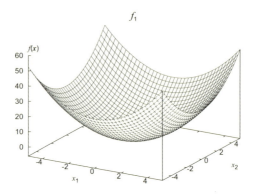

Figure 4. Graph of f_1

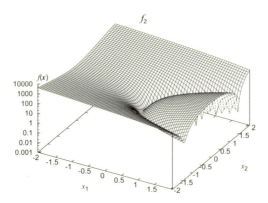

Figure 5. Graph of f_2

Table 1 shows the features of the functions.

5.2 Experimental Conditions

Functions f_1 to f_4 are optimized using rand, current-to and current-to-rand strategies to compare the performance of mutation strategies for IEC with pairwise comparison. Original functions f_1 to f_4 have optimal solutions at the center of search space or near the center. In order to know the ability of finding solutions far from the center, the optimal solutions are shifted by giving offset values $0.2u_i$, $0.4u_i$ and $0.8u_i$. So, 4 cases with offset 0, 0.2, 0.4 and 0.8 u_i are examined for each function. The dimensions of the problems are $D = 5$, 10, 20 and 30. Individuals with population size $N = 12$ are evolved in 50 generations. Thus, the maximum number of function evaluations $FE_{\max} = 600$. In order to know accurate average performance, 1000 trials are performed.

The four algorithms of DE with $F = 0.5$ and $CR = 0.5$, DE with $F = 0.5$ and $CR = 0.9$, DE with $F = 0.7$ and $CR = 0.9$, and JADE with an archive are compared with varying the mutation

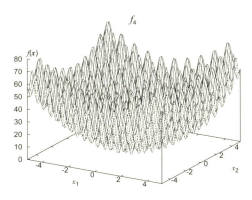

Figure 6. Graphs of f_4

Table 1. Features of test problems

Function	modality	surface	dependency of variables	ill-scale
f_1	unimodal	smooth	—	—
f_2	unimodal	steep	strong	—
f_3	unimodal	steep	strong	strong
f_4	multimodal	bumpy	—	—

strategy as rand, current-to, and current-to-rand. The parameters for JADE are: the archive size $N_A = N$ and a weight for updating means c=0.1.

5.3 Experimental Results

Table 2 – 5, Table 6 – 9, Table 10 – 13 and Table 14 – 17 show the results of 5, 10, 20 and 30 dimension problems with varying offset values as 0, 0.2, 0.4 and 0.8 u_i. Each problem with an offset is solved by four algorithms with changing mutation strategies as rand, current-to and current-to-rand. The best results among all mutations strategies of all algorithms are highlighted by bold fonts.

As for problems of 5 dimensions, JADE with rand strategy attained best results in 5 cases over all functions, DE with $F = 0.7$ and $CR = 0.9$ using current-to-rand strategy attained best results in 6 cases over 2 functions, JADE with current-to-rand strategy attained best results in 3 cases over 2 functions, and DE with $F = 0.5$ and $CR = 0.5$ using current-to-rand strategy attained best results in 2 cases of f_4. DE with $F = 0.5$ and $CR = 0.9$ could not attain good results. Also, current-to strategy could not attain good results.

As for problems of 10 dimensions, JADE with current-to-rand strategy attained best results in 10 cases over all functions, JADE with rand strategy attained best results in 5 cases over all functions, and DE with $F = 0.5$ and $CR = 0.5$ using current-to-rand strategy attained best result in 1 case of f_4. DE with $F = 0.5$ and $CR = 0.9$ and DE with $F = 0.7$ and $CR = 0.9$ could not attain good results. Also, current-to strategy could not attain good results.

As for problems of 20 dimensions, JADE with current-to-rand strategy attained best results

Table 2. Results in 5 dimensions by standard DEs with F=0.5 and CR=0.5

func.	offset	rand	current-to	current-to-rand
f_1	0.0	1.686e-03 ± 6.99e-03	1.878e-01 ± 1.25e-01	7.198e-03 ± 3.63e-02
	0.2	1.763e-03 ± 1.58e-02	2.085e-01 ± 1.43e-01	1.874e-02 ± 1.01e-01
	0.4	2.515e-03 ± 1.70e-02	2.532e-01 ± 1.64e-01	6.773e-02 ± 2.94e-01
	0.8	4.441e-02 ± 3.51e-01	5.058e-01 ± 3.59e-01	1.205e+00 ± 2.38e+00
f_2	0.0	3.761e+00 ± 2.96e+00	5.793e+00 ± 2.73e+00	2.707e+00 ± 1.09e+00
	0.2	3.385e+00 ± 2.09e+00	5.885e+00 ± 2.53e+00	3.043e+00 ± 1.21e+00
	0.4	3.347e+00 ± 1.95e+00	6.235e+00 ± 3.03e+00	3.789e+00 ± 2.31e+00
	0.8	4.417e+00 ± 3.48e+00	9.367e+00 ± 6.51e+00	1.573e+01 ± 8.27e+01
f_3	0.0	3.761e+00 ± 2.96e+00	5.793e+00 ± 2.73e+00	2.707e+00 ± 1.09e+00
	0.2	3.385e+00 ± 2.09e+00	5.885e+00 ± 2.53e+00	3.043e+00 ± 1.21e+00
	0.4	3.347e+00 ± 1.95e+00	6.235e+00 ± 3.03e+00	3.789e+00 ± 2.31e+00
	0.8	4.417e+00 ± 3.48e+00	9.367e+00 ± 6.51e+00	1.573e+01 ± 8.27e+01
f_4	0.0	7.414e+00 ± 2.79e+00	1.499e+01 ± 4.31e+00	**5.417e+00 ± 2.12e+00**
	0.2	7.428e+00 ± 2.80e+00	1.496e+01 ± 4.53e+00	**5.602e+00 ± 2.28e+00**
	0.4	7.637e+00 ± 2.87e+00	1.610e+01 ± 4.80e+00	6.717e+00 ± 2.65e+00
	0.8	8.272e+00 ± 3.33e+00	1.876e+01 ± 5.51e+00	1.309e+01 ± 6.17e+00

Table 3. Results in 5 dimensions by standard DEs with F=0.5 and CR=0.9

func.	offset	rand	current-to	current-to-rand
f_1	0.0	7.441e-02 ± 3.32e-01	3.187e-01 ± 1.98e-01	1.369e-01 ± 3.06e-01
	0.2	7.125e-02 ± 2.21e-01	3.502e-01 ± 2.21e-01	2.837e-01 ± 6.13e-01
	0.4	1.383e-01 ± 5.04e-01	4.429e-01 ± 2.84e-01	1.003e+00 ± 1.78e+00
	0.8	1.068e+00 ± 2.27e+00	7.496e-01 ± 5.07e-01	8.602e+00 ± 8.27e+00
f_2	0.0	2.864e+00 ± 1.50e+00	6.910e+00 ± 3.49e+00	2.812e+00 ± 1.05e+00
	0.2	3.069e+00 ± 1.74e+00	7.123e+00 ± 3.58e+00	3.873e+00 ± 5.36e+00
	0.4	3.672e+00 ± 3.50e+00	7.658e+00 ± 4.26e+00	7.854e+00 ± 2.78e+01
	0.8	1.314e+01 ± 4.10e+01	1.206e+01 ± 9.24e+00	1.818e+02 ± 4.29e+02
f_3	0.0	2.864e+00 ± 1.50e+00	6.910e+00 ± 3.49e+00	2.812e+00 ± 1.05e+00
	0.2	3.069e+00 ± 1.74e+00	7.123e+00 ± 3.58e+00	3.873e+00 ± 5.36e+00
	0.4	3.672e+00 ± 3.50e+00	7.658e+00 ± 4.26e+00	7.854e+00 ± 2.78e+01
	0.8	1.314e+01 ± 4.10e+01	1.206e+01 ± 9.24e+00	1.818e+02 ± 4.29e+02
f_4	0.0	1.140e+01 ± 4.38e+00	2.160e+01 ± 5.27e+00	9.161e+00 ± 3.30e+00
	0.2	1.139e+01 ± 4.35e+00	2.201e+01 ± 5.53e+00	9.619e+00 ± 3.38e+00
	0.4	1.185e+01 ± 4.42e+00	2.258e+01 ± 5.65e+00	1.197e+01 ± 4.82e+00
	0.8	1.395e+01 ± 6.10e+00	2.527e+01 ± 6.41e+00	2.447e+01 ± 1.08e+01

Table 4. Results in 5 dimensions by standard DEs with F=0.7 and CR=0.9

func.	offset	rand	current-to	current-to-rand
f_1	0.0	1.955e-02 ± 4.62e-02	6.552e-01 ± 4.28e-01	6.797e-03 ± 3.56e-02
	0.2	2.002e-02 ± 4.92e-02	7.061e-01 ± 4.65e-01	8.216e-03 ± 4.16e-02
	0.4	2.053e-02 ± 3.23e-02	8.055e-01 ± 4.78e-01	2.749e-02 ± 1.60e-01
	0.8	6.735e-02 ± 2.75e-01	1.348e+00 ± 8.40e-01	3.662e-01 ± 1.06e+00
f_2	0.0	3.126e+00 ± 1.57e+00	1.162e+01 ± 8.57e+00	**2.633e+00 ± 1.34e+00**
	0.2	3.111e+00 ± 1.39e+00	1.182e+01 ± 8.59e+00	**2.628e+00 ± 1.17e+00**
	0.4	3.188e+00 ± 1.68e+00	1.329e+01 ± 9.56e+00	**2.954e+00 ± 1.84e+00**
	0.8	4.468e+00 ± 3.91e+00	2.396e+01 ± 2.15e+01	6.025e+00 ± 1.04e+01
f_3	0.0	3.126e+00 ± 1.57e+00	1.162e+01 ± 8.57e+00	**2.633e+00 ± 1.34e+00**
	0.2	3.111e+00 ± 1.39e+00	1.182e+01 ± 8.59e+00	**2.628e+00 ± 1.17e+00**
	0.4	3.188e+00 ± 1.68e+00	1.329e+01 ± 9.56e+00	**2.954e+00 ± 1.84e+00**
	0.8	4.468e+00 ± 3.91e+00	2.396e+01 ± 2.15e+01	6.025e+00 ± 1.04e+01
f_4	0.0	1.583e+01 ± 4.91e+00	2.423e+01 ± 5.85e+00	1.396e+01 ± 4.12e+00
	0.2	1.611e+01 ± 4.94e+00	2.406e+01 ± 6.01e+00	1.384e+01 ± 4.05e+00
	0.4	1.623e+01 ± 4.97e+00	2.502e+01 ± 6.40e+00	1.415e+01 ± 4.31e+00
	0.8	1.706e+01 ± 5.48e+00	2.760e+01 ± 6.75e+00	1.683e+01 ± 5.52e+00

Table 5. Results in 5 dimensions by JADE

func.	offset	rand	current-to	current-to-rand
f_1	0.0	1.516e-03 ± 1.77e-03	1.227e-01 ± 8.47e-02	**6.699e-04 ± 4.58e-03**
	0.2	1.638e-03 ± 1.81e-03	1.295e-01 ± 9.65e-02	**1.215e-03 ± 1.79e-02**
	0.4	**1.703e-03 ± 2.01e-03**	1.523e-01 ± 1.11e-01	6.063e-03 ± 5.20e-02
	0.8	**2.819e-03 ± 4.99e-03**	2.851e-01 ± 2.04e-01	1.460e-01 ± 6.35e-01
f_2	0.0	3.835e+00 ± 2.42e+00	5.344e+00 ± 2.28e+00	2.730e+00 ± 1.17e+00
	0.2	3.482e+00 ± 2.10e+00	5.232e+00 ± 2.40e+00	2.871e+00 ± 1.19e+00
	0.4	3.448e+00 ± 2.04e+00	5.601e+00 ± 2.55e+00	3.325e+00 ± 1.67e+00
	0.8	**3.975e+00 ± 2.91e+00**	7.433e+00 ± 4.69e+00	6.171e+00 ± 9.40e+00
f_3	0.0	3.837e+00 ± 2.42e+00	5.344e+00 ± 2.28e+00	2.730e+00 ± 1.17e+00
	0.2	3.482e+00 ± 2.10e+00	5.232e+00 ± 2.40e+00	2.871e+00 ± 1.19e+00
	0.4	3.447e+00 ± 2.04e+00	5.601e+00 ± 2.55e+00	3.325e+00 ± 1.67e+00
	0.8	**3.975e+00 ± 2.91e+00**	7.433e+00 ± 4.69e+00	6.171e+00 ± 9.40e+00
f_4	0.0	7.469e+00 ± 2.69e+00	1.351e+01 ± 4.07e+00	5.644e+00 ± 2.14e+00
	0.2	7.493e+00 ± 2.75e+00	1.378e+01 ± 4.04e+00	5.904e+00 ± 2.31e+00
	0.4	7.452e+00 ± 2.73e+00	1.402e+01 ± 4.24e+00	**6.444e+00 ± 2.52e+00**
	0.8	**7.782e+00 ± 2.90e+00**	1.637e+01 ± 5.20e+00	9.825e+00 ± 4.88e+00

Table 6. Results in 10 dimensions by standard DEs with F=0.5 and CR=0.5

func.	offset	rand	current-to	current-to-rand
f_1	0.0	2.777e-01 ± 2.26e-01	5.912e+00 ± 2.28e+00	2.287e-01 ± 3.09e-01
	0.2	2.789e-01 ± 3.25e-01	6.219e+00 ± 2.42e+00	3.449e-01 ± 4.81e-01
	0.4	3.203e-01 ± 3.72e-01	7.647e+00 ± 3.08e+00	1.082e+00 ± 1.34e+00
	0.8	9.711e-01 ± 1.55e+00	1.398e+01 ± 5.72e+00	9.978e+00 ± 7.09e+00
f_2	0.0	3.265e+01 ± 2.52e+01	7.809e+01 ± 4.51e+01	1.264e+01 ± 7.82e+00
	0.2	2.844e+01 ± 2.00e+01	8.228e+01 ± 4.97e+01	1.433e+01 ± 7.75e+00
	0.4	3.003e+01 ± 2.71e+01	1.049e+02 ± 6.71e+01	2.210e+01 ± 1.45e+01
	0.8	5.230e+01 ± 5.41e+01	2.660e+02 ± 1.78e+02	1.376e+02 ± 2.46e+02
f_3	0.0	3.265e+01 ± 2.52e+01	7.809e+01 ± 4.51e+01	1.264e+01 ± 7.82e+00
	0.2	2.844e+01 ± 2.00e+01	8.228e+01 ± 4.97e+01	1.433e+01 ± 7.75e+00
	0.4	3.003e+01 ± 2.71e+01	1.049e+02 ± 6.71e+01	2.210e+01 ± 1.45e+01
	0.8	5.230e+01 ± 5.41e+01	2.660e+02 ± 1.78e+02	1.376e+02 ± 2.46e+02
f_4	0.0	4.349e+01 ± 8.14e+00	6.770e+01 ± 1.09e+01	**3.516e+01 ± 6.91e+00**
	0.2	4.360e+01 ± 8.05e+00	6.888e+01 ± 1.10e+01	3.676e+01 ± 7.09e+00
	0.4	4.356e+01 ± 8.41e+00	7.280e+01 ± 1.18e+01	4.062e+01 ± 8.33e+00
	0.8	4.716e+01 ± 8.88e+00	8.818e+01 ± 1.56e+01	6.469e+01 ± 1.41e+01

Table 7. Results in 10 dimensions by standard DEs with F=0.5 and CR=0.9

func.	offset	rand	current-to	current-to-rand
f_1	0.0	1.465e+00 ± 1.40e+00	1.344e+01 ± 4.75e+00	1.809e+00 ± 1.39e+00
	0.2	1.714e+00 ± 1.61e+00	1.411e+01 ± 4.81e+00	3.107e+00 ± 2.31e+00
	0.4	2.932e+00 ± 2.84e+00	1.575e+01 ± 5.71e+00	8.518e+00 ± 5.36e+00
	0.8	1.182e+01 ± 9.73e+00	2.642e+01 ± 1.20e+01	4.403e+01 ± 1.81e+01
f_2	0.0	2.334e+01 ± 1.95e+01	1.616e+02 ± 9.21e+01	1.387e+01 ± 8.23e+00
	0.2	2.490e+01 ± 2.25e+01	1.782e+02 ± 1.01e+02	2.220e+01 ± 3.18e+01
	0.4	4.026e+01 ± 5.60e+01	2.263e+02 ± 1.41e+02	7.409e+01 ± 1.10e+02
	0.8	2.505e+02 ± 4.45e+02	5.809e+02 ± 4.92e+02	1.555e+03 ± 1.61e+03
f_3	0.0	2.334e+01 ± 1.95e+01	1.616e+02 ± 9.21e+01	1.387e+01 ± 8.23e+00
	0.2	2.490e+01 ± 2.25e+01	1.782e+02 ± 1.01e+02	2.220e+01 ± 3.18e+01
	0.4	4.026e+01 ± 5.60e+01	2.263e+02 ± 1.41e+02	7.409e+01 ± 1.10e+02
	0.8	2.505e+02 ± 4.45e+02	5.809e+02 ± 4.92e+02	1.555e+03 ± 1.61e+03
f_4	0.0	5.165e+01 ± 9.97e+00	8.741e+01 ± 1.19e+01	4.493e+01 ± 8.10e+00
	0.2	5.248e+01 ± 1.04e+01	8.888e+01 ± 1.23e+01	4.795e+01 ± 8.51e+00
	0.4	5.459e+01 ± 1.12e+01	9.363e+01 ± 1.33e+01	5.632e+01 ± 1.14e+01
	0.8	6.873e+01 ± 1.61e+01	1.135e+02 ± 2.07e+01	9.990e+01 ± 2.28e+01

Table 8. Results in 10 dimensions by standard DEs with F=0.7 and CR=0.9

func.	offset	rand	current-to	current-to-rand
f_1	0.0	2.104e+00 ± 1.35e+00	2.135e+01 ± 7.12e+00	6.811e-01 ± 6.98e-01
	0.2	2.189e+00 ± 1.53e+00	2.189e+01 ± 7.23e+00	9.224e-01 ± 9.49e-01
	0.4	2.756e+00 ± 1.97e+00	2.492e+01 ± 8.40e+00	1.703e+00 ± 1.79e+00
	0.8	6.239e+00 ± 4.85e+00	3.906e+01 ± 1.40e+01	7.932e+00 ± 6.41e+00
f_2	0.0	4.913e+01 ± 5.10e+01	3.129e+02 ± 1.65e+02	2.082e+01 ± 1.92e+01
	0.2	4.476e+01 ± 4.13e+01	3.353e+02 ± 1.86e+02	2.114e+01 ± 1.77e+01
	0.4	5.532e+01 ± 6.09e+01	4.534e+02 ± 2.66e+02	3.084e+01 ± 3.42e+01
	0.8	1.711e+02 ± 2.15e+02	1.094e+03 ± 7.90e+02	1.521e+02 ± 2.12e+02
f_3	0.0	4.913e+01 ± 5.10e+01	3.129e+02 ± 1.65e+02	2.082e+01 ± 1.92e+01
	0.2	4.476e+01 ± 4.13e+01	3.353e+02 ± 1.86e+02	2.114e+01 ± 1.77e+01
	0.4	5.532e+01 ± 6.09e+01	4.534e+02 ± 2.66e+02	3.084e+01 ± 3.42e+01
	0.8	1.711e+02 ± 2.15e+02	1.094e+03 ± 7.90e+02	1.521e+02 ± 2.12e+02
f_4	0.0	6.525e+01 ± 1.16e+01	9.876e+01 ± 1.38e+01	5.585e+01 ± 9.08e+00
	0.2	6.554e+01 ± 1.10e+01	9.980e+01 ± 1.44e+01	5.664e+01 ± 8.74e+00
	0.4	6.763e+01 ± 1.12e+01	1.048e+02 ± 1.49e+01	6.015e+01 ± 1.05e+01
	0.8	7.618e+01 ± 1.42e+01	1.254e+02 ± 2.14e+01	7.495e+01 ± 1.51e+01

Table 9. Results in 10 dimensions by JADE

func.	offset	rand	current-to	current-to-rand
f_1	0.0	2.747e-01 ± 1.77e-01	3.599e+00 ± 1.58e+00	**1.242e-01 ± 1.98e-01**
	0.2	2.855e-01 ± 2.44e-01	3.930e+00 ± 1.66e+00	**1.922e-01 ± 3.63e-01**
	0.4	**3.139e-01 ± 2.31e-01**	4.813e+00 ± 2.06e+00	4.783e-01 ± 8.47e-01
	0.8	**5.476e-01 ± 6.87e-01**	8.938e+00 ± 3.93e+00	4.465e+00 ± 4.92e+00
f_2	0.0	3.115e+01 ± 2.61e+01	5.686e+01 ± 3.40e+01	**1.184e+01 ± 6.13e+00**
	0.2	2.772e+01 ± 2.25e+01	5.918e+01 ± 3.33e+01	**1.272e+01 ± 6.18e+00**
	0.4	2.802e+01 ± 2.20e+01	7.865e+01 ± 5.22e+01	**1.717e+01 ± 9.74e+00**
	0.8	**4.625e+01 ± 4.46e+01**	1.837e+02 ± 1.28e+02	5.967e+01 ± 8.19e+01
f_3	0.0	3.115e+01 ± 2.61e+01	5.686e+01 ± 3.40e+01	**1.184e+01 ± 6.13e+00**
	0.2	2.772e+01 ± 2.25e+01	5.918e+01 ± 3.33e+01	**1.272e+01 ± 6.18e+00**
	0.4	2.802e+01 ± 2.20e+01	7.865e+01 ± 5.22e+01	**1.717e+01 ± 9.74e+00**
	0.8	**4.625e+01 ± 4.46e+01**	1.837e+02 ± 1.28e+02	5.967e+01 ± 8.19e+01
f_4	0.0	4.293e+01 ± 8.14e+00	6.167e+01 ± 1.02e+01	3.557e+01 ± 6.90e+00
	0.2	4.268e+01 ± 8.07e+00	6.330e+01 ± 1.01e+01	**3.672e+01 ± 7.10e+00**
	0.4	4.284e+01 ± 8.21e+00	6.581e+01 ± 1.08e+01	**3.983e+01 ± 8.09e+00**
	0.8	**4.544e+01 ± 8.87e+00**	7.842e+01 ± 1.40e+01	5.579e+01 ± 1.27e+01

Table 10. Results in 20 dimensions by standard DEs with $F=0.5$ and $CR=0.5$

func.	offset	rand	current-to	current-to-rand
f_1	0.0	7.449e+00 ± 2.70e+00	5.481e+01 ± 1.21e+01	2.643e+00 ± 1.52e+00
	0.2	7.547e+00 ± 2.73e+00	5.886e+01 ± 1.32e+01	3.888e+00 ± 2.28e+00
	0.4	8.972e+00 ± 3.37e+00	7.112e+01 ± 1.61e+01	9.557e+00 ± 5.00e+00
	0.8	1.754e+01 ± 7.58e+00	1.250e+02 ± 2.93e+01	5.461e+01 ± 1.81e+01
f_2	0.0	3.196e+02 ± 1.77e+02	9.340e+02 ± 3.20e+02	6.912e+01 ± 4.31e+01
	0.2	2.921e+02 ± 1.59e+02	1.056e+03 ± 3.97e+02	7.857e+01 ± 4.48e+01
	0.4	3.272e+02 ± 2.02e+02	1.573e+03 ± 6.38e+02	1.405e+02 ± 8.08e+01
	0.8	7.608e+02 ± 5.00e+02	4.701e+03 ± 2.15e+03	1.040e+03 ± 9.17e+02
f_3	0.0	3.196e+02 ± 1.77e+02	9.340e+02 ± 3.20e+02	6.912e+01 ± 4.31e+01
	0.2	2.921e+02 ± 1.59e+02	1.056e+03 ± 3.97e+02	7.857e+01 ± 4.48e+01
	0.4	3.272e+02 ± 2.02e+02	1.573e+03 ± 6.38e+02	1.405e+02 ± 8.08e+01
	0.8	7.608e+02 ± 5.00e+02	4.701e+03 ± 2.15e+03	1.040e+03 ± 9.17e+02
f_4	0.0	1.511e+02 ± 1.62e+01	2.180e+02 ± 2.08e+01	**1.205e+02 ± 1.28e+01**
	0.2	1.517e+02 ± 1.57e+01	2.241e+02 ± 2.14e+01	**1.247e+02 ± 1.33e+01**
	0.4	1.537e+02 ± 1.67e+01	2.420e+02 ± 2.56e+01	1.388e+02 ± 1.54e+01
	0.8	1.694e+02 ± 1.96e+01	3.152e+02 ± 3.94e+01	2.097e+02 ± 2.75e+01

Table 11. Results in 20 dimensions by standard DEs with $F=0.5$ and $CR=0.9$

func.	offset	rand	current-to	current-to-rand
f_1	0.0	1.243e+01 ± 5.32e+00	8.806e+01 ± 1.62e+01	9.767e+00 ± 3.76e+00
	0.2	1.490e+01 ± 6.73e+00	9.226e+01 ± 1.73e+01	1.632e+01 ± 6.49e+00
	0.4	2.435e+01 ± 1.02e+01	1.106e+02 ± 2.34e+01	3.941e+01 ± 1.28e+01
	0.8	7.752e+01 ± 2.73e+01	1.990e+02 ± 4.74e+01	1.583e+02 ± 3.43e+01
f_2	0.0	1.984e+02 ± 1.36e+02	1.631e+03 ± 5.21e+02	7.600e+01 ± 4.85e+01
	0.2	2.154e+02 ± 1.46e+02	1.922e+03 ± 6.88e+02	1.297e+02 ± 9.35e+01
	0.4	4.281e+02 ± 3.48e+02	3.065e+03 ± 1.46e+03	4.916e+02 ± 4.22e+02
	0.8	2.613e+03 ± 1.97e+03	1.076e+04 ± 5.98e+03	7.787e+03 ± 4.68e+03
f_3	0.0	1.984e+02 ± 1.36e+02	1.631e+03 ± 5.21e+02	7.600e+01 ± 4.85e+01
	0.2	2.154e+02 ± 1.46e+02	1.922e+03 ± 6.88e+02	1.297e+02 ± 9.35e+01
	0.4	4.281e+02 ± 3.48e+02	3.065e+03 ± 1.46e+03	4.916e+02 ± 4.22e+02
	0.8	2.613e+03 ± 1.97e+03	1.076e+04 ± 5.98e+03	7.787e+03 ± 4.68e+03
f_4	0.0	1.522e+02 ± 1.86e+01	2.529e+02 ± 2.14e+01	1.302e+02 ± 1.37e+01
	0.2	1.567e+02 ± 1.91e+01	2.598e+02 ± 2.30e+01	1.403e+02 ± 1.51e+01
	0.4	1.689e+02 ± 2.20e+01	2.839e+02 ± 2.79e+01	1.689e+02 ± 2.07e+01
	0.8	2.342e+02 ± 3.48e+01	3.892e+02 ± 5.24e+01	2.999e+02 ± 3.93e+01

Table 12. Results in 20 dimensions by standard DEs with $F=0.7$ and $CR=0.9$

func.	offset	rand	current-to	current-to-rand
f_1	0.0	2.435e+01 ± 9.67e+00	1.066e+02 ± 1.75e+01	8.730e+00 ± 3.64e+00
	0.2	2.629e+01 ± 9.61e+00	1.123e+02 ± 1.86e+01	1.091e+01 ± 4.60e+00
	0.4	3.411e+01 ± 1.26e+01	1.348e+02 ± 2.51e+01	2.101e+01 ± 8.86e+00
	0.8	7.664e+01 ± 2.67e+01	2.389e+02 ± 5.12e+01	7.133e+01 ± 2.48e+01
f_2	0.0	4.843e+02 ± 3.29e+02	2.167e+03 ± 5.45e+02	1.662e+02 ± 1.24e+02
	0.2	4.669e+02 ± 2.95e+02	2.814e+03 ± 1.06e+03	1.747e+02 ± 1.14e+02
	0.4	7.499e+02 ± 5.26e+02	5.062e+03 ± 2.16e+03	3.462e+02 ± 2.33e+02
	0.8	2.926e+03 ± 1.78e+03	1.619e+04 ± 7.84e+03	2.114e+03 ± 1.56e+03
f_3	0.0	4.843e+02 ± 3.29e+02	2.167e+03 ± 5.45e+02	1.662e+02 ± 1.24e+02
	0.2	4.669e+02 ± 2.95e+02	2.814e+03 ± 1.06e+03	1.747e+02 ± 1.14e+02
	0.4	7.499e+02 ± 5.26e+02	5.062e+03 ± 2.16e+03	3.462e+02 ± 2.33e+02
	0.8	2.926e+03 ± 1.78e+03	1.619e+04 ± 7.84e+03	2.114e+03 ± 1.56e+03
f_4	0.0	1.888e+02 ± 2.26e+01	2.779e+02 ± 2.37e+01	1.582e+02 ± 1.55e+01
	0.2	1.924e+02 ± 2.21e+01	2.858e+02 ± 2.40e+01	1.636e+02 ± 1.69e+01
	0.4	2.051e+02 ± 2.34e+01	3.114e+02 ± 3.14e+01	1.790e+02 ± 1.90e+01
	0.8	2.572e+02 ± 3.66e+01	4.257e+02 ± 5.45e+01	2.460e+02 ± 3.50e+01

Table 13. Results in 20 dimensions by JADE

func.	offset	rand	current-to	current-to-rand
f_1	0.0	7.570e+00 ± 2.87e+00	3.098e+01 ± 8.32e+00	**2.538e+00 ± 1.55e+00**
	0.2	7.671e+00 ± 2.81e+00	3.449e+01 ± 9.13e+00	**3.437e+00 ± 2.10e+00**
	0.4	8.814e+00 ± 3.53e+00	4.364e+01 ± 1.17e+01	**7.554e+00 ± 4.25e+00**
	0.8	**1.457e+01 ± 5.77e+00**	8.552e+01 ± 2.24e+01	4.148e+01 ± 1.67e+01
f_2	0.0	3.096e+02 ± 1.78e+02	5.209e+02 ± 2.30e+02	**5.880e+01 ± 3.41e+01**
	0.2	2.808e+02 ± 1.57e+02	6.091e+02 ± 2.61e+02	**6.900e+01 ± 3.98e+01**
	0.4	3.295e+02 ± 2.11e+02	9.197e+02 ± 4.02e+02	**1.243e+02 ± 8.05e+01**
	0.8	7.240e+02 ± 4.89e+02	2.897e+03 ± 1.28e+03	**7.011e+02 ± 6.44e+02**
f_3	0.0	3.096e+02 ± 1.78e+02	5.209e+02 ± 2.30e+02	**5.880e+01 ± 3.41e+01**
	0.2	2.808e+02 ± 1.57e+02	6.091e+02 ± 2.61e+02	**6.900e+01 ± 3.98e+01**
	0.4	3.295e+02 ± 2.11e+02	9.197e+02 ± 4.02e+02	**1.243e+02 ± 8.05e+01**
	0.8	7.240e+02 ± 4.89e+02	2.897e+03 ± 1.28e+03	**7.011e+02 ± 6.44e+02**
f_4	0.0	1.508e+02 ± 1.65e+01	1.909e+02 ± 1.98e+01	1.217e+02 ± 1.25e+01
	0.2	1.502e+02 ± 1.60e+01	1.959e+02 ± 2.06e+01	1.258e+02 ± 1.33e+01
	0.4	1.518e+02 ± 1.66e+01	2.136e+02 ± 2.21e+01	**1.374e+02 ± 1.54e+01**
	0.8	**1.641e+02 ± 1.88e+01**	2.719e+02 ± 3.33e+01	1.954e+02 ± 2.68e+01

Table 14. Results in 30 dimensions by standard DEs with F=0.5 and CR=0.5

func.	offset	rand	current-to	current-to-rand
f_1	0.0	3.096e+01 ± 8.36e+00	1.350e+02 ± 2.00e+01	**8.186e+00 ± 2.97e+00**
	0.2	3.153e+01 ± 8.48e+00	1.422e+02 ± 2.23e+01	1.184e+01 ± 4.49e+00
	0.4	3.683e+01 ± 9.94e+00	1.728e+02 ± 2.74e+01	2.615e+01 ± 9.29e+00
	0.8	6.746e+01 ± 1.93e+01	3.070e+02 ± 5.28e+01	1.246e+02 ± 2.86e+01
f_2	0.0	1.155e+03 ± 4.92e+02	2.668e+03 ± 6.52e+02	1.840e+02 ± 1.07e+02
	0.2	1.024e+03 ± 4.32e+02	3.217e+03 ± 9.73e+02	2.025e+02 ± 1.00e+02
	0.4	1.217e+03 ± 5.38e+02	5.337e+03 ± 1.78e+03	3.969e+02 ± 1.90e+02
	0.8	2.905e+03 ± 1.38e+03	1.684e+04 ± 5.95e+03	2.928e+03 ± 2.09e+03
f_3	0.0	1.155e+03 ± 4.92e+02	2.668e+03 ± 6.52e+02	1.840e+02 ± 1.07e+02
	0.2	1.024e+03 ± 4.32e+02	3.217e+03 ± 9.73e+02	2.025e+02 ± 1.00e+02
	0.4	1.217e+03 ± 5.38e+02	5.337e+03 ± 1.78e+03	3.969e+02 ± 1.90e+02
	0.8	2.905e+03 ± 1.38e+03	1.684e+04 ± 5.95e+03	2.928e+03 ± 2.09e+03
f_4	0.0	2.862e+02 ± 2.33e+01	3.912e+02 ± 2.82e+01	**2.180e+02 ± 1.73e+01**
	0.2	2.853e+02 ± 2.34e+01	4.048e+02 ± 2.90e+01	2.261e+02 ± 1.75e+01
	0.4	2.913e+02 ± 2.43e+01	4.430e+02 ± 3.43e+01	2.523e+02 ± 2.13e+01
	0.8	3.314e+02 ± 3.23e+01	5.992e+02 ± 6.05e+01	3.821e+02 ± 3.86e+01

Table 15. Results in 30 dimensions by standard DEs with F=0.5 and CR=0.9

func.	offset	rand	current-to	current-to-rand
f_1	0.0	3.153e+01 ± 9.75e+00	1.745e+02 ± 2.29e+01	1.983e+01 ± 5.92e+00
	0.2	3.846e+01 ± 1.19e+01	1.852e+02 ± 2.49e+01	3.334e+01 ± 9.74e+00
	0.4	6.249e+01 ± 1.83e+01	2.256e+02 ± 3.48e+01	7.820e+01 ± 1.84e+01
	0.8	1.815e+02 ± 4.39e+01	4.217e+02 ± 6.98e+01	2.913e+02 ± 4.64e+01
f_2	0.0	4.977e+02 ± 2.88e+02	3.554e+03 ± 7.64e+02	1.873e+02 ± 1.11e+02
	0.2	5.777e+02 ± 3.28e+02	4.768e+03 ± 1.51e+03	3.081e+02 ± 1.79e+02
	0.4	1.211e+03 ± 7.21e+02	8.605e+03 ± 3.22e+03	1.154e+03 ± 7.87e+02
	0.8	7.800e+03 ± 4.64e+03	3.360e+04 ± 1.42e+04	1.560e+04 ± 7.74e+03
f_3	0.0	4.977e+02 ± 2.88e+02	3.554e+03 ± 7.64e+02	1.873e+02 ± 1.11e+02
	0.2	5.777e+02 ± 3.28e+02	4.768e+03 ± 1.51e+03	3.081e+02 ± 1.79e+02
	0.4	1.211e+03 ± 7.21e+02	8.605e+03 ± 3.22e+03	1.154e+03 ± 7.87e+02
	0.8	7.800e+03 ± 4.64e+03	3.360e+04 ± 1.42e+04	1.560e+04 ± 7.74e+03
f_4	0.0	2.629e+02 ± 2.48e+01	4.319e+02 ± 2.83e+01	2.238e+02 ± 1.81e+01
	0.2	2.711e+02 ± 2.66e+01	4.475e+02 ± 3.07e+01	2.415e+02 ± 2.02e+01
	0.4	3.022e+02 ± 3.18e+01	4.923e+02 ± 4.17e+01	2.938e+02 ± 2.83e+01
	0.8	4.405e+02 ± 5.52e+01	7.047e+02 ± 7.33e+01	5.197e+02 ± 5.49e+01

Table 16. Results in 30 dimensions by standard DEs with F=0.7 and CR=0.9

func.	offset	rand	current-to	current-to-rand
f_1	0.0	7.300e+01 ± 3.41e+01	1.913e+02 ± 2.26e+01	2.328e+01 ± 7.03e+00
	0.2	7.217e+01 ± 2.45e+01	2.032e+02 ± 2.53e+01	3.038e+01 ± 9.47e+00
	0.4	9.197e+01 ± 2.52e+01	2.526e+02 ± 3.71e+01	5.587e+01 ± 1.52e+01
	0.8	2.046e+02 ± 4.92e+01	4.742e+02 ± 7.11e+01	1.742e+02 ± 4.12e+01
f_2	0.0	1.368e+03 ± 8.04e+02	3.894e+03 ± 7.50e+02	4.218e+02 ± 2.76e+02
	0.2	1.332e+03 ± 7.25e+02	5.698e+03 ± 1.75e+03	4.684e+02 ± 2.58e+02
	0.4	2.171e+03 ± 1.13e+03	1.200e+04 ± 4.11e+03	9.803e+02 ± 5.08e+02
	0.8	9.420e+03 ± 4.69e+03	4.490e+04 ± 1.72e+04	6.482e+03 ± 3.61e+03
f_3	0.0	1.368e+03 ± 8.04e+02	3.894e+03 ± 7.50e+02	4.218e+02 ± 2.76e+02
	0.2	1.332e+03 ± 7.25e+02	5.698e+03 ± 1.75e+03	4.684e+02 ± 2.58e+02
	0.4	2.171e+03 ± 1.13e+03	1.200e+04 ± 4.11e+03	9.803e+02 ± 5.08e+02
	0.8	9.420e+03 ± 4.69e+03	4.490e+04 ± 1.72e+04	6.482e+03 ± 3.61e+03
f_4	0.0	3.335e+02 ± 3.86e+01	4.575e+02 ± 2.98e+01	2.691e+02 ± 2.05e+01
	0.2	3.383e+02 ± 3.69e+01	4.738e+02 ± 3.28e+01	2.791e+02 ± 2.33e+01
	0.4	3.648e+02 ± 3.60e+01	5.269e+02 ± 4.13e+01	3.136e+02 ± 2.78e+01
	0.8	4.908e+02 ± 5.71e+01	7.592e+02 ± 7.57e+01	4.585e+02 ± 5.23e+01

Table 17. Results in 30 dimensions by JADE

func.	offset	rand	current-to	current-to-rand
f_1	0.0	3.060e+01 ± 8.71e+00	7.408e+01 ± 1.51e+01	8.697e+00 ± 3.48e+00
	0.2	3.162e+01 ± 8.54e+00	8.362e+01 ± 1.75e+01	**1.172e+01 ± 4.43e+00**
	0.4	3.493e+01 ± 9.54e+00	1.088e+02 ± 2.34e+01	**2.346e+01 ± 8.79e+00**
	0.8	**5.874e+01 ± 1.64e+01**	2.167e+02 ± 4.19e+01	1.059e+02 ± 2.90e+01
f_2	0.0	1.121e+03 ± 4.88e+02	1.476e+03 ± 5.34e+02	**1.580e+02 ± 8.70e+01**
	0.2	1.036e+03 ± 4.39e+02	1.750e+03 ± 6.32e+02	**1.877e+02 ± 9.00e+01**
	0.4	1.257e+03 ± 5.83e+02	2.853e+03 ± 1.07e+03	**3.644e+02 ± 1.93e+02**
	0.8	3.060e+03 ± 1.49e+03	9.737e+03 ± 3.43e+03	**2.164e+03 ± 1.22e+03**
f_3	0.0	1.121e+03 ± 4.88e+02	1.476e+03 ± 5.34e+02	**1.580e+02 ± 8.70e+01**
	0.2	1.036e+03 ± 4.39e+02	1.750e+03 ± 6.32e+02	**1.877e+02 ± 9.00e+01**
	0.4	1.257e+03 ± 5.83e+02	2.853e+03 ± 1.07e+03	**3.644e+02 ± 1.93e+02**
	0.8	3.060e+03 ± 1.49e+03	9.737e+03 ± 3.43e+03	**2.164e+03 ± 1.22e+03**
f_4	0.0	2.840e+02 ± 2.55e+01	3.332e+02 ± 2.70e+01	2.208e+02 ± 1.68e+01
	0.2	2.839e+02 ± 2.45e+01	3.461e+02 ± 2.90e+01	**2.258e+02 ± 1.79e+01**
	0.4	2.887e+02 ± 2.50e+01	3.815e+02 ± 3.32e+01	**2.506e+02 ± 2.28e+01**
	0.8	**3.218e+02 ± 3.04e+01**	5.162e+02 ± 5.33e+01	3.660e+02 ± 3.86e+01

in 12 cases over all functions, JADE with rand strategy attained best results in 2 cases over 2 functions, and DE with $F = 0.5$ and $CR = 0.5$ using current-to-rand strategy attained best results in 2 cases of f_4. DE with $F = 0.5$ and $CR = 0.9$ and DE with $F = 0.7$ and $CR = 0.9$ could not attain good results. Also, current-to strategy could not attain good results.

As for problems of 30 dimensions, JADE with current-to-rand strategy attained best results in 12 cases over all functions, JADE with rand strategy attained best results in 2 cases over 2 functions, and DE with $F = 0.5$ and $CR = 0.5$ attained best results in 2 cases over 2 functions. DE with $F = 0.5$ and $CR = 0.9$ and DE with $F = 0.7$ and $CR = 0.9$ could not attain good results. Also, current-to strategy could not attain good results.

As a summary, JADE with current-to-rand strategy attained best results in 37 cases, JADE with rand strategy attained best results in 14 cases, DE with $F = 0.5$ and $CR = 0.5$ attained best results in 7 cases, DE with $F = 0.7$ and $CR = 0.9$ attained best results in 6 cases, and DE with $F = 0.5$ and $CR = 0.9$ attained no best results. Thus, it is thought that JADE with current-to-rand strategy is the best method to attain stable results.

6. Conclusion

IDE using the pairwise comparison has been proposed to reduce fatigue of a user. In this study, mutation strategy and parameter settings of IDE are studied to improve the efficiency of the IDE. A comparative study on standard DEs and JADE which is one of the most successful method on the adaptive parameter control in DE is performed. When the pairwise comparison is used, the order relation of solutions cannot be obtained and best strategy or current-to-pbest strategy cannot be utilized. Therefore, three strategies of rand, current-to and current-to-rand strategy are adopted in standard DEs with some F and CR values and JADE. The algorithms are applied to optimization of various functions including unimodal function, a function with ridge structure, an ill-scaled function and a multimodal function with big-valley. It is shown that JADE with current-to-rand strategy attained most stable results. It is thought that JADE is effective to IDE.

In the future, we will estimate goodness of solutions from the results of pairwise comparison, select the base vector according to the estimated goodness and improve the performance of IDE.

Acknowledgment

This study is supported by JSPS KAKENHI Grant Numbers 24500177, 26350443 and the 2014 Research Fund (ChosaKenkyu-Hi) of the Center for the Co-creation of Hiroshima's Future, Hiroshima Shudo University.

References

[1] Takagi, H., "Interactive evolutionary computation: Fusion of the capabilities of EC optimization and human evaluation", *Proceedings of the IEEE*, Vol. 89, No. 9, pp. 1275–1296 (2001).

[2] Takagi, H. and Pallez, D., "Paired comparison-based interactive differential evolution", *Proc. of the 2009 World Congress on Nature & Biologically Inspired Computing*, IEEE (2009), pp. 475–480.

[3] Funaki, R. and Takagi, H., "Application of Gravity Vectors and Moving Vectors for the Acceleration of Both Differential Evolution and Interactive Differential Evolution", *Proc.*

of the 2011 International Conference on Genetic and Evolutionary Computing (2011), pp. 287–290.

[4] Storn, R. and Price, K., "Minimizing the Real Functions of the ICEC'96 Contest by Differential Evolution", *Proc. of the International Conference on Evolutionary Computation* (1996), pp. 842–844.

[5] Storn, R. and Price, K., "Differential Evolution – A Simple and Efficient Heuristic for Global Optimization over Continuous Spaces", *Journal of Global Optimization*, Vol. 11, pp. 341–359 (1997).

[6] Takahama, T. and Sakai, S., "Differential Evolution with Dynamic Strategy and Parameter Selection by Detecting Landscape Modality", *Proc. of the 2012 IEEE Congress on Evolutionary Computation* (2012), pp. 2114–2121.

[7] Wang, Y., Cai, Z. and Zhang, Q., "Differential Evolution With Composite Trial Vector Generation Strategies and Control Parameters", *IEEE Transactions on Evolutionary Computation*, Vol. 15, No. 1, pp. 55–66 (2011).

[8] Liu, J. and Lampinen, J., "A Fuzzy Adaptive Differential Evolution Algorithm", *Soft Comput.*, Vol. 9, No. 6, pp. 448–462 (2005).

[9] Takahama, T. and Sakai, S., "Fuzzy C-Means Clustering and Partition Entropy for Species-Best Strategy and Search Mode Selection in Nonlinear Optimization by Differential Evolution", *Proc. of the 2011 IEEE International Conference on Fuzzy Systems* (2011), pp. 290–297.

[10] Takahama, T. and Sakai, S., "Large Scale Optimization by Differential Evolution with Landscape Modality Detection and a Diversity Archive", *Proc. of the 2012 IEEE Congress on Evolutionary Computation* (2012), pp. 2842–2849.

[11] Teo, J., "Exploring Dynamic Self-Adaptive Populations in Differential Evolution", *Soft Comput.*, Vol. 10, No. 8, pp. 673–686 (2006).

[12] Qin, A., Huang, V. and Suganthan, P., "Differential Evolution Algorithm With Strategy Adaptation for Global Numerical Optimization", *IEEE Transactions on Evolutionary Computation*, Vol. 13, No. 2, pp. 398–417 (2009).

[13] Brest, J., Greiner, S., Boskovic, B., Mernik, M. and Zumer, V., "Self-Adapting Control Parameters in Differential Evolution: A Comparative Study on Numerical Benchmark Problems", *IEEE Transaction on Evolutionary Computation*, Vol. 10, No. 6, pp. 646–657 (2006).

[14] Zhang, J. and Sanderson, A. C., "JADE: Adaptive Differential Evolution With Optional External Archive", *IEEE Transactions on Evolutionary Computation*, Vol. 13, No. 5, pp. 945–958 (2009).

[15] Islam, S. M., Das, S., Ghosh, S., Roy, S. and Suganthan, P. N., "An Adaptive Differential Evolution Algorithm With Novel Mutation and Crossover Strategies for Global Numerical Optimization", *IEEE Transactions on Systems, Man, and Cybernetics, Part B: Cybernetics*, Vol. 42, No. 2, pp. 482–500 (2012).

Chapter 7

On Some Properties of Harmonic Polynomials in the Case of $\mathfrak{so}(p,2)$: Irreducible Decomposition and Integral Formulas

Ryoko Wada[*] *and Yoshio Agaoka*[**]
[*]*Faculty of Economic Sciences, Hiroshima Shudo University,*
1-1 Ozuka-Higashi 1-chome, Asaminami-Ku, Hiroshima, Japan 731-3195,
[**]*Department of Mathematics, Graduate School of Science, Hiroshima University,*
7-1 Kagamiyama 1-chome, Higashi-Hiroshima, Japan 739-8521.

Abstract

Kostant-Rallis generalized classical harmonic polynomials on $\mathbf{C}^p$ to a more wide class of polynomials from the Lie algebraic viewpoint. From their viewpoint, classical harmonic polynomials on $\mathbf{C}^p$ can be identified with the harmonic polynomials on a space canonically associated with the Lie algebra $\mathfrak{so}(p,1)$. In our previous paper we consider some properties of generalized harmonic polynomials in the case $\mathfrak{so}(p,2)$, which is the case of real rank 2, and show some results about harmonic polynomials of degree≤ 4. In this paper we give the irreducible decomposition of these harmonic polynomials for general degree, and also show integral formulas including some reproducing formulas for special cases.

Key Words:

Harmonic polynomial, Spherical harmonics, Reproducing kernel, Special function

1. Introduction

Let $\mathfrak{g}$ be a complex semisimple Lie algebra and let $\mathfrak{g}_\mathbf{R}$ be a noncompact real form of $\mathfrak{g}$. We fix a maximal compact subalgebra $\mathfrak{k}_\mathbf{R}$ of $\mathfrak{g}_\mathbf{R}$, and let $\mathfrak{g}_\mathbf{R} = \mathfrak{k}_\mathbf{R} + \mathfrak{p}_\mathbf{R}$ be a Cartan decomposition of $\mathfrak{g}_\mathbf{R}$. We denote by $\mathfrak{g} = \mathfrak{k} + \mathfrak{p}$ its complexification. We express the adjoint group of $\mathfrak{k}$ as K, i.e., $K = \exp \operatorname{ad} \mathfrak{k} \subset GL(\mathfrak{p})$. Kostant-Rallis [4] introduced harmonic polynomials on $\mathfrak{p}$ and stated some results. In view of [4], classical harmonic polynomials on $\mathbf{C}^p$ correspond to the harmonic polynomials on $\mathfrak{p}$ in the case of $\mathfrak{g}_\mathbf{R} = \mathfrak{so}(p,1)$.

In [7], [8] we considered the reproducing formulas of the harmonic polynomials in the cases of real rank 1, i.e., the case $\mathfrak{g}_\mathbf{R} = \mathfrak{so}(p,1)$ ($p \geq 2$), $\mathfrak{su}(p,1)$, $\mathfrak{sp}(p,1)$ ($p \geq 1$) or $\mathfrak{f}_{4(-20)}$. In [9], we considered the case $\mathfrak{g}_\mathbf{R} = \mathfrak{so}(p,2)$, which is the case of the classical real rank 2 and explicitly gave the irreducible decomposition of the space of harmonic polynomials of degree≤ 4, including their generators, and showed the reproducing formulas for some cases.

In this paper, we will give the $\mathfrak{k}_\mathbf{R}$-irreducible decomposition of the space of harmonic polynomials of general dimension in the case $\mathfrak{g}_\mathbf{R} = \mathfrak{so}(p,2)$ and give the examples of reproducing formulas of harmonic polynomials of degree≤ 4.

2. Preliminaries

In this section we fix several notations and review the definitions and some known results. Let p be an integer satisfying $p \geq 3$ and n be a non-negative integer. We denote by $H_n(\mathbf{C}^p)$ the space of harmonic polynomials on $\mathbf{C}^p$ of degree n, i.e., the space of polynomials f on $\mathbf{C}^p$ of degree n satisfying $\sum_{j=1}^{p} \frac{\partial^2}{\partial z_j^2} f(z) = 0$. We denote by $H_{n,p}$ the space of spherical harmonics of degree n in dimension p, i.e., $H_{n,p} = H_n(\mathbf{C}^p)|_{S^{p-1}}$, where S^{p-1} is the unit sphere in $\mathbf{R}^p$.

For $z, \zeta \in \mathbf{C}^p$ we put $z \cdot \zeta = {}^t z \zeta$, $z^2 = z \cdot z$. It is known that

$$\dim H_{n,p} = \frac{(2n+p-2)(n+p-3)!}{n!(p-2)!} \tag{2.1}$$

for $n \geq 0$. Let $P_{n,p}$ be the Legendre polynomials of degree n and dimension p. $P_{n,p}(t)$ is a polynomial of degree n in t and it is valid that

$$P_{n,p}(t) = \frac{(p-3)! n!}{(n+p-3)!} C_n^{\frac{p-2}{2}}(t),$$

where $C_n^\nu(t)$ is the Gegenbauer function.

The following proposition is known.

Proposition 2.1 (cf. [5]). (1) *It is valid that*

$$P_{n,p}(1) = 1 \quad (n = 0, 1, 2, \cdots). \tag{2.2}$$

(2) *Suppose* $P_{n,p}(t) = \sum_{k=1}^{n} C_{k,p} t^k$. *Then we have*

$$C_{n,p} = \frac{2^n \, \Gamma(n + \frac{p}{2})}{n! \, \Gamma(\frac{p}{2}) \dim H_{n,p}}. \tag{2.3}$$

It is known that $H_{n,p}$ is spanned by the set $\{P_{n,p}(\,\cdot\, a); a \in S^{p-1}\}$ for every degree n. For $z, \zeta \in \mathbf{C}^p$ we define $h_\zeta(z) = (z \cdot \zeta)^n$. It is also known that $H_n(\mathbf{C}^p)$ is spanned by the set $\{h_\alpha; \alpha \in \mathbf{C}^p, \alpha^2 = 0\}$.

For $z, w \in \mathbf{C}^p$ we define

$$\widetilde{P}_{n,p}(z,w) = (z^2)^{n/2} (\overline{w}^2)^{n/2} P_{n,p}\left(\frac{z \cdot \overline{w}}{(z^2)^{1/2}(\overline{w}^2)^{1/2}}\right).$$

Remark that $\widetilde{P}_{n,p}(z,w)$ is a homogeneous harmonic polynomial of z of degree n for any fixed $w \in \mathbf{C}^p$, and $\widetilde{P}_{n,p}(z,w)$ is the unique element of $H_n(\mathbf{C}^p)$ such that $\widetilde{P}_{n,p}(s, w_0) = P_{n,p}(s \cdot w_0)$ for fixed $s, w_0 \in S^{p-1}$.

In the following we denote by $SO(p)$ the special orthogonal group of degree p, and dh denotes the Haar measure on $SO(p)$. We put $e_j = {}^t(0 \cdots 0 \overset{j}{1} 0 \cdots 0)$, $e_0 = e_1 + ie_2$. The following formulas are known.

Proposition 2.2 (cf. [2], [5], [10]). (1) *For any $f_m \in H_m(\mathbf{C}^p)$, $g_n \in H_{n,p}$ and any $x \in S^{p-1}$, it is valid that*

$$\delta_{n,m} f_m(x) = \dim H_{n,p} \int_{SO(p)} f_m(he_1) P_{n,p}(x \cdot he_1) dh, \qquad (2.4)$$

$$\int_{SO(p)} f_m(he_1) \overline{g_n(he_1)} dh = 0 \quad (n \neq m). \qquad (2.5)$$

(2) *Suppose f is continuous on the interval $[-1,1]$. Then for any $h_n \in H_{n,p}$ and any $x \in S^{p-1}$ we have*

$$\int_{SO(p)} f(x \cdot he_1) h_n(he_1) dh = \lambda h_n(x), \qquad (2.6)$$

where

$$\lambda = \frac{\Gamma(\frac{p}{2})}{\sqrt{\pi}\, \Gamma(\frac{p-1}{2})} \int_{-1}^{1} f(t) P_{n,p}(t)(1-t^2)^{(p-3)/2} dt$$

(*Funk-Hecke formula*).

(3) *For $s, s_0 \in S^{p-1}$ the following formula is valid.*

$$\int_{SO(p)} (he_0 \cdot s)^n \overline{(he_0 \cdot s_0)^m} dh = \delta_{n,m} 2^n \lambda_{n,p} P_{n,p}(s \cdot s_0), \qquad (2.7)$$

where $\lambda_{n,p} = \frac{n! \Gamma(p/2)}{2^n \Gamma(n+p/2)}$.

(4) *For any $f_n \in H_n(\mathbf{C}^p)$ and any $z \in \mathbf{C}^p$, it is valid that*

$$2^n \delta_{n,m} f_n(z) = \dim H_{n,p} \int_{SO(p)} f_n(he_0) \overline{(he_0 \cdot \bar{z})^m} dh. \qquad (2.8)$$

For more details on spherical harmonics, see [2], [5], etc.

From now, let $\mathfrak{g} = \mathfrak{k} + \mathfrak{p}$, $\mathfrak{g}_\mathbf{R} = \mathfrak{k}_\mathbf{R} + \mathfrak{p}_\mathbf{R}$ and K be as stated in Introduction, and we put $K_\mathbf{R} = \exp \operatorname{ad} \mathfrak{k}_\mathbf{R}$.

Let $S(\mathfrak{p})$ be the symmetric algebra over $\mathfrak{p}$ and we denote by S the spaces of polynomials on $\mathfrak{p}$. For $X \in \mathfrak{p}$ let $\partial(X)$ denote the differential operator defined by

$$(\partial(X)f)(Y) = \frac{d}{dt} f(Y + tX) \big|_{t=0} \qquad (f \in S,\ Y \in \mathfrak{p}).$$

The mapping $X \to \partial(X)$ extends to an isomorphism of $S(\mathfrak{p})$ onto the algebra of all differential operators on $\mathfrak{p}$ with complex coefficients. For $f \in S$ and $g \in K$, an element $\rho(g)f$ of S is defined by $\rho(g)f(X) = f(g^{-1}X)$ ($X \in \mathfrak{p}$). Let J denote the ring of K-invariant polynomials on $\mathfrak{p}$ and we put $J_+ = \{f \in J\,;\, f(0) = 0\}$.

Let $I(\mathfrak{p})$ be the set of K-invariants in $S(\mathfrak{p})$ and we put $I_+(\mathfrak{p}) = \{u \in I(\mathfrak{p})\,;\, \partial(u)1 = 0\}$, i.e., $I_+(\mathfrak{p}) \subset I(\mathfrak{p})$ is the set of K-invariants without constant term.

According to the definition in [4], $f \in S$ is harmonic if and only if $\partial(u)f = 0$ for any $u \in I_+(\mathfrak{p})$. We denote by S_n the space of homogeneous polynomials on $\mathfrak{p}$ of degree n, and $\mathcal{H}_n$ the space of homogeneous harmonic polynomials of degree n. Remark that K acts on S_n and $\mathcal{H}_n$. We regard $K_{\mathbf{R}} \subset K$ and $\mathfrak{p}_{\mathbf{R}} \subset \mathfrak{p}$ in the following.

We put $\mathcal{N} = \{X \in \mathfrak{p}\, ; P(X) = 0 \text{ for any } P \in J_+\}$. The following facts are known:

Proposition 2.3 (cf. [4]).
(1) If we put $(J_+S)_n = S_n \cap J_+S$, it is valid that
$$S_n = \mathcal{H}_n \oplus (J_+S)_n. \tag{2.9}$$

(2) The space $\mathcal{H}_n$ is spanned by $\{B(\ ,Y)^n\, ; Y \in \mathcal{N}\}$, where $B(X,Y)$ $(X,Y \in \mathfrak{g})$ is the Killing form of $\mathfrak{g}$.

For details on harmonic polynomials on $\mathfrak{p}$, see [1], [4].

Now we consider the case $\mathfrak{g}_{\mathbf{R}} = \mathfrak{so}(p,2)$. From now we assume that $p \geq 4$. We have
$$\mathfrak{k} = \left\{ \begin{pmatrix} A & 0 \\ 0 & B \end{pmatrix} \in M(p+2, \mathbf{C})\, ; A \in \mathfrak{so}(p,\mathbf{C}),\, B \in \mathfrak{so}(2,\mathbf{C}) \right\},$$
$$\mathfrak{p} = \left\{ \begin{pmatrix} 0 & X \\ {}^tX & 0 \end{pmatrix} \in M(p+2, \mathbf{C})\, ; X \text{ is a complex } p \times 2 \text{ matrix} \right\},$$
$$K_{\mathbf{R}} = \left\{ \mathrm{Ad}\begin{pmatrix} A & 0 \\ 0 & B \end{pmatrix}\, ; A \in SO(p),\, B \in SO(2) \right\},$$

and $\mathfrak{g} = \mathfrak{k} + \mathfrak{p}$. For $\widetilde{X} = \begin{pmatrix} 0 & X \\ {}^tX & 0 \end{pmatrix} \in \mathfrak{p}$, and $g = \mathrm{Ad}\begin{pmatrix} A & 0 \\ 0 & B \end{pmatrix} \in K_{\mathbf{R}}$ ($A \in SO(p), B \in SO(2)$) we have $g\widetilde{X} = \begin{pmatrix} 0 & AX^tB \\ {}^t(AX^tB) & 0 \end{pmatrix}$. For $\widetilde{X} = \begin{pmatrix} 0 & X \\ {}^tX & 0 \end{pmatrix} \in \mathfrak{p}$ and $X = (x\ y)$ $(x, y \in \mathbf{C}^p)$, two polynomials

$$P(\widetilde{X}) = \frac{1}{2}\mathrm{Tr}(\widetilde{X}^2) = x^2 + y^2,$$
$$Q(\widetilde{X}) = \det({}^tXX) = x^2y^2 - (x \cdot y)^2$$

give the generators of J. Then $\mathcal{H}_n = \{f \in S_n; P(D)f = Q(D)f = 0\}$, where
$$P(D) = \Delta_x + \Delta_y,$$
$$Q(D) = \Delta_x \Delta_y - \left(\sum_{j=1}^p \frac{\partial^2}{\partial x_j \partial y_j} \right)^2,$$
$$\Delta_x = \sum_{j=1}^p \left(\frac{\partial}{\partial x_j} \right)^2,\ \Delta_y = \sum_{j=1}^p \left(\frac{\partial}{\partial y_j} \right)^2.$$

For $\widetilde{X} = \begin{pmatrix} 0 & X \\ {}^tX & 0 \end{pmatrix} \in \mathfrak{p}$, we put $\begin{pmatrix} z \\ w \end{pmatrix} = \begin{pmatrix} x + iy \\ x - iy \end{pmatrix} \in \mathbf{C}^{2p}$ and we define the linear bijective mapping $\Psi : \mathfrak{p} \longrightarrow \mathbf{C}^{2p}$ by $\Psi(\widetilde{X}) = \begin{pmatrix} z \\ w \end{pmatrix}$. We denote by $S_n(\mathbf{C}^{2p})$ the space of homogeneous polynomials on $\mathbf{C}^{2p}$ with degree n and we put

$$\mathcal{H}_n(\mathbf{C}^{2p}) = \left\{ f\left(\begin{pmatrix} z \\ w \end{pmatrix}\right) \in S_n(\mathbf{C}^{2p});\, \Delta_z \Delta_w f = 0 \text{ and } \Sigma_{j=1}^p \frac{\partial^2 f}{\partial z_j \partial w_j} = 0 \right\}.$$

Since we have $P(\widetilde{X}) = P \circ \Psi^{-1}\left(\begin{pmatrix} z \\ w \end{pmatrix}\right) = z \cdot w$ and $Q(\widetilde{X}) = Q \circ \Psi^{-1}\left(\begin{pmatrix} z \\ w \end{pmatrix}\right) = \frac{1}{4}\{z^2 w^2 - (z \cdot w)^2\}$, we can see that $f \in \mathcal{H}_n$ if and only if $f \circ \Psi^{-1} \in \mathcal{H}_n(\mathbf{C}^{2p})$.

3. Irreducible Decomposition of $\mathcal{H}_n$

In this section we give the $K_\mathbf{R}$-irreducible decomposition of the space $\mathcal{H}_n$ for general n in case $\mathfrak{g}_\mathbf{R} = \mathfrak{so}(p,2)$.

We review the symbols expressing the irreducible representation space of the group $K_\mathbf{R}$ (for details see [9]). Since $K_\mathbf{R}$ is isomorphic to $SO(p) \times SO(2)$, its irreducible representation space is expressed as $W \otimes V$, where W and V are $SO(p)$- and $SO(2)$-irreducible spaces, respectively. The $SO(p)$-irreducible space W canonically corresponds to the standard symbol $\sum n_i \Lambda_i$, where $\Lambda_1 \sim \Lambda_p$ are the highest weights of $SO(p)$. The $SO(2)$-irreducible space is always 1-dimensional, and we express it simply as V_k, where k is an integer. Thus any $K_\mathbf{R}$-irreducible space is symbolically expressed as $(\sum n_i \Lambda_i) \otimes V_k$, where $n_1, n_2, \cdots$ are non-negative integers and $k \in \mathbf{Z}$. Actually, only the symbols of the form $(n_1 \Lambda_1 + n_2 \Lambda_2) \otimes V_k$ appear in $\mathcal{H}_n$ as we will see in the next theorem.

Our main purpose of this section is to prove the following theorem:

Theorem 3.1. $K_\mathbf{R}$-*irreducible direct sum decomposition of the space $\mathcal{H}_n$ is symbolically given by*

$$\sum_{\substack{p+2q=n, \\ p \geq 0, q \geq 0}} (p\Lambda_1 + q\Lambda_2) \otimes (V_{n-2q} + V_{n-2q-2} + \cdots + V_{-(n-2q-2)} + V_{-(n-2q)})$$

$$+ \sum_{\substack{p+2q \leq n-2, \\ p \geq 0,\, q \geq 0, \\ p \equiv n \,(\mathrm{mod}\, 2)}} (p\Lambda_1 + q\Lambda_2) \otimes (V_{n-2q} + V_{n-2q-2} + \cdots + V_{n-2p-2q} \\ + V_{-(n-2p-2q)} + \cdots + V_{-(n-2q-2)} + V_{-(n-2q)}).$$

In particular, the number of irreducible components is equal to

$$\begin{cases} \frac{1}{12}(n+1)(n+2)(n+3) & (n \text{ is odd}), \\ \frac{1}{12}(n+2)(n^2+4n+6) & (n \text{ is even}). \end{cases}$$

Note that the above sum $(p\Lambda_1 + q\Lambda_2) \otimes (V_{n-2q} + \cdots + V_{-(n-2q)})$ etc. actually means

$$(p\Lambda_1 + q\Lambda_2) \otimes V_{n-2q} + \cdots + (p\Lambda_1 + q\Lambda_2) \otimes V_{-(n-2q)},$$

which is a sum of $n - 2q + 1$ irreducible components.

The multiplicity of each irreducible component is at most 2, and the multiplicity 2 case occurs if and only if $p + 2q \leq n - 2$ and $p + q \geq n/2$ for the space V_k with $|k| \leq 2p + 2q - n$.

Proof. We divide the proof into two cases according as the parity of n. We here treat the case n is odd. The $n =$ even case can be treated in a similar way.

First we decompose the representation space S_n into the irreducible factor under the action of the group $GL(p, \mathbf{C}) \times GL(2, \mathbf{C})$. As is well known that the character of the $GL(p, \mathbf{C})$-irreducible representation space is expressed by the Schur function $T_{n_1, n_2, \cdots, n_p}$ with $n_1 \geq n_2 \geq \cdots \geq n_p \geq 0$. (Usually, the Schur function is expressed as $S_{n_1, n_2, \cdots, n_p}$. But we use this notation because two symbols S_n and $S_{n,0,\cdots,0}$ are quite confusing.) Similarly we denote the character of the group $GL(2, \mathbf{C})$ by U_{ab} with $a \geq b \geq 0$. Then, since the space S_n is isomorphic to the space $S^n(\mathbf{C}^p \otimes \mathbf{C}^2)$ as a $GL(p, \mathbf{C}) \times GL(2, \mathbf{C})$-representation space, it is irreducibly decomposed as

$$S_n = T_n U_n + T_{n-1,1} U_{n-1,1} + T_{n-2,2} U_{n-2,2} + \cdots + T_{\frac{n+1}{2},\frac{n-1}{2}} U_{\frac{n+1}{2},\frac{n-1}{2}}.$$

Next, we decompose the spaces T_{ab} and U_{ab} with $a > b \geq 0$ and $a + b = n$ into $SO(p)$- and $SO(2)$-irreducible factors. As for the space U_{ab}, it is $a-b+1$-dimensional and is decomposed into the sum of 1-dimensional spaces

$$U_{ab} = V_{a-b} + V_{a-b-2} + V_{a-b-4} + \cdots + V_{-(a-b)}.$$

In order to decompose the space T_{ab} into $SO(p)$-irreducible subspaces, we must review the theory of Koike-Terada [3], concerning the branching rule of $GL(p) \to SO(p)$.

According to [3] the space T_{ab} is decomposed as

$$T_{ab} = \sum_{\substack{2c+2d+e+f=n, \\ c \geq d \geq 0, \, e \geq f \geq 0}} LR^{(a,b)}_{(2c,2d),(e,f)} \{(e-f)\Lambda_1 + f\Lambda_2\}.$$

Here, LR means the Littlewood-Richardson coefficient restricted to the range depth$\leq$ 2, i.e., we have for the partitions (p, q) and (r, s) with $p \geq q \geq 0$, $r \geq s \geq 0$

$$T_{pq} T_{rs} = \sum_{\substack{t+u=p+q+r+s, \\ t \geq u \geq 0}} LR^{(t,u)}_{(p,q),(r,s)} T_{tu}.$$

Hence we have clearly $2c, e \leq a$ and $2d, f \leq b$. Now we find a condition such that $LR^{(a,b)}_{(2c,2d),(e,f)} \neq 0$ for a given partition (a, b). By drawing the Young diagram, we can easily find that this condition is equivalent to

$$2d + e - a + 2c \leq 2c,$$
$$a - 2c \geq f,$$
$$e - a + 2c \geq 0.$$

We fix (a, b) and (c, d) with $0 \leq 2c \leq a$, $0 \leq 2d \leq b$ and $c \geq d$. Then the partition (e, f) must satisfy the conditions

$$e + f = a + b - 2c - 2d,$$
$$0 \leq f \leq a - 2c \leq e \leq a - 2d.$$

These conditions are equivalent to

$$f = a + b - 2c - 2d - e,$$
$$\max\{a - 2c, b - 2d\} \leq e \leq \min\{a - 2d, a + b - 2c - 2d\}.$$

Thus we have the $SO(p)$-irreducible decomposition
$$T_{ab} = \sum \{(2c + 2d + 2e - a - b)\Lambda_1 + (a + b - 2c - 2d - e)\Lambda_2\},$$
where the summation is taken over the range
$$0 \le 2c \le a, \ 0 \le 2d \le b, \ d \le c,$$
$$\max\{a - 2c, b - 2d\} \le e \le \min\{a - 2d, a + b - 2c - 2d\}.$$
By replacing the symbols $p = a - 2c$, $q = b - 2d$ and $r = a + b - 2c - 2d - e$, we can rewrite the above simply as
$$T_{ab} = \sum_{\begin{cases} 0 \le p \le a, \ 0 \le q \le b, \\ 0 \le r \le p, q, \\ p - r \le a - b, \\ p \equiv a, \ q \equiv b \pmod 2 \end{cases}} \{(p + q - 2r)\Lambda_1 + r\Lambda_2\}.$$

For our purpose, we must express this decomposition in the form of a generating function. In the following we express the $SO(p) \times SO(2)$-irreducible component $(p\Lambda_1 + q\Lambda_2) \otimes V_k$ as a monomial $x^p y^q z^k$. Then for the pair (a,b) with $a > b \ge 0$, $a + b = n$, we have
$$T_{ab}U_{ab} = \sum x^{p+q-2r} y^r (z^{a-b} + z^{a-b-2} + \cdots + z^{-(a-b)}),$$
where the summation is taken over the same range as above. We calculate this summation. Then, in case a is odd and b is even, we have
$$T_{ab}U_{ab} = \frac{x(1 - x^{a-b+1})(z^{-(a-b)} - z^{a-b+2})\{(x^2 - y^2) - (1 - y)(x^2 + y)x^{b+2} + (1 - x^2)y^{b+3}\}}{(1 - x^2)^2(1 - y)(1 - z^2)(x^2 - y^2)},$$
and in case a is even and b is odd, we have
$$T_{ab}U_{ab} = \frac{x(1 - x^{a-b+1})(z^{-(a-b)} - z^{a-b+2})\{(x^2 - y^2) - (1 - y^2)x^{b+3} + (1 - x^2)y^{b+3}\}}{(1 - x^2)^2(1 - y)(1 - z^2)(x^2 - y^2)}.$$

Now assume $n \equiv 1 \pmod 4$. Then we have
$$S_n = T_n U_n + T_{n-1,1} U_{n-1,1} + T_{n-2,2} U_{n-2,2} + \cdots + T_{\frac{n+1}{2},\frac{n-1}{2}} U_{\frac{n+1}{2},\frac{n-1}{2}},$$
where $(n+1)/2$ is odd and $(n-1)/2$ is even. To calculate the generating function of S_n, in the above $T_{ab}U_{ab}$'s, we divide the terms in the parenthesis $\{(x^2 - y^2) - \cdots + (1 - x^2)y^{b+3}\}$ of the numerators of $T_{ab}U_{ab}$ into three parts. After some calculations, we know that the sum of first terms in $T_{ab}U_{ab}$ containing $(x^2 - y^2)$ is equal to
$$\frac{x}{(1 - x^2)^2(1 - y)(1 - z^2)} \left\{ z^{-n} \frac{1 - z^{n+1}}{1 - z^2} - z^3 \frac{1 - z^{n+1}}{1 - z^2} \right.$$
$$\left. - x^2 z^{-n} \frac{x^{n+1} - z^{n+1}}{x^2 - z^2} + x^2 z^3 \frac{1 - x^{n+1}z^{n+1}}{1 - x^2 z^2} \right\}$$
$$= \frac{xz^{-n}(1 - z^{n+1})(1 - z^{n+3})}{(1 - x^2)^2(1 - y)(1 - z^2)^2} - \frac{x^3 z^{-n}(x^{n+1} - z^{n+1})}{(1 - x^2)^2(1 - y)(1 - z^2)(x^2 - z^2)}$$
$$+ \frac{x^3 z^3 (1 - x^{n+1} z^{n+1})}{(1 - x^2)^2(1 - y)(1 - z^2)(1 - x^2 z^2)}. \quad (3.1)$$

(We take the summation for $b = 0, 1, \cdots, (n-1)/2$, since the first terms in $T_{ab}U_{ab}$ containing $(x^2 - y^2)$ are common for both cases $b =$ even and odd.) Calculations of the sum of second terms containing $-(1-y)(x^2+y)x^{b+2}$ and $-(1-y^2)x^{b+3}$ are a little more complicated because we must add alternatively the terms according as the parity of a and b. The sum for the cases a are odd is equal to

$$-\frac{x(x^2+y)}{(1-x^2)^2(1-z^2)(x^2-y^2)}\left\{x^2z^{-n}\frac{1-x^{(n+3)/2}z^{n+3}}{1-x^2z^4} - x^2z^3\frac{x^{(n+3)/2}-z^{n+3}}{x^2-z^4}\right.$$
$$\left. -x^{(n+7)/2}z^{-n}\frac{x^{(n+3)/2}-z^{n+3}}{x^2-z^4} + x^{(n+7)/2}z^3\frac{1-x^{(n+3)/2}z^{n+3}}{1-x^2z^4}\right\},$$

and the sum for the cases a are even is equal to

$$-\frac{x(1+y)}{(1-x^2)^2(1-z^2)(x^2-y^2)}\left\{x^4z^{-n+2}\frac{1-x^{(n-1)/2}z^{n-1}}{1-x^2z^4} - x^4z^5\frac{x^{(n-1)/2}-z^{n-1}}{x^2-z^4}\right.$$
$$\left. -x^{(n+11)/2}z^{-n+2}\frac{x^{(n-1)/2}-z^{n-1}}{x^2-z^4} + x^{(n+11)/2}z^5\frac{1-x^{(n-1)/2}z^{n-1}}{1-x^2z^4}\right\}.$$

We add these two expressions. Then we obtain

$$-\frac{x^3z^{-n}(x^2yz^2+x^2z^2+x^2+y)}{(1-x^2)^2(1-z^2)(1-x^2z^4)(x^2-y^2)} + \frac{x^{n+6}z^{n+4}(x^2z^2+yz^2+y+1)}{(1-x^2)^2(1-z^2)(1-x^2z^4)(x^2-y^2)}$$
$$-\frac{x^3z^{n+4}(x^2z^2+x^2y+yz^2+x^2)}{(1-x^2)^2(1-z^2)(x^2-y^2)(x^2-z^4)} + \frac{x^{n+6}z^{-n}(yz^2+x^2+z^2+y)}{(1-x^2)^2(1-z^2)(x^2-y^2)(x^2-z^4)}.$$
(3.2)

Finally we add the third terms concerning $(1-x^2)y^{b+3}$. By a similar calculations as above, we have

$$\frac{xy^3}{(1-x^2)(1-y)(1-z^2)(x^2-y^2)}\left\{z^{-n}\frac{1-y^{(n+1)/2}z^{n+1}}{1-yz^2} - z^3\frac{y^{(n+1)/2}-z^{n+1}}{y-z^2}\right.$$
$$\left. -x^2z^{-n}\frac{x^{n+1}-y^{(n+1)/2}z^{n+1}}{x^2-yz^2} + x^2z^3\frac{x^{n+1}z^{n+1}-y^{(n+1)/2}}{x^2z^2-y}\right\}$$
$$= \frac{xy^3z^{-n}(1-y^{(n+1)/2}z^{n+1})}{(1-x^2)(1-y)(1-z^2)(1-yz^2)(x^2-y^2)}$$
$$- \frac{xy^3z^3(y^{(n+1)/2}-z^{n+1})}{(1-x^2)(1-y)(1-z^2)(x^2-y^2)(y-z^2)}$$
$$- \frac{x^3y^3z^{-n}(x^{n+1}-y^{(n+1)/2}z^{n+1})}{(1-x^2)(1-y)(1-z^2)(x^2-y^2)(x^2-yz^2)}$$
$$+ \frac{x^3y^3z^3(x^{n+1}z^{n+1}-y^{(n+1)/2})}{(1-x^2)(1-y)(1-z^2)(x^2-y^2)(x^2z^2-y)}. \quad (3.3)$$

We add these three partial sums (3.1)–(3.3). Then we have

$$\frac{xz^3(1+z^2)}{(1-y)(1-z^2)^2(1-x^2z^2)(x^2-z^2)} + \frac{x^{n+8}z^{n+10}}{(1-x^2)(1-z^2)(1-x^2z^2)(1-x^2z^4)(x^2z^2-y)}$$
$$+ \frac{xz^{-n}}{(1-x^2)(1-z^2)^2(1-x^2z^4)(1-yz^2)} + \frac{x^{n+8}z^{-n}}{(1-x^2)(1-z^2)(x^2-z^2)(z^4-x^2)(x^2-yz^2)}$$
$$+ \frac{xz^{n+10}}{(1-x^2)(1-z^2)^2(z^4-x^2)(z^2-y)} - \frac{xy^{(n+9)/2}z^3(1+z^2)}{(1-y)(1-yz^2)(z^2-y)(x^2z^2-y)(x^2-yz^2)}. \quad (3.4)$$

This expression gives the generating function of the $SO(p) \times SO(2)$-irreducible decomposition of the space S_n for the case $n \equiv 1 \pmod 4$. In a similar way we can obtain the generating function of S_n for the case $n \equiv 3 \pmod 4$.

To prove Theorem 3.1, we next calculate the generating function of the space $\mathcal{H}_n$. For this purpose, we use the formula of Kostant on the decomposition of the space S_n:

$$S_n = \mathcal{H}_n \oplus (J_+S)_n$$

(for details, see [9; p.83]). In our case the ring of K-invariant polynomials J is generated by two elements with degree 2 and 4. Hence by using the above formula repeatedly, we obtain the direct sum decomposition

$$S_n \cong \mathcal{H}_n + \mathcal{H}_{n-2} + 2(\mathcal{H}_{n-4} + \mathcal{H}_{n-6}) + 3(\mathcal{H}_{n-8} + \mathcal{H}_{n-10}) + \cdots$$
$$+ \begin{cases} \frac{n-1}{4}(\mathcal{H}_5 + \mathcal{H}_3) + \frac{n+3}{4}\mathcal{H}_1 & (n \equiv 1 \pmod 4), \\ \frac{n+1}{4}(\mathcal{H}_3 + \mathcal{H}_1) & (n \equiv 3 \pmod 4), \end{cases}$$

as a representation space.

Now we show Theorem 3.1 by induction on n. In case $n = 1$ we have $\mathcal{H}_1 = (\Lambda_1) \otimes (V_1 + V_{-1})$. Since $n = 1$, we have $p = 1$ and $q = 0$ in the summation of Theorem 3.1, and hence the theorem holds in this case.

We assume that Theorem 3.1 holds for $n = 1, 3, \cdots, m-2$ for some odd integer m with $m \geq 3$. Then by this assumption, the generating function of $\mathcal{H}_n$ is equal to

$$\sum_{\substack{p+2q=n,\\ p \geq 1, q \geq 0}} x^p y^q (z^{n-2q} + z^{n-2q-2} + \cdots + z^{-(n-2q-2)} + z^{-(n-2q)})$$

$$+ \sum_{\substack{p+2q \leq n-2,\\ p \geq 1, q \geq 0,\\ p = \text{odd}}} x^p y^q (z^{n-2q} + z^{n-2q-2} + \cdots + z^{n-2p-2q} + z^{-(n-2p-2q)} + \cdots + z^{-(n-2q-2)} + z^{-(n-2q)}).$$

for odd integers n with $1 \leq n \leq m-2$. After some calculations, we know that the first summation in the above sum is equal to

$$\frac{x^{n+2}z^{-n} - xy^{(n+1)/2}z}{(1-z^2)(x^2-yz^2)} - \frac{x^{n+2}z^{n+4} - xy^{(n+1)/2}z^3}{(1-z^2)(x^2z^2-y)}.$$

As for the second summation, by the change of the symbol p, it is equal to

$$\sum x^{2p+1} y^q (z^{n-2q} + z^{n-2q-2} + \cdots + z^{n-4p-2q-2}$$
$$+ z^{-(n-4p-2q-2)} + \cdots + z^{-(n-2q-2)} + z^{-(n-2q)},$$

where the summation is taken over the range $p, q \geq 0$ and $p + q \leq (n-3)/2$. (In case $n = 1$ the summation is reduced to 0.) Then it is equal to

$$\sum x^{2p+1} y^q z^{-(n-2q)} (1 + z^{2n-4p-4q-2}) \frac{1 - z^{4p+4}}{1 - z^2}$$
$$= \frac{xz^{-n}}{1 - z^2} \sum (x^2)^p (yz^2)^q + \frac{xz^{n-2}}{1 - z^2} \sum (x^2 z^{-4})^p (yz^{-2})^q$$
$$- \frac{xz^{-n+4}}{1 - z^2} \sum (x^2 z^4)^p (yz^2)^q - \frac{xz^{n+2}}{1 - z^2} \sum (x^2)^p (yz^{-2})^q.$$

By using the formula

$$\sum_{p+q \leq (n-3)/2} a^p b^q = \frac{1}{(1-a)(1-b)} - \frac{a^{(n+1)/2}}{(1-a)(a-b)} + \frac{b^{(n+1)/2}}{(1-b)(a-b)},$$

we can calculate these summations. We finally add these terms according as the type of exponents of x, z, y, i.e., we separately gather five terms involving $x^n z^n$, z^{-n}, $x^n z^{-n}$, z^n and $y^{(n+1)/2}$. Then the final expression is given as follows:

$$\frac{x^{n+2} z^{n+4} (1 - x^4 z^4)}{(1-x^2)(1-z^2)(1-x^2 z^4)(x^2 z^2 - y)} + \frac{xz^{-n}(1 - z^4)}{(1-x^2)(1-z^2)(1-x^2 z^4)(1 - yz^2)}$$
$$- \frac{x^{n+2} z^{-n} (x^4 - z^4)}{(1-x^2)(1-z^2)(x^2 - z^4)(x^2 - yz^2)} + \frac{xz^{n+4}(1 - z^4)}{(1-x^2)(1-z^2)(x^2 - z^4)(y - z^2)}$$
$$+ \frac{xy^{(n+3)/2} z^3 (1 - y^2)(1 + z^2)}{(1 - yz^2)(y - z^2)(x^2 z^2 - y)(x^2 - yz^2)}. \tag{3.5}$$

This gives the generating function of $\mathcal{H}_n$ for $n \leq m - 2$.

Under these preparations, we show that the generating function of $\mathcal{H}_m$ is given by the above expression (3.5) where n is replaced by m. We already know the generating function of the space S_m for odd m, and also know the direct sum decomposition $S_m = \mathcal{H}_m + \mathcal{H}_{m-2} + 2(\mathcal{H}_{m-4} + \mathcal{H}_{m-6}) + \cdots$. Thus it suffices to show that the sum of generating functions $\mathcal{H}_m, \mathcal{H}_{m-2}, 2\mathcal{H}_{m-4}, 2\mathcal{H}_{m-6}, \cdots$ is equal to that of S_m, assuming (3.5) holds for the case $n = m$.

We first treat the case $m \equiv 1 \pmod 4$. We calculate the sum $\mathcal{H}_m + \mathcal{H}_{m-2} + 2(\mathcal{H}_{m-4} + \mathcal{H}_{m-6}) + \cdots$ for five terms in (3.5) separately. As for the first term, we have

$$x^{m+2} z^{m+4} + x^m z^{m+2} + 2(x^{m-2} z^m + x^{m-4} z^{m-2}) + \cdots + \frac{m-1}{4}(x^7 z^9 + x^5 z^7) + \frac{m+3}{4} x^3 z^5$$
$$= \frac{m+3}{4} \frac{x^3 z^5}{1 - x^4 z^4} - \frac{x^7 z^9 (1 - x^{m+3} z^{m+3})}{(1 - x^4 z^4)^2} + \frac{m-1}{4} \frac{x^5 z^7}{1 - x^4 z^4} - \frac{x^9 z^{11}(1 - x^{m-1} z^{m-1})}{(1 - x^4 z^4)^2}.$$

Hence the sum of first terms is equal to

$$\frac{1}{(1-x^2)(1-z^2)(1-x^2z^4)(x^2z^2-y)}\left\{\frac{m+3}{4}x^3z^5+\frac{m-1}{4}x^5z^7\right.$$
$$\left.-\frac{x^7z^9(1-x^{m+1}z^{m+1})}{1-x^2z^2}\right\}. \qquad (3.6)$$

Similarly, we can calculate the remaining four summations according to the order in (3.5). The results are respectively given as follows:

$$\frac{x}{(1-x^2)(1-z^2)(1-x^2z^4)(1-yz^2)}\left\{\frac{z^{-m}(1-z^{m+1})}{1-z^2}-\frac{m+3}{4}z^3-\frac{m-1}{4}z\right\}, \qquad (3.7)$$

$$\frac{-1}{(1-x^2)(1-z^2)(x^2-z^4)(x^2-yz^2)}\left\{\frac{x^7z^{-m}(x^{m+1}-z^{m+1})}{x^2-z^2}\right.$$
$$\left.-\frac{m+3}{4}x^3z^3-\frac{m-1}{4}x^5z\right\}, \qquad (3.8)$$

$$\frac{x}{(1-x^2)(1-z^2)(x^2-z^4)(y-z^2)}\left\{\frac{m+3}{4}z^5+\frac{m-1}{4}z^7-\frac{z^9(1-z^{m+1})}{1-z^2}\right\}, \qquad (3.9)$$

and

$$\frac{xz^3(1+z^2)}{(1-yz^2)(y-z^2)(x^2z^2-y)(x^2-yz^2)}\left\{\frac{m+3}{4}y^2+\frac{m-1}{4}y^3-\frac{y^4(1-y^{(m+1)/2})}{1-y}\right\}. \qquad (3.10)$$

We must add these five expressions (3.6)–(3.10). We first calculate sum of terms not involving the symbol m. It is equal to

$$\frac{x^3z^5}{(1-x^2)(1-z^2)(1-x^2z^4)(x^2z^2-y)}\left\{\frac{3}{4}-\frac{x^2z^2}{4}-\frac{x^4z^4}{1-x^2z^2}\right\}$$
$$+\frac{xz}{(1-x^2)(1-z^2)(1-x^2z^4)(1-yz^2)}\left\{\frac{-1}{1-z^2}-\frac{3z^2}{4}+\frac{1}{4}\right\}$$
$$-\frac{x^3z}{(1-x^2)(1-z^2)(x^2-z^4)(x^2-yz^2)}\left\{\frac{-x^4}{x^2-z^2}-\frac{3z^2}{4}+\frac{x^2}{4}\right\}$$
$$+\frac{xz^5}{(1-x^2)(1-z^2)(x^2-z^4)(y-z^2)}\left\{\frac{3}{4}-\frac{z^2}{4}-\frac{z^4}{1-z^2}\right\}$$
$$+\frac{xz^3(1+z^2)y^2}{(1-yz^2)(y-z^2)(x^2z^2-y)(x^2-yz^2)}\left\{\frac{3}{4}-\frac{y}{4}-\frac{y^2}{1-y}\right\}.$$

Surprisingly, it just coincides with the expression

$$\frac{xz^3(1+z^2)}{(1-y)(1-z^2)^2(1-x^2z^2)(x^2-z^2)},$$

which is the first term of S_m in (3.4).

The term involving $x^m z^m$ appears only in the first sum (3.6), and it is equal to

$$\frac{x^{m+8} z^{m+10}}{(1-x^2)(1-z^2)(1-x^2z^2)(1-x^2z^4)(x^2z^2-y)}.$$

This expression just coincides with the second term of S_n in (3.4), if we replace n by m. The terms involving z^{-m}, $x^m z^{-m}$, z^m and $y^{(m+1)/2}$ also appear only in one place of the above (3.6)–(3.10), and they also coincides with the third, fourth, fifth and sixth terms of S_n in (3.4), respectively. Finally, we consider the terms in (3.6)–(3.10) possessing m as a coefficient. By dividing $m/4$, it becomes

$$\frac{x^3 z^5 (1+x^2 z^2)}{(1-x^2)(1-z^2)(1-x^2 z^4)(x^2 z^2 - y)} - \frac{xz(1+z^2)}{(1-x^2)(1-z^2)(1-x^2 z^4)(1-yz^2)}$$
$$+ \frac{x^3 z(x^2 + z^2)}{(1-x^2)(1-z^2)(x^2 - z^4)(x^2 - yz^2)} + \frac{xz^5(1+z^2)}{(1-x^2)(1-z^2)(x^2 - z^4)(y - z^2)}$$
$$+ \frac{xy^2 z^3 (1+y)(1+z^2)}{(1-yz^2)(y-z^2)(x^2 z^2 - y)(x^2 - yz^2)}.$$

It is surprising again that this expression reduces to 0 after direct calculations. Therefore, summarizing these results, it follows that the generating function of $\mathcal{H}_m$ has the desired expression.

The case $m \equiv 3 \pmod{4}$ can be treated in the same way, and thus the induction is completed. Hence the proof of Theorem 3.1 is completed for the case n is odd.

We can similarly prove the theorem for the case n is even. q.e.d.

4. Irreducible Subspaces of $\mathcal{H}_n$ for $n \leq 4$

In this section we show the $K_{\mathbf{R}}$-irreducible subspaces of the space $\mathcal{H}_n$ for $n \leq 4$ and give some integral formulas on some orbits of them.

For $\widetilde{X} = \begin{pmatrix} 0 & X \\ {}^t X & 0 \end{pmatrix} \in \mathfrak{p}$ and $X = (x\ y)$ and $g = \mathrm{Ad} \begin{pmatrix} A & 0 \\ 0 & R(\theta) \end{pmatrix} \in K_{\mathbf{R}}$ $(A \in SO(p))$, where $R(\theta) = \begin{pmatrix} \cos\theta & -\sin\theta \\ \sin\theta & \cos\theta \end{pmatrix}$, we have

$$\Psi(g\widetilde{X}) = \begin{pmatrix} e^{-i\theta} Az \\ e^{i\theta} Aw \end{pmatrix}$$

and it is valid that for $f \in S(\mathfrak{p})$

$$\int_{K_{\mathbf{R}}} f(g\widetilde{X}_0) dg = \frac{1}{2\pi} \int_0^{2\pi} \int_{SO(p)} f \circ \Psi^{-1}\left(\begin{pmatrix} e^{-i\theta} h z_0 \\ e^{i\theta} h w_0 \end{pmatrix}\right) dh d\theta,$$

where $\widetilde{X}_0 = \Psi^{-1}\left(\begin{pmatrix} z_0 \\ w_0 \end{pmatrix}\right) \in \mathfrak{p}$. We put

$$\widetilde{E}_0 = \Psi^{-1}\left(\begin{pmatrix} e_1 + ie_2 \\ e_3 + ie_4 \end{pmatrix}\right), \quad \widetilde{E}_1 = \Psi^{-1}\left(\begin{pmatrix} e_1 \\ e_1 \end{pmatrix}\right), \quad \widetilde{E}_2 = \Psi^{-1}\left(\begin{pmatrix} e_1 \\ e_2 + ie_3 \end{pmatrix}\right),$$
$$\widetilde{E}_3 = \Psi^{-1}\left(\begin{pmatrix} e_2 + ie_3 \\ e_1 \end{pmatrix}\right), \quad \widetilde{E}_4 = \Psi^{-1}\left(\begin{pmatrix} e_1 + ie_2 \\ e_1 + ie_2 \end{pmatrix}\right), \quad \widetilde{E}_5 = \Psi^{-1}\left(\begin{pmatrix} e_1 \\ e_2 \end{pmatrix}\right),$$
$$\widetilde{E}_6 = \Psi^{-1}\left(\begin{pmatrix} e_1 \\ e_1 + ie_2 \end{pmatrix}\right), \quad \widetilde{E}_7 = \Psi^{-1}\left(\begin{pmatrix} e_1 + ie_2 \\ e_1 \end{pmatrix}\right).$$

Let $\alpha, \beta \in \mathbf{C}^p$ satisfy $\alpha^2 = \beta^2 = \alpha \cdot \beta = \alpha \cdot \overline{\beta} = 0$. For $f \in \mathcal{H}_n$ we denote by $\langle f \rangle$ the subspace generated by the set $\{f(gX)\,;\, g \in K_{\mathbf{R}}\}$. In the following we identify $f \in \mathcal{H}_n$ and $f \circ \Psi^{-1} \in H_n(\mathbf{C}^p)$.

Example 4.1 (cf. [9]). We put $\mathcal{H}_{1,1} = \langle z \cdot a\,;\, a \in \mathbf{C}^p, \rangle$ and $\mathcal{H}_{1,2} = \langle w \cdot b\,;\, b \in \mathbf{C}^p \rangle$. Then $\mathcal{H}_{1,1}$ and $\mathcal{H}_{1,2}$ are subspaces of $\mathcal{H}_1$, and $\mathcal{H}_1 = \mathcal{H}_{1,1} \oplus \mathcal{H}_{1,2}$ gives the $K_{\mathbf{R}}$-irreducible decomposition of $\mathcal{H}_1$. We have $\dim \mathcal{H}_{1,1} = \dim \mathcal{H}_{1,2} = p$ and $\dim \mathcal{H}_1 = 2p$. The highest weights of $\mathcal{H}_{1,1}$ and $\mathcal{H}_{1,2}$ are $(\Lambda_1) \otimes V_1$ and $(\Lambda_1) \otimes V_{-1}$, respectively.

Example 4.2 (cf. [9]). We define $\mathcal{H}_{2,k}$ ($1 \leq k \leq 6$) as in the following table:

	generating element	highest weight	dimension
$\mathcal{H}_{2,1}$	$(z \cdot \alpha)^2$	$(2\Lambda_1) \otimes V_2$	$(p-1)(p+2)/2$
$\mathcal{H}_{2,2}$	$(z \cdot \alpha)(w \cdot \alpha)$	$(2\Lambda_1) \otimes V_0$	$(p-1)(p+2)/2$
$\mathcal{H}_{2,3}$	$(w \cdot \alpha)^2$	$(2\Lambda_1) \otimes V_{-2}$	$(p-1)(p+2)/2$
$\mathcal{H}_{2,4}$	$(z \cdot \alpha)(w \cdot \beta) - (z \cdot \beta)(w \cdot \alpha)$	$(\Lambda_2) \otimes V_0$	$p(p-1)/2$
$\mathcal{H}_{2,5}$	z^2	$(0) \otimes V_2$	1
$\mathcal{H}_{2,6}$	w^2	$(0) \otimes V_{-2}$	1

Then $\dim \mathcal{H}_2 = (p+1)(2p-1)$ and $\mathcal{H}_2 = \oplus_{1 \leq k \leq 6} \mathcal{H}_{2,k}$ gives the $K_{\mathbf{R}}$-irreducible decomposition of $\mathcal{H}_2$. Let $\widetilde{X} = \Psi^{-1}\left(\begin{pmatrix} z \\ w \end{pmatrix}\right)$, $\widetilde{X}' = \Psi^{-1}\left(\begin{pmatrix} z' \\ w' \end{pmatrix}\right) \in \mathfrak{p}$. From (2.2)–(2.6) we have the following integral formulas.

(1) For $k = 1, 2, 3$ we can express $\mathcal{H}_{2,k} = \langle (z \cdot \alpha)^{3-k}(w \cdot \alpha)^{k-1} \rangle$ and we put

$$K_{2,k}(\widetilde{X}, \widetilde{X}') = \frac{1}{4} \dim \mathcal{H}_{2,k}\, (z \cdot \overline{z}')^{3-k}(w \cdot \overline{w}')^{k-1}.$$

It is clear that $K_{2,k}(\ , g\widetilde{E}_4) \in \mathcal{H}_{2,k}$ for any $g \in K_{\mathbf{R}}$. Then we have the following reproducing formula:

$$f(\widetilde{X}) = \int_{K_{\mathbf{K}}} f(g\widetilde{E}_4) K_{2,k}(\widetilde{X}, g\widetilde{E}_4) dg \quad (f \in \mathcal{H}_{2,k}). \tag{4.1}$$

For $\widetilde{X}' \in K_{\mathbf{R}} \widetilde{E}_1$ it is valid that $K_{2,k}(\ , \widetilde{X}') \notin \mathcal{H}_{2,k}$. In this case we have the following formula:

$$\frac{1}{4} \lambda_{2,p} \dim \mathcal{H}_{2,k} f(\widetilde{X}) = \int_{K_{\mathbf{R}}} f(g\widetilde{E}_1) K_{2,k}(\widetilde{X}, g\widetilde{E}_1) dg. \tag{4.2}$$

(2) For the space $\mathcal{H}_{2,4} = \langle (z \cdot \alpha)(w \cdot \beta) - (z \cdot \beta)(w \cdot \alpha) \rangle$ we define

$$K_{2,4}(\widetilde{X}, \widetilde{X}') = \frac{1}{2} \dim \mathcal{H}_{2,4}\{(z \cdot \overline{z}')(w \cdot \overline{w}') - (w \cdot \overline{z}')(z \cdot \overline{w}')\}.$$

For any $g \in K_{\mathbf{R}}$ $K_{2,4}(\ ,g\widetilde{E}_2)$ belongs to $\mathcal{H}_{2,k}$. Then $K_{2,4}(\widetilde{X},\widetilde{X}')$ is the reproducing kernel of $\mathcal{H}_{2,4}$ and we have

$$f(\widetilde{X}) = \int_{K_{\mathbf{R}}} f(g\widetilde{E}_2) K_{2,4}(\widetilde{X},g\widetilde{E}_2) dg. \qquad (4.3)$$

(3) We put $\mathcal{H}_{2,5} = \langle z^2 \rangle$. We define

$$K_{2,5}(\widetilde{X},\widetilde{X}') = z^2 \overline{z}'^2.$$

It is clear that $K_{2,5}(\ ,\widetilde{X}_0)$ belongs to $\mathcal{H}_{2,5}$ for any $\widetilde{X}_0 \in \mathfrak{p}$. Then we have the following reproducing formula of $\mathcal{H}_{2,5}$:

$$f(\widetilde{X}) = \int_{K_{\mathbf{R}}} f(g\widetilde{E}_1) K_{2,5}(\widetilde{X},g\widetilde{E}_1) dg. \qquad (4.4)$$

(4) We put $\mathcal{H}_{2,6} = \langle w^2 \rangle$. We define

$$K_{2,6}(\widetilde{X},\widetilde{X}') = w^2 \overline{w}'^2.$$

Then it is valid that $K_{2,6}(X,g\widetilde{E}_1) \in \mathcal{H}_{2,6}$ for any $g \in K_{\mathbf{R}}$ and we have the following reproducing formula of $\mathcal{H}_{2,6}$:

$$f(\widetilde{X}) = \int_{K_{\mathbf{R}}} f(g\widetilde{X}_0) K_{2,6}(\widetilde{X},g\widetilde{X}_0) dg. \qquad (4.5)$$

Example 4.3 (cf. [9]). We define $\mathcal{H}_{3,k}$ ($1 \leq k \leq 10$) as in the following table:

	generating element	highest weight	dimension
$\mathcal{H}_{3,1}$	$(z \cdot \alpha)^3$	$(3\Lambda_1) \otimes V_3$	$p(p-1)(p+4)/6$
$\mathcal{H}_{3,2}$	$(z \cdot \alpha)^2 (w \cdot \alpha)$	$(3\Lambda_1) \otimes V_1$	$p(p-1)(p+4)/6$
$\mathcal{H}_{3,3}$	$(z \cdot \alpha)(w \cdot \alpha)^2$	$(3\Lambda_1) \otimes V_{-1}$	$p(p-1)(p+4)/6$
$\mathcal{H}_{3,4}$	$(w \cdot \alpha)^3$	$(3\Lambda_1) \otimes V_{-3}$	$p(p-1)(p+4)/6$
$\mathcal{H}_{3,5}$	$(z \cdot \alpha)(z \cdot \beta)(w \cdot \alpha) - (w \cdot \beta)(z \cdot \alpha)^2$	$(\Lambda_1 + \Lambda_2) \otimes V_1$	$p(p-2)(p+2)/3$
$\mathcal{H}_{3,6}$	$(w \cdot \alpha)(w \cdot \beta)(z \cdot \alpha) - (z \cdot \beta)(w \cdot \alpha)^2$	$(\Lambda_1 + \Lambda_2) \otimes V_{-1}$	$p(p-2)(p+2)/3$
$\mathcal{H}_{3,7}$	$(z \cdot \alpha) z^2$	$(\Lambda_1) \otimes V_3$	p
$\mathcal{H}_{3,8}$	$(p+1)z^2(w \cdot \alpha) - 2(z \cdot w)(z \cdot \alpha)$	$(\Lambda_1) \otimes V_1$	p
$\mathcal{H}_{3,9}$	$(p+1)w^2(z \cdot \alpha) - 2(z \cdot w)(w \cdot \alpha)$	$(\Lambda_1) \otimes V_{-1}$	p
$\mathcal{H}_{3,10}$	$(w \cdot \alpha)w^2$	$(\Lambda_1) \otimes V_{-3}$	p

Then $\dim \mathcal{H}_3 = \frac{2}{3}p(p+2)(2p-1)$ and $\mathcal{H}_3 = \oplus_{1 \leq k \leq 10} \mathcal{H}_{3,k}$ gives the $K_\mathbf{R}$-irreducible decomposition. Remark that $\mathcal{H}_{3,8}$, $\mathcal{H}_{1,1}$ and $\mathcal{H}_{3,9}$, $\mathcal{H}_{1,-1}$ are equivalent as representation spaces, respectively.

(1) For $k = 1, 2, 3, 4$ we put $\mathcal{H}_{3,k} = \langle (z \cdot \alpha)^{4-k}(w \cdot \alpha)^{k-1} \rangle$ and

$$K_{3,k}(\widetilde{X}, \widetilde{X}') = \frac{1}{8} \dim \mathcal{H}_{3,k} \, (z \cdot \overline{z}')^{4-k}(w \cdot \overline{w}')^{k-1}.$$

For any $\widetilde{X}' \in K_\mathbf{R}\widetilde{E}_4$ we have $K_{3,k}(\,, \widetilde{X}') \in \mathcal{H}_{3,k}$. Then we have for any $f \in \mathcal{H}_{3,k}$

$$f(\widetilde{X}) = \int_{K_\mathbf{R}} f(g\widetilde{E}_4) K_{3,k}(\widetilde{X}, g\widetilde{E}_4) dg. \qquad (4.6)$$

(4.6) is the reproducing formula of $\mathcal{H}_{3,k}$. Though $K_{3,k}(\,, g\widetilde{E}_1)$ is not an element of $\mathcal{H}_{3,k}$ ($g \in K_\mathbf{R}$), the following formula holds:

$$f(\widetilde{X}) = \frac{1}{8} \lambda_{3,p} \dim \mathcal{H}_{3,k} \int_{K_\mathbf{R}} f(g\widetilde{E}_1) K_{3,k}(\widetilde{X}, g\widetilde{E}_1) dg. \qquad (4.7)$$

(2) We put $\mathcal{H}_{3,7} = \langle (z \cdot \alpha) z^2 \rangle$ and

$$K_{3,7}(\widetilde{X}, \widetilde{X}') = \dim \mathcal{H}_{3,7} \, z^2 \overline{z}'^2 (z \cdot \overline{z}').$$

It is easy to see that $K_{3,7}(\,, g\widetilde{E}_1) \in \mathcal{H}_{3,7}$ for any $g \in K_\mathbf{R}$. Then we have for any $f \in \mathcal{H}_{3,7}$

$$f(\widetilde{X}) = \int_{K_\mathbf{R}} f(g\widetilde{E}_1) K_{3,7}(\widetilde{X}, g\widetilde{E}_1) dg, \qquad (4.8)$$

and (4.8) is the reproducing formula of $\mathcal{H}_{3,7}$.

(3) We put
$$\mathcal{H}_{3,8} = \langle (p+1) z^2 (w \cdot \alpha) - 2(z \cdot w)(z \cdot \alpha) \rangle$$
and
$$\mathcal{H}_{3,9} = \langle (p+1) w^2 (z \cdot \alpha) - 2(z \cdot w)(w \cdot \alpha) \rangle.$$

We define

$$K_{3,8}(\widetilde{X}, \widetilde{X}') = \frac{\dim \mathcal{H}_{3,8}}{p-1} \{(p+1) z^2 \overline{z}'^2 (w \cdot \overline{w}') - 2(z \cdot w)(\overline{z}' \cdot \overline{w}')(z \cdot \overline{z}')\}$$

and

$$K_{3,9}(\widetilde{X}, \widetilde{X}') = \frac{\dim \mathcal{H}_{3,9}}{p-1} \{(p+1) w^2 \overline{z}'^2 (z \cdot \overline{z}') - 2(z \cdot z)(\overline{w}' \cdot \overline{w}')(z \cdot \overline{w}')\}.$$

For any $g \in K_{\mathbf{R}}$ we have $K_{3,8}(\ ,g\widetilde{E}_1) \in \mathcal{H}_{3,8}$ and $K_{3,9}(\ ,g\widetilde{E}_1) \in \mathcal{H}_{3,9}$. Then we have for any $f \in \mathcal{H}_{3,8}$ and $h \in \mathcal{H}_{3,9}$

$$f(\widetilde{X}) = \int_{K_{\mathbf{R}}} f(g\widetilde{E}_1) K_{3,8}(\widetilde{X},g\widetilde{E}_1) dg, \qquad (4.9)$$

$$h(\widetilde{X}) = \int_{K_{\mathbf{R}}} h(g\widetilde{E}_1) K_{3,9}(\widetilde{X},g\widetilde{E}_1) dg. \qquad (4.10)$$

(4.9) and (4.10) are the reproducing formulas of $\mathcal{H}_{3,8}$ and $\mathcal{H}_{3,9}$, respectively.

(4) We put $\mathcal{H}_{3,10} = \langle (w \cdot \alpha)w^2 \rangle$ and

$$K_{3,10}(\widetilde{X},\widetilde{X}') = \dim \mathcal{H}_{3,10}\, w^2\, \overline{w}'^2 (z \cdot \overline{w}').$$

Then we have $K_{3,10}(\ ,\widetilde{X}') \in \mathcal{H}_{3,10}$ for any $\widetilde{X}' \in K_{\mathbf{R}}\widetilde{E}_1$ and it is valid that

$$f(\widetilde{X}) = \int_{K_{\mathbf{R}}} f(g\widetilde{E}_1) K_{3,10}(\widetilde{X},g\widetilde{E}_1) dg. \qquad (4.11)$$

(4.11) is the reproducing formula of $\mathcal{H}_{3,10}$.

Example 4.4 (cf. [9]). We define $\mathcal{H}_{4,k}$ ($1 \leq k \leq 19$) as in the following table:

	generating element	highest weight	dimension
$\mathcal{H}_{4,1}$	$(z \cdot \alpha)^4$	$(4\Lambda_1) \otimes V_4$	$p(p-1)(p+1)(p+6)/24$
$\mathcal{H}_{4,2}$	$(z \cdot \alpha)^3(w \cdot \alpha)$	$(4\Lambda_1) \otimes V_2$	$p(p-1)(p+1)(p+6)/24$
$\mathcal{H}_{4,3}$	$(z \cdot \alpha)^2(w \cdot \alpha)^2$	$(4\Lambda_1) \otimes V_0$	$p(p-1)(p+1)(p+6)/24$
$\mathcal{H}_{4,4}$	$(z \cdot \alpha)(w \cdot \alpha)^3$	$(4\Lambda_1) \otimes V_{-2}$	$p(p-1)(p+1)(p+6)/24$
$\mathcal{H}_{4,5}$	$(w \cdot \alpha)^4$	$(4\Lambda_1) \otimes V_{-4}$	$p(p-1)(p+1)(p+6)/24$
$\mathcal{H}_{4,6}$	$(z \cdot \alpha)^2(z \cdot \beta)(w \cdot \beta) - (z \cdot \beta)^2(z \cdot \alpha)(w \cdot \alpha)$	$(2\Lambda_1 + \Lambda_2) \otimes V_2$	$(p-1)(p-2)(p+1)(p+4)/8$
$\mathcal{H}_{4,7}$	$(z \cdot \alpha)^2(w \cdot \beta)^2 - (z \cdot \beta)^2(w \cdot \alpha)^2$	$(2\Lambda_1 + \Lambda_2) \otimes V_0$	$(p-1)(p-2)(p+1)(p+4)/8$
$\mathcal{H}_{4,8}$	$(w \cdot \alpha)^2(w \cdot \beta)(z \cdot \beta) - (w \cdot \beta)^2(w \cdot \alpha)(z \cdot \alpha)$	$(2\Lambda_1 + \Lambda_2) \otimes V_{-2}$	$(p-1)(p-2)(p+1)(p+4)/8$
$\mathcal{H}_{4,9}$	$\{(z \cdot \alpha)(w \cdot \beta) - (w \cdot \alpha)(z \cdot \beta)\}^2$	$(2\Lambda_2) \otimes V_0$	$p(p-3)(p+1)(p+2)/12$
$\mathcal{H}_{4,10}$	$(z \cdot \alpha)^2 z^2$	$(2\Lambda_1) \otimes V_4$	$(p-1)(p+2)/2$
$\mathcal{H}_{4,11}$	$(p+2)(z \cdot \alpha)(w \cdot \alpha)z^2 - 2(z \cdot \alpha)^2(z \cdot w)$	$(2\Lambda_1) \otimes V_2$	$(p-1)(p+2)/2$
$\mathcal{H}_{4,12}$	$(p+2)(z \cdot \alpha)^2 w^2 - 4(z \cdot \alpha)(w \cdot \alpha)(z \cdot w)$	$(2\Lambda_1) \otimes V_0$	$(p-1)(p+2)/2$
$\mathcal{H}_{4,13}$	$(p+2)(w \cdot \alpha)^2 z^2 - 4(w \cdot \alpha)(z \cdot \alpha)(z \cdot w)$	$(2\Lambda_1) \otimes V_0$	$(p-1)(p+2)/2$
$\mathcal{H}_{4,14}$	$(p+2)(w \cdot \alpha)(z \cdot \alpha)w^2 - 2(w \cdot \alpha)^2(z \cdot w)$	$(2\Lambda_1) \otimes V_{-2}$	$(p-1)(p+2)/2$
$\mathcal{H}_{4,15}$	$(w \cdot \alpha)^2 w^2$	$(2\Lambda_1) \otimes V_{-4}$	$(p-1)(p+2)/2$
$\mathcal{H}_{4,16}$	$\{(z \cdot \alpha)(w \cdot \beta) - (w \cdot \alpha)(z \cdot \beta)\} z^2$	$(\Lambda_2) \otimes V_2$	$p(p-1)/2$
$\mathcal{H}_{4,17}$	$\{(z \cdot \alpha)(w \cdot \beta) - (w \cdot \alpha)(z \cdot \beta)\} w^2$	$(\Lambda_2) \otimes V_{-2}$	$p(p-1)/2$
$\mathcal{H}_{4,18}$	$(z^2)^2$	$(0) \otimes V_4$	1
$\mathcal{H}_{4,19}$	$(w^2)^2$	$(0) \otimes V_{-4}$	1

Then $\dim \mathcal{H}_4 = \frac{1}{6}(p+1)(4p^3 + 8p^2 - 9p + 6) - 2$ and $\mathcal{H}_4 = \oplus_{1 \leq k \leq 19} \mathcal{H}_{4,k}$ gives the $K_{\mathbf{R}}$-irreducible decomposition. Remark that $\mathcal{H}_{4,12}$, $\mathcal{H}_{4,13}$ and $\mathcal{H}_{2,2}$ are equivalent as representation spaces. Furthermore we have $\mathcal{H}_{4,11} \simeq \mathcal{H}_{2,1}$ and $\mathcal{H}_{4,14} \simeq \mathcal{H}_{2,3}$.

(1) For $k = 1, 2, 3, 4, 5$ we put $\mathcal{H}_{4,k} = \langle (z \cdot \alpha)^{5-k} (w \cdot \alpha)^{k-1} \rangle$ and

$$K_{4,k}(\widetilde{X}, \widetilde{X}') = \frac{1}{16} \dim \mathcal{H}_{4,k} (z \cdot \overline{z}')^{5-k} (w \cdot \overline{w}')^{k-1}.$$

It is clear that $K_{4,k}(\ , g\widetilde{E}_4) \in \mathcal{H}_{4,k}$ for any $g \in K_{\mathbf{R}}$. Then we have for any $f \in \mathcal{H}_{4,k}$

$$f(\widetilde{X}) = \int_{K_{\mathbf{R}}} f(g\widetilde{E}_4) K_{4,k}(\widetilde{X}, g\widetilde{E}_4) dg. \tag{4.12}$$

(4.12) is the reproducing formula of $\mathcal{H}_{4,k}$. We also have

$$\frac{1}{16} \lambda_{4,p} \dim \mathcal{H}_{4,k} f(\widetilde{X}) = \int_{K_{\mathbf{R}}} f(g\widetilde{E}_1) K_{4,k}(\widetilde{X}, g\widetilde{E}_1) dg, \tag{4.13}$$

but $K_{4,k}(\ , g\widetilde{E}_1) \notin \mathcal{H}_{4,k}$ for $g \in K_{\mathbf{R}}$.

(2) We put
$$\mathcal{H}_{4,6} = \langle (z \cdot \alpha)^2 (z \cdot \beta)(w \cdot \alpha) - (w \cdot \beta)(z \cdot \alpha)^3 \rangle$$
and
$$\mathcal{H}_{4,8} = \langle (w \cdot \alpha)^2 (z \cdot \beta)(z \cdot \alpha) - (z \cdot \beta)(w \cdot \alpha)^3 \rangle.$$

We define

$$K_{4,6}(\widetilde{X}, \widetilde{X}') = \frac{p(p+2)}{(p-2)(p+1)} \dim \mathcal{H}_{4,6} \{(z \cdot \overline{w}')(z \cdot \overline{z}')^2 (w \cdot \overline{z}') - (w \cdot \overline{w}')(z \cdot \overline{z}')^3\},$$

$$K_{4,8}(\widetilde{X}, \widetilde{X}') = \frac{p(p+2)}{(p-2)(p+1)} \dim \mathcal{H}_{4,8} \{(w \cdot \overline{z}')(w \cdot \overline{w}')^2 (z \cdot \overline{w}') - (z \cdot \overline{z}')(w \cdot \overline{w}')^3\}.$$

For any $f \in \mathcal{H}_{4,6}$ and $h \in \mathcal{H}_{4,8}$ we have

$$f(\widetilde{X}) = \int_{K_{\mathbf{R}}} f(g\widetilde{E}_5) K_{4,6}(\widetilde{X}, g\widetilde{E}_5) dg, \tag{4.14}$$

$$h(\widetilde{X}) = \int_{K_{\mathbf{R}}} h(g\widetilde{E}_5) K_{4,8}(\widetilde{X}, g\widetilde{E}_5) dg. \tag{4.15}$$

Because we have $K_{4,6}(\ , g\widetilde{E}_5) \notin \mathcal{H}_{4,6}$ and $K_{4,8}(\ , g\widetilde{E}_5) \notin \mathcal{H}_{4,8}$ for $g \in K_{\mathbf{R}}$, (4.14) and (4.15) are not reproducing formulas of $\mathcal{H}_{4,6}$ and $\mathcal{H}_{4,8}$.

(3) We put $\mathcal{H}_{4,10} = \langle (z \cdot \alpha)^2 z^2 \rangle$ and we define

$$K_{4,10}(\widetilde{X}, \widetilde{X}') = \dim \mathcal{H}_{4,10} \, z^2 \overline{z}'^2 \widetilde{P}_{2,p}(z, \overline{z}').$$

For any $\widetilde{X}' \in \mathfrak{p}$ $K_{4,10}(\ ,\widetilde{X}')$ belongs to $\mathcal{H}_{4,10}$. Then we have for any $f \in \mathcal{H}_{4,10}$

$$f(\widetilde{X}) = \int_{K_\mathbf{R}} f(g\widetilde{E}_1)K_{4,10}(\widetilde{X},g\widetilde{E}_1)dg, \qquad (4.16)$$

and (4.16) is a reproducing formula of $\mathcal{H}_{4,10}$.

(4) We put

$$\mathcal{H}_{4,11} = \langle (p+2)(z\cdot\alpha)(w\cdot\alpha)z^2 - 2(z\cdot\alpha)^2(z\cdot w)\rangle$$

and

$$\mathcal{H}_{4,14} = \langle (p+2)(w\cdot\alpha)(z\cdot\alpha)w^2 - 2(w\cdot\alpha)^2(w\cdot z)\rangle.$$

We define

$$K_{4,11}(\widetilde{X},\widetilde{X}')$$
$$= \frac{1}{8}\dim\mathcal{H}_{4,11}\{-(p+2)z^2(\overline{z}'\cdot\overline{w}')(z\cdot\overline{z}')(w\cdot\overline{z}') + 2(z\cdot w)(\overline{z}'\cdot\overline{w}')(z\cdot\overline{z}')^2\},$$

$$K_{4,14}(\widetilde{X},\widetilde{X}')$$
$$= \frac{1}{8}\dim\mathcal{H}_{4,14}\{-(p+2)w^2(\overline{w}'\cdot\overline{z}')(w\cdot\overline{w}')(z\cdot\overline{w}') + 2(w\cdot z)(\overline{w}'\cdot\overline{z}')(w\cdot\overline{w}')^2\}.$$

Then we have $K_{4,11}(\ ,g\widetilde{E}_7) \in \mathcal{H}_{4,11}$ and $K_{4,14}(\ ,g\widetilde{E}_6) \in \mathcal{H}_{4,14}$ for any $g \in K_\mathbf{R}$. Then we have for any $f \in \mathcal{H}_{4,11}$ and $h \in \mathcal{H}_{4,14}$

$$f(\widetilde{X}) = \int_{K_\mathbf{R}} f(g\widetilde{E}_7)K_{4,11}(\widetilde{X},g\widetilde{E}_7)dg, \qquad (4.17)$$

$$h(\widetilde{X}) = \int_{K_\mathbf{R}} h(g\widetilde{E}_6)K_{4,14}(\widetilde{X},g\widetilde{E}_6)dg. \qquad (4.18)$$

(4.17) and (4.18) are reproducing formulas of $\mathcal{H}_{4,11}$ and $\mathcal{H}_{4,14}$, respectively.

(5) We put

$$\mathcal{H}_{4,12} = \langle (p+2)(z\cdot\alpha)^2 w^2 - 4(z\cdot\alpha)(w\cdot\alpha)(z\cdot w)\rangle$$

and

$$\mathcal{H}_{4,13} = \langle (p+2)(w\cdot\alpha)^2 z^2 - 4(w\cdot\alpha)(z\cdot\alpha)(z\cdot w)\rangle.$$

Remark that $\mathcal{H}_{4,12} \cong \mathcal{H}_{4,13}$. We define

$$K_{4,12}(\widetilde{X},\widetilde{X}') = \frac{\dim\mathcal{H}_{4,12}}{4p}\{(p+2)(z\cdot\overline{z}')^2 w^2\overline{w}'^2 - 4(z\cdot w)\overline{w}'^2(z\cdot\overline{z}')(w\cdot\overline{z}')\}$$

and

$$K_{4,13}(\widetilde{X},\widetilde{X}') = \frac{\dim\mathcal{H}_{4,13}}{4p}\{(p+2)(w\cdot\overline{w}')^2 z^2\overline{z}'^2 - 4(w\cdot z)\overline{z}'^2(w\cdot\overline{z}')(z\cdot\overline{w}')\}$$

We can see that $K_{4,12}(\ ,g\widetilde{E}_7) \in \mathcal{H}_{4,12}$ and $K_{4,13}(\ ,g\widetilde{E}_6) \in \mathcal{H}_{4,13}$. Then we have for any $f \in \mathcal{H}_{4,12}$ and $h \in \mathcal{H}_{4,13}$ the following reproducing formulas of $\mathcal{H}_{4,12}$ and $\mathcal{H}_{4,13}$:

$$f(\widetilde{X}) = \int_{K_\mathbf{R}} f(g\widetilde{E}_7) K_{4,12}(\widetilde{X}, g\widetilde{E}_7) dg, \qquad (4.19)$$

$$h(\widetilde{X}) = \int_{K_\mathbf{R}} h(g\widetilde{E}_6) K_{4,13}(\widetilde{X}, g\widetilde{E}_6) dg. \qquad (4.20)$$

(6) We put $\mathcal{H}_{4,15} = \langle (w \cdot \alpha)^2 w^2 \rangle$ and we define

$$K_{4,15}(\widetilde{X}, \widetilde{X}') = \dim \mathcal{H}_{4,15}\, w^2 \overline{w}'^2 \widetilde{P}_{2,p}(w, \overline{w}').$$

For any $\widetilde{X}_0 \in \mathfrak{p}$ we have $K_{4,15}(\ ,\widetilde{X}_0) \in \mathcal{H}_{4,15}$. Then we have the following reproducing formula of $\mathcal{H}_{4,15}$:

$$f(\widetilde{X}) = \int_{K_\mathbf{R}} f(g\widetilde{E}_1) K_{4,15}(\widetilde{X}, g\widetilde{E}_1) dg \qquad (4.21)$$

for any $f \in \mathcal{H}_{4,15}$.

(7) We have

$$\mathcal{H}_{4,16} = \langle \{(z \cdot \alpha)(w \cdot \beta) - (w \cdot \alpha)(z \cdot \beta)\} z^2 \rangle$$

and

$$\mathcal{H}_{4,17} = \langle \{(z \cdot \alpha)(w \cdot \beta) - (w \cdot \alpha)(z \cdot \beta)\} w^2 \rangle.$$

We define

$$K_{4,16}(\widetilde{X}, \widetilde{X}') = \frac{1}{2} \dim \mathcal{H}_{4,16} \{(z \cdot \overline{z}')(w \cdot \overline{w}') - (z \cdot \overline{w}')(w \cdot \overline{z}')\} z^2 \overline{z}'^2,$$

$$K_{4,17}(\widetilde{X}, \widetilde{X}') = \frac{1}{2} \dim \mathcal{H}_{4,17} \{(w \cdot \overline{w}')(z \cdot \overline{z}') - (w \cdot \overline{z}')(z \cdot \overline{w}')\} w^2 \overline{w}'^2.$$

For $g \in K_\mathbf{R}$ $K_{4,16}(\ ,g\widetilde{E}_2)$ belongs to $\mathcal{H}_{4,16}$ and $K_{4,17}(\ ,g\widetilde{E}_3)$ belongs to $\mathcal{H}_{4,17}$. Then we have for any $f \in \mathcal{H}_{4,16}$ and $h \in \mathcal{H}_{4,17}$

$$f(\widetilde{X}) = \int_{K_\mathbf{R}} f(g\widetilde{E}_2) K_{4,16}(\widetilde{X}, g\widetilde{E}_2) dg, \qquad (4.22)$$

$$h(\widetilde{X}) = \int_{K_\mathbf{R}} h(g\widetilde{E}_3) K_{4,17}(\widetilde{X}, g\widetilde{E}_3) dg. \qquad (4.23)$$

(4.22) and (4.23) are reproducing formulas of $\mathcal{H}_{4,16}$ and $\mathcal{H}_{4,17}$.

(10) We put $\mathcal{H}_{4,18} = \langle (z^2)^2 \rangle$ and $\mathcal{H}_{4,19} = \langle (w^2)^2 \rangle$. We define

$$K_{4,18}(\widetilde{X}, \widetilde{X}') = (z^2)^2(\overline{z}'^2)^2,$$
$$K_{4,19}(X, \widetilde{X}') = (w^2)^2(\overline{w}'^2)^2.$$

For any $\widetilde{X}_0 \in \mathfrak{p}$ $K_{4,18}(\ ,\widetilde{X}_0) \in \mathcal{H}_{4,18}$ and $K_{4,19}(\ ,\widetilde{X}_0) \in \mathcal{H}_{4,19}$. Then we have for any $f \in \mathcal{H}_{4,18}$ and $h \in \mathcal{H}_{4,19}$

$$f(\widetilde{X}) = \int_{K_\mathbf{R}} f(g\widetilde{E}_1) K_{4,18}(\widetilde{X}, g\widetilde{E}_1) dg, \tag{4.24}$$

$$h(\widetilde{X}) = \int_{K_\mathbf{R}} f(g\widetilde{E}_1) K_{4,19}(\widetilde{X}, g\widetilde{E}_1) dg, \tag{4.25}$$

and (4.24) and (4.25) are reproducing formulas of $\mathcal{H}_{4,18}$ and $\mathcal{H}_{4,19}$.

References

[1] S. Helgason, Groups and Geometric Analysis, *Academic Press Inc.*, Orlando, 1984.

[2] K. Ii, On a Bargmann-type transform and a Hilbert space of holomorphic functions, *Tôhoku Math. J.*, **38** (1986), 57–69.

[3] K. Koike and I. Terada, Young-diagrammatic methods for the representation theory of the classical groups of type B_n, C_n, D_n, *J. Algebra*, **107** (1987), 466–511.

[4] B. Kostant and S. Rallis, Orbits and representations associated with symmetric spaces, *Amer. J. Math.*, **93** (1971), 753–809.

[5] C. Müller, Spherical Harmonics, *Lecture Notes in Math.*, **17** (1966), Springer-Verlag.

[6] M. Takeuchi, Modern Spherical Functions, *Translations of Mathematical Monographs* vol.**135**, Amer. Math. Soc., 1994.

[7] R. Wada, Explicit formulas for the reproducing kernels of the space of harmonic polynomials in the case of classical real rank 1, *Scientiae Mathematicae Japonicae*, **65** (2007), 384–406.

[8] R. Wada and Y. Agaoka, The reproducing kernels of the space of harmonic polynomials in the case of real rank 1, in "Microlocal Analysis and Complex Fourier Analysis" (Ed. T. Kawai, K. Fujita), 297–316, *World Scientific*, New Jersey (2002).

[9] R. Wada and Y. Agaoka, Some properties of harmonic polynomials in the case of $\mathfrak{so}(p,2)$, in "Legal Informatics, Economic Science and Mathematical Research" (Ed. M. Kitahara, C. Czerkawski), 81–88, *Kyushu University Press*, (2014).

[10] R. Wada and M. Morimoto, A uniqueness set for the differential operator $\Delta_z + \lambda^2$, *Tokyo J. Math.*, **10** (1987), 93–105.

Contributors

Munenori KITAHARA, Professor, *Hiroshima Shudo University*

Munenori Kitahara (LL.M) is Professor of legal informatics (Rechtsinformatik) at the Faculty of Economic Sciences and the Graduate School of Economic Sciences in Hiroshima Shudo University, Japan. He lectures "Research on Information Society," "Legal Informatics," and "Personal Data Protection Management System." He was a guest professor at the Legal Informatics Institute of Hannover University in Germany (1999-2000).

He was a research member of legal expert systems (Legal Expert System Les-2, Lecture Note in Computer Science, No.264, Springer Verlag 1987). He is also a member of IVR. He presented several papers: "The Impact of the Computer on the Interpretation of Law (ARSP Beiheft 39, 1991), "Personal Data Processing and Business Ethics"(IVR 22nd World Congress, Granada, Spain 2005), "Ethics of Cyberspace: Information Ethics and Information Moral" (IVR 23rd World Congress, Krakow, Poland 2007), "The Right to Data Protection in Digital Society" (IVR 24th World Congress, Beijin, China 2009), "The Fusion of Law and Information Technology" and "Law and Technology Security Standard" (IVR 25th World Congress, Frankfurt am Main, Germany 2011), "The Information Society Law in Japan" (The 3rd International Seminar on Information Law 2010, Ionian University, Corfu, Greece). "The Information Society Law : The Fusion of Law and Information Technology" (The 5th International Conference on Information Law and Ethics 2012, Ionian University, Corfu). "Law and Technology: The Fusion of Law and Information Technology" and "Law and Technology: Legal Justice through Deploying Information Technology in Law" (IVR 26th World Congress, Belo Horizonte, Brazil 2013). He also published a paper titled "Legal Justice through the Fusion of Law and Information Technology" (*Legal Informatics, Economic Science and Mathematical Research*, Kyushu Univ. Press 2014).

His latest research is "Systematizing and Networking Information Society Law." The legal system consists of twelve legal groups and some fifty acts which have been related to information, information devices and information networks. He also proposes networking the legal system, and the fusion of law and information technology. He is researching on realizing a legal justice through using information technology.

Takeshi OGAWA, Assistant Professor, *Hiroshima Shudo University*

Takeshi Ogawa (Doctor of Economics) is Assistant Professor of mathematics for economics at the Faculty of Economic Sciences in Hiroshima Shudo University, Japan. He lectures "Introduction to Economic Mathematics: I and II", "Computer-Aided Economics: I and II", and "Basic Analysis: I and II". He was a Research Fellow at the Graduate School of Economics in Nagoya University (2011-2012).

He was a research assistant of RIETI (The Research Institute of Economy, Trade and Industry) (2008-2010, 2011-2012). He is also a member of JSRSAI (the Japan Society of the Regional Science Association International). He had presented a paper in JSRSAI: "the Joint Production and the Patterns of Specialization (Best Presentation Award of JSRSAI, 2009)". He also had published several papers: "Classification of the Frontier in the Three-country, Three-good Ricardian Model" (Economics Bulletin, 2012), "Application of Jones' inequality to the n-country, m-good, Ricardo and Graham model" (Economics Bulletin, 2013), "Shared Renewable Resource: Gains from Trade and Trade Policy" (with Yasuhiro Takarada and Weijia Dong, Review of International Economics, 2013), and "Consumer Heterogeneity and Gains from Trade in Renewable Resource Trading" (SSRN Working Paper, 2014). Moreover, he also published a manual for Microsoft Mathematics (MS Math), which is useful free software about mathematical education from Microsoft. The manual "Leverage in economics education of Microsoft Mathematics" (Economic Science Research [Faculty of Economic Sciences, Hiroshima Shudo University], 2014) shows the way using MS Math for economic education. Recently, he has also presented several papers: "International Trade and Each Country's Management of Shared Renewable Resource" (JSIE [Japan Society of International Economics] Kansai, Osaka 2014; JIFRS [Japan International Fisheries Research Society], Tokyo 2014; SWET [Summer Workshop on Economic Theory], Otaru 2014), "Analysis with Illustration of Patterns of Specialization with Ricardian-Leontief Model" (JSME Kinki Area, Osaka 2014), "Consumer Heterogeneity and Gains from Trade in Renewable Resource Trading" (ETSG [European Trade Study Group], Munich [Germany] 2014; JEA [Japanese Economic Association], Fukuoka 2014; the 14th EAEA [East Asian Economic Association], Bangkok [Thailand] 2014). Now he is financially supported by JSPS KAKENHI Grant-in-Aid for Young Scientists (B) (2012-2015).

His latest research is "Three-Good Ricardian Model with Joint Production: A Schematic Reconsideration": The analysis for Ricardian-Graham model with three-good cases. He focuses a suitable definition of by-product for the Ricardian model, suitable setting for using illustration for three-good Ricardian model with joint production, and classification (with 48 illustrations) about two-country, three-good Ricardian model.

Kouhei IYORI, Associate Professor, *Hiroshima Shudo University*

Kouhei Iyori (Ph.D) is Associate Professor at the Faculty of Economic Sciences and the Graduate School of Economic Sciences in Hiroshima Shudo University, Japan. He lectures "Simulation Theory". He was a postdoctoral research fellow of the Japan Society for the Promotion of Science (JSPS), and visiting researcher at the Faculty of Economics in Kyoto Sangyo University (2003-2006).

He is a member of iSCIe, Institute of Systems, Control and Information Engineers. His fields of interest are experimental economics, computational economics and simulations. He published several papers: "The application of cellular automata to the consumer's theory: simulating a duopolistic market" (with Sobei H. Oda, Ken Miura and Kanji Ueda, Simulated Evolution and Learning, Springer, 1999), "Price Competition Between Middlemen: An Experimental Study" (with Kazuhito Ogawa and Sobeo H. Oda, Gaming, Simulations, and Society: Research Scope and Perspective, Springer, 2005), and "Prisoner's Dilemma Network: Experiments and Simulations" (System Sciences for Economics and Informatics, Kyushu University Press, 2007).

Takashi YANO, Associate Professor, *Hiroshima Shudo University*

Takashi Yano is Associate Professor of Economic Sciences at Hiroshima Shudo University. He obtained a Ph.D. in Media and Governance from Keio University in 2010. His research field is international economics and applied econometrics, particularly, large-scale econometric modeling. Some of his papers can be found in the following journals: Developing Economies, Journal of Econometric Study of Northeast Asia, Carbon Management and Energy Policy.

Hiroyuki KOSAKA, Professor Emeritus, *Keio University*

Hiroyuki Kosaka is Professor Emeritus at the Faculty of Policy Management, Keio University. His research area is applied econometrics, policy coordination, qualitative game theory and peace science. Currently, he has been working on multi-country/multi-sectoral modeling. He published many papers on applied econometrics and a book titled *Model Analysis on Global System*. He received a doctorate in engineering from Keio University in 1983.

Michinori SAKAGUCHI, *Professor, Hiroshima Shudo University*

Michinori Sakaguchi graduated from Hiroshima University, Japan in 1969 and received the Ph.D. degree in mathematics from Hiroshima University in 1980. He has worked at Hiroshima Shudo University since 1974 and he is now a professor. His current search interests are dynamic programming and linear programming in operations research, especially analysis of inventory models. He is a member of

Mathematical Society of Japan, the Operations Research Society of Japan and Production Operations Management Society.

Masanori KODAMA, *Emeritus Professor, Hiroshima Shudo University*

Masanori Kodama was born in Hiroshima, Japan, on April 22, 1932. He received the B.S. degree in physics from Hiroshima University in 1955, and the M.S. and Ph. D. degrees in mathematics from Kyusyu University, in 1960 and 1968 respectively. He is now Honorary Professor of Kyushu University and Hiroshima Shudo University. His fields of interest include dynamic inventory problem and operations research. He is a member of JPSM, the Mathematical Society of Japan and so on.

Setsuko SAKAI, *Professor, Hiroshima Shudo University*

Setsuko Sakai graduated from the Faculty of Education, Fukui University, 1979. She finished her doctoral course of Informatics and Mathematical Science at Osaka University in 1984. She became a lecturer at the College of Business Administration and Information Science, Koshien University, in 1986, and then an associate professor of the Faculty of Education, Fukui University, in 1990. Since 1998, she has been with the Faculty of Commercial Sciences of Hiroshima Shudo University, where she is a professor in the Department of Business Administration. She is currently working on game theory, decision making, fuzzy mathematical programming, optimization of fuzzy control by genetic algorithms and CAI. She is a member of the Operations Research Society of Japan, Japan Society for Fuzzy Theory and Intelligent Informatics, and the Japan Society for Production Management. She holds a D.Eng.degree. She has published papers such as "Tuning fuzzy control rules by α constrained method which solves constrained nonlinear optimization problems"(1999) and "Reducing the Number of Function Evaluations in Differential Evolution by Estimated Comparison Method using an Approximation Model with Low Accuracy"(2008) in The Transactions of the Institute of Electronics, Information and Communication Engineers, "Fast and Stable Constrained Optimization by the ε Constrained Differential Evolution", in Pacific Journal of Optimization (2009) and so on. She has also published papers in such journals as IEEE Transactions on Evolutionary Computation, Journal of Optimization Theory and its Applications, Transactions of the Japanese Society for Artificial Intelligence etc.

Tetsuyuki TAKAHAMA, *Professor, Hiroshima City University*

Tetsuyuki Takahama graduated from the Department of Electrical Engineering II, Kyoto University, in 1982. He finished his doctoral course in 1987. He became an assistant professor, and then a lecturer, at Fukui University in 1994. Since 1998, he has been with the Faculty of Information Science of Hiroshima City University, where he is an associate professor in the Department of Intelligent Systems. He is currently working on nonlinear optimization methods, learning of fuzzy control rules, machine learning, inference, CAI, and natural language processing. He is a member of the Information Processing Society of Japan, the Japan Society for Artificial Intelligence, the Japanese Society of Information and Systems in Education, the Association for Natural Language Processing and IEEE. He holds a D.Eng.degree. He has published papers such as "Structural Optimization by Genetic Algorithm with Degeneration (GAd)", in The Transactions of the Institute of Electronics, Information and Communication Engineers (2003), "Constrained Optimization by Applying the α Constrained Method to the Nonlinear Simplex Method with Mutations", in IEEE Transactions on Evolutionary Computation (2005), "Efficient Constrained Optimization by the Constrained Differential Evolution Using an Approximation Model with Low Accuracy", in Transactions of the Japanese Society for Artificial Intelligence (2009) and so on. He has also published papers in such journals as Information Processing Society of Japan Journal, International Journal of Innovative Computing, Information and Control Journal of Japan Society for Fuzzy Theory and Systems etc.

Ryoko WADA, *Professor, Hiroshima Shudo University*

Ryoko Wada is a Professor at the Faculty and Graduate School of Economic Sciences of Hiroshima Shudo University. She received the Doctor Degree of Science from Sophia University, Japan, in 1988. Her major research areas are harmonic analysis on homogeneous spaces. Especially she is engaged in topics on integral representations of harmonic polynomials. She also presented at a paper titled "Fantappié Transformations of Analytic Functionals on the Truncated Complex Sphere", M.Kitahara/K.Morioka (eds.), Social Systems Solutions by Legal Informatics, Economic Sciences and Computer Sciences, Kyushu Univ. Press (2010).

Yoshio AGAOKA, *Professor, Hiroshima University*

Yoshio Agaoka is a Professor at the Graduate School of Science of Hiroshima University. He graduated from Kyoto University (Faculty of Science) in 1977, and entered the Graduate School of Science, received the Doctor Degree of Science from Kyoto University in 1985. His major research areas are Differential Geometry, Representation Theory and Discrete Geometry. Especially he is engaged in topics on local isometric imbeddings of Riemannian symmetric spaces, decomposition formula of plethysms and classification of tilings of the two-dimensional sphere, etc. Recently, he is mainly engaged in the subject on elementary geometry from the viewpoint of classical invariant theory.

Series of Monographs of Contemporary Social Systems Solutions
Produced by
the Faculty of Economic Sciences, Hiroshima Shudo University

190 × 265 mm   5,000 yen (tax not included)

Volume 1   Social Systems Solutions by Legal Informatics, Economic Sciences and Computer Sciences

Edited by Munenori Kitahara and Kazunori Morioka   160 pages   ISBN 978-4-7985-0011-9

Preface

Chapter 1   The Concept of Personal Data Protection in Information Society   ⋯ *Munenori Kitahara*

Chapter 2   On the Evaluation System of Public Sector   ⋯ *Kazunori Morioka*

Chapter 3   Effects of Property Right Restriction: An Analysis Using a Product Differentiation Model   ⋯ *Koshiro Ota*

Chapter 4   Tax Coordination between Asymmetric Regions in a Repeated Game Setting   ⋯ *Chikara Yamaguchi*

Chapter 5   The Household Production and Comsumer Behavior   ⋯ *Hiroaki Teramoto*

Chapter 6   Modeling a Sequencing Problem for a Mixed-model Assembly Line   ⋯ *Shusaku Hiraki, Hugejile and Zhuqi Xu*

Chapter 7   Long-run Superneutrality of Money in Japanese Economy   ⋯ *Md. Jahanur Rahman*

Chapter 8   A Parametric Study on Estimated Comparison in Differential Evolution with Rough Approximation Model   ⋯ *Setsuko Sakai and Tetsuyuki Takahama*

Chapter 9   Fantappié Transformations of Analytic Functionals on the Truncated Complex Sphere   ⋯ *Ryoko Wada*

Volume 2   The New Viewpoints and New Solutions of Economic Sciences in the Information Society

Edited by Shusaku Hiraki and Nan Zhang   160 pages   ISBN 978-4-7985-0055-3

Preface

Chapter 1   Economic Evaluation of the Recovery Process from a Great Disaster in Japan: The Case of Hanshin-Awaji Earthquake   ⋯ *Toshihisa Toyoda*

Chapter 2   The Economic Analysis of Altruistic Consumer Behavior   ⋯ *Hiroaki Teramoto*

Chapter 3   External Debt Default and Renegotiation Economics   ⋯ *Chris Czerkawski*

Chapter 4   Statistical Observations on the External Flow of Funds between China and the U.S.   ⋯ *Nan Zhang*

Chapter 5   Trade Flows in ASEAN plus Alpha   ⋯ *Sithanonxay Suvannaphakdy and Toshihisa Toyoda*

Chapter 6   Inventory Policies Under Time-varying Demand   ⋯ *Michinori Sakaguchi*

Chapter 7   RIDE: Differential Evolution with a Rotation-Invariant Crossover Operation for Nonlinear Optimization   ⋯ *Setsuko Sakai and Tetsuyuki Takahama*

Chapter 8   The Network of Information Society Law   ⋯ *Munenori Kitahara*

Chapter 9   The Function of the Copyright Mechanism: The Coordination of Interests of an Inventor and an Improver   ⋯ *Koshiro Ota*

Volume 3 Social Systems Solutions Applied by Economic Sciences and Mathematical Solutions

Edited by Minenori Kitahara and Chris Czerkawski   156 pages ISBN 978-4-7985-0078-2

Preface

Chapter 1	The Collaboration of Law and InformationTechnology	⋯ *Munenori Kitahara*
Chapter 2	The Australian Broadband Policy: Theory and Reality	⋯ *Koshiro Ota*
Chapter 3	Evaluating the Impact of Mining Foreign Capital Inflows on the Lao Economy	⋯ *Phouphet Kyophilavong and Toshihisa Toyoda*
Chapter 4	Empirical Study of the Impact of the Thai Economy on the Lao Electricity Export	⋯ *Thongphet Lamphayphan, Chris Czerkawski and Toshihisa Toyoda*
Chapter 5	Calculating CO_2 Emissions for Coastal Shipping of Finished Cars by Pure Car Carriers in Japan	⋯ *Min Zhang, Shusaku Hiraki and Yoshiaki Ishihara*
Chapter 6	A Statistical Model for Global-Flow-of-Funds Analysis	⋯ *Nan Zhang*
Chapter 7	The Reproducing Kernels of the Space of Harmonic Polynomials	⋯ *Ryoko Wada*
Chapter 8	A Comparative Study on Neighborhood Structures for Speciation in Species-Based Differential Evolution	⋯ *Setsuko Sakai and Tetsuyuki Takahama*

Volume 4 Social Systems Solutions through Economic Sciences

Edited by Munenori Kitahara and Chris Czerkawski   156 pages ISBN 978-4-7985-0097-3

Preface

Chapter 1	Law and Technology: Privacy Protection through Technology	⋯ *Munenori Kitahara*
Chapter 2	The Signaling Role of Promotions in Japan —A Pseud-Panel Data Analysis	⋯ *Kazuaki Okamura*
Chapter 3	The Chinese Spring Festival Model's Design and Application	⋯ *Gang Shi and Nan Zhang*
Chapter 4	Money and Real Output in Laos: An Econometric Analysis	⋯ *Inthiphone Xaiyavong and Chris Czerkawski*
Chapter 5	Literature Review on Ship Scheduling and Routing	⋯ *Min Zhang, Shusaku Hiraki and Yoshiaki Ishihara*
Chapter 6	Optimal Ordering Policies in a Multi-item Inventory Model	⋯ *Michinori Sakaguchi and Masanori Kodama*
Chapter 7	A Comparative Study on Graph-Based Speciation Methods for Species-Based Differential Evolution	⋯ *Setsuko Sakai and Tetsuyuki Takahama*
Chapter 8	Sino-Japanese Compounds	⋯ *Paul Jensen*

Volume 5   **Legal Informatics, Economic Science and Mathematical Research**

Edited by Munenori Kitahara and Chris Czerkawski   104 pages   ISBN 4-978-7985-0125-3

Preface

Chapter 1   Legal Justice through the Fusion of Law and Information Technology
⋯*Munenori Kitahara*

Chapter 2   The Role of International Transportation in Trade and the Environment
⋯*Takeshi Ogawa*

Chapter 3   A Comparative Study on Estimation Methods of Landscape Modality for Evolutionary Algorithms   ⋯*Setsuko Sakai and Tetsuyuki Takahama*

Chapter 4   Some Properties of Harmonic Polynomials in the Case of $\mathfrak{so}(p, 2)$
⋯*Ryoko Wada and Yoshio Agaoka*